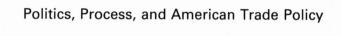

Politics, Process, and American Trade Policy

Politics, Process, and American Trade Policy

Sharyn O'Halloran

Ann Arbor

THE UNIVERSITY OF MICHIGAN PRESS

Copyright © by the University of Michigan 1994
All rights reserved
Published in the United States of America by
The University of Michigan Press
Manufactured in the United States of America
♾ Printed on acid-free paper

1997   1996   1995   1994   4 3 2 1

A CIP catalogue record for this book is available from the British Library.

Library of Congress Cataloging-in-Publication Data

O'Halloran, Sharyn, 1963–
        Politics, process, and American trade policy / Sharyn O'Halloran.
        p.   cm.
        Revision of the author's thesis (Ph.D.)—University of California,
    San Diego.
        Includes bibliographical references (p.   ) and index.
        ISBN 0-472-10516-7 (acid-free paper)
        1. United States—Commercial policy.   I. Title.
    HF1455.037   1994
    382'.3'0973—dc20   94-19986
                                                                      CIP

For my sister, Jeanne

Contents

Preface

This is a study of American politics and the institutions that structure policy-making. As students of the legislative process know, the multitude of factors influencing the formation of public policy is staggering. The interactions among voters, interest groups, and the various branches of government can overwhelm even the veteran observer. The aim of this book is to provide a unified framework for thinking about how policy is made. Its subject is American trade legislation from the beginning of the republic to present day. Its focus is the decision-making process.

How is trade policy made? There are many ways to approach this question. The main emphasis might be placed on interest groups that seek favorable policies and legislators' reactions to them. Emphasis could equally be placed on the executive and administrative agencies that have come to dominate the daily workings of trade policy. Each of these approaches certainly captures an important element of how policy is made, but before they can be effectively evaluated, we must first ask: What procedures define the decision-making process, and what effect do they have on public policy?

The choice of institutions is a political one and is crucial to determining outcomes. Consequently, any understanding of public policy must begin with process, and any discussion of process must begin with who has the constitutional power to make policy. As the Constitution grants Congress the authority to regulate foreign commerce, analysis of trade policy must begin with the legislative branch. This might seem a simple point, but most previous studies of trade policy have failed to recognize its significance.

If Congress is the logical starting point of analysis, then a number of further questions immediately follow. What are the preferences of legislators regarding trade policy? And given these preferences, how do they choose the institutions that structure decision making? Part of my project is to relate the wealth of detailed procedures that Congress employs to regulate trade policy to theories of institutional design. I recognize the ever present danger of becoming mired in detail when dealing with the specifics of legislation. I therefore attempt to provide a theoretical context in which to understand these procedures and their effect on policy outcomes.

The purpose of this book, then, is to lay the cornerstone for an institution-based approach to trade policy by drawing on a large body of recent theoretical investigations into the study of procedure. Affectionately called the New Economics of Organizations (NEO) or the New Institutional-ism, this line of research begins with a few basic assumptions and then derives a set of testable propositions about the effects of institutions on policy out-comes. My analysis builds on diverse literatures in American politics that emphasize legislative organization, the internal decision-making procedures of Congress, and the relation between the legislative and executive branches. In many ways, this book can be viewed as a user-friendly application of the central tenets of NEO. I identify the common assumptions in this research tradition and then apply these techniques, by now familiar to many, to the study of trade policy.

One advantage of my approach is that I can explain trade policy in a consistent and integrated fashion over time, whereas previous studies, reason-ing backward from outcomes to process, have interpreted trade policy as disparate and ad hoc. In fact, one of the main points of this book is that a single set of procedures may lead to apparently different outcomes under differing initial conditions. Sometimes it may seem as if the president domi-nates policy outcomes, sometimes as if Congress is the victor, and sometimes a compromise is the most obvious solution. The point is not to determine which branch dominates, but rather to realize that there is a common logic, derived from constitutional imperatives, that underlies all policy outcomes.

To a large extent, my project is an attempt to reconcile the more theoreti-cally based analyses of American politics with the largely empirical studies of trade policy. Given the wealth of detailed empirical literature, it is important that the models I analyze provide predictions consistent with this evidence. For the project to be of interest, these predictions should provide insights that have not been generated previously and pose new challenges to the prevailing wisdom. It is left for the reader to judge whether this book succeeds on either account. But in any case, I believe that it is important that theory and empiri-cal evidence be tightly linked. Otherwise, our theories may lack empirical relevance and our empirical analyses may not rest on firm theoretical foundations.

This study began as my dissertation at the University of California, San Diego, and has benefited from the guidance of my advisors Gary Cox, Gary Jacobson, and Mathew McCubbins. Vincent Crawford and Lawrence Krause also served on my committee and supplied insightful suggestions. Jeanne O'Halloran provided careful and diligent research assistance. Karla Ewalt, David Geddes, Judy McTigue, and Brian Sala commented on an early draft.

Most of the revisions to the manuscript were completed at Stanford University. The logical flow of the argument was greatly improved by discus-sions with Richard Brody, John Ferejohn, Keith Krehbiel, Susanne Lohmann, John Londregan, Helen Milner, Roger Noll, Doug Rivers, Dani Rodrik, Geoff Rothwell, Charles Stewart, and Barry Weingast. David Brady gave extremely encouraging and helpful comments on an earlier version of the manuscript. My greatest debt, however, is to my colleague David Epstein, who painstakingly read several drafts. I would also like to thank my parents, Sally and James O'Halloran, and my sisters, Christina, Jeanne, and Dyane, for their encouragement.

This research and data collection were made possible through the generous financial support of the National Science Foundation Grant SES-8913940; the Social Science Research Council Fellowship in Foreign Policy Studies; and the Center for Economic Policy Research and the Public Policy Program at Stanford University. All remaining errors and omissions are my responsibility alone.

CHAPTER 1

Introduction

The procedure through which Congress functions is a fruitful point at which to begin. . . . This may be said without pretending that the term "procedure" comprises the whole of the elusive concept included in the expression "the process of law making," for the procedure itself determines the final results at many points.
                    —E. E. Schattschneider, *Politics, Pressure, and the Tariff*

When Schattschneider penned these words over half a century ago, he could not have foreseen that his insights would lay the foundation for a future generation of legislative scholars. His point was a simple one: that decision-making procedures greatly influence outcomes. In his seminal study of the 1930 Smoot-Hawley Tariff Act, Schattschneider concluded that the legislative process, and in particular the committee system, gave producer interests disproportionate influence in shaping policy. These forces led inevitably to legislative logrolls with predictably high tariffs and disastrous results. His basic logic remains true today: a process that places unbalanced pressures on Congress will lead to skewed policies.

The notion that institutions matter is a basic premise of current congressional scholarship. Following Schattschneider's lead, much work has concentrated on the policy implications of various institutional arrangements, such as the committee seniority system, open and closed rules, committee gatekeeping powers, and party leadership. What Schattschneider failed to realize, however, is that these procedures are themselves a political choice and as such can be changed to suit legislators' needs. Thus Schattschneider's prediction that trade policy would be eternally plagued by logrolls was disproved even as his book went to press. In the 1934 Reciprocal Trade Agreements Act Congress changed the procedure for setting tariffs by shifting authority to the executive branch.

This book is an attempt to update Schattschneider's original project by examining the institutions that underlie trade policy making, identifying the political basis for these procedures, and elucidating their effects on trade policy. Unlike Schattschneider's work, which was a detailed case study, I examine trade policy from the beginning of the republic to the present. Although the substance of trade policy may have changed over the years, its underlying logic has remained the same.

1.1. American Politics and Trade Policy in Perspective

On April 8, 1789, Representative James Madison (Va.) introduced a resolution to impose duties on specified articles for the express purpose of raising revenues and protecting industry. Foreshadowing the great political divide of the nineteenth and early twentieth centuries, the first law enacted by Congress was a tariff bill.[1]

The first bill was far from the last concerning trade. The first twenty Congresses saw the passage of more than twenty duty acts. During this period, tariff revenues comprised, on average, nearly 90 percent of total federal income. In the second party system, the protective tariff became the primary issue dividing the Whigs and Democrats. Secessionist rumblings from South Carolina were quieted only by the passage of the Compromise Tariff Act of 1833. The harmony was short-lived, however, as the tariff was a major issue in the demise of the Whigs, the birth of the Republican party, and the outbreak of the Civil War. By the late 1860s high tariffs became synonymous with Republicanism, and by the 1872 presidential election the tariff had become the litmus test for political affiliation.

Throughout the late nineteenth and early twentieth centuries, the tariff was a major issue in every national election. During this period, the fate of the tariff oscillated wildly, whenever partisan control of national government changed hands. Grover Cleveland drew the dividing line clearly in his 1887 presidential message, committing the Democratic party to opposing a protective tariff. The Republican victory in the subsequent election led to the passage of the protectionist 1890 McKinley Tariff Act. On returning to power in 1892, the Democrats enacted the 1894 Wilson "Free Trade" Act. The swing to the Republicans in 1896 was followed by the protectionist Dingley Tariff Act of 1897. Throughout the early twentieth century, the tariff continued to change with the political parties, until 1934, when the Democratic Congress enacted the Reciprocal Trade Agreements Act and swung the tariff pendulum decisively toward rate reduction.[2]

---

1. Duty Act of July 4, 1789, 1 Stat. 24.

2. For example, the Payne-Aldrich Tariff Act of 1909 incorporated the Republican platform shift from the protective tariff to an equalization of the costs of production between foreign and domestic producers. Following the Democratic victory in 1912, the tariff rate was lowered in the Underwood Tariff Act of 1913. The 1920 presidential election returned the Republicans to power and tariff policy was again reversed in the Fordney-McCumber Act of 1922. President Hoover signed into law the infamous 1930 Smoot-Hawley Tariff Act, which increased duties on over

Two hundred years after the first tariff bill, trade legislation continues to be a dominant issue on the contemporary political agenda. Although the tariff is no longer the central subject of debate, new trade conflicts involving non-tariff barriers, export subsidies, and market access have emerged. The unprecedented trade deficits in the 1980s have continued into the 1990s, accentuating conflict and creating new demands for import protection. The turbulent battles over the North American Free Trade Agreement (NAFTA) show the delicate equilibrium between free trade and protectionist concerns in the current political landscape.

The history of American trade legislation can be summarized by the tariff trends presented in figure 1.1. The time series show the variations in two measures of protectionism from 1821 to 1990. The first series, labeled Dutiable Imports, records the value of duties collected as a percentage of the value of dutiable imports. The second series, labeled Total Imports, records the value of duties collected as a percentage of the total value of imports.[3]

Several facts are immediately apparent from these trends. The most obvious is that since the 1830s, except during the Civil War, the average duty on total imports has declined. Although the 1930 tariff act resulted in the highest tariff rates in the twentieth century, it would have been considered a rather liberal trade law fifty years earlier. Further, the trends show that although the average tariff on dutiable imports was about 60 percent in the early 1930s, only 20 percent of the value of total imports was affected. Thus, the tariff burden was concentrated in a few select goods. Second, beginning with the 1890s, the wild swings in the tariff taper off. For example, the mean level of protection on all goods from 1821 to 1890 is 30.5 percent with a standard deviation of 10.2 percent; the mean tariff between 1890 and 1934 is 18.8 percent with a standard deviation of 6.6 percent; and in the contemporary era, the mean tariff is 7.4 percent with a standard deviation of 3.9 percent. Third, the means of these ratios are closest when the tariff is employed for revenue purposes, as in the beginning of the 1800s and during the Civil War, whereas the means of these ratios are furthest apart during the late 1800s and the early 1930s, both highly politicized periods in American trade history.

Although trade issues play a central role in American politics, relatively few studies focus on trade policy making. Prominent exceptions include Schattschneider's (1935) classic study on the 1930 Smoot-Hawley Tariff Act referenced above; Bauer, Pool, and Dexter's (1963) study of the 1955 renewal of the Reciprocal Trade Agreements Act; and, more recently, Pastor (1980)

25,000 specified commodities. For an overview of American tariff history, see Stanwood 1903, Taussig 1931, Terrill 1973, and Setser 1969.

3. Since the value of dutiable imports can be no greater than the value of total imports, the first statistic will always exceed the second. Potential weaknesses of these measures as proxies for protectionism are discussed in chapters 4 and 5.

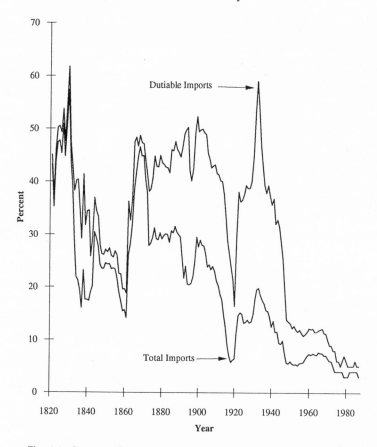

Fig. 1.1. Average duty on dutiable and total imports, 1821–1990

and Destler's (1986a) pioneering work on congressional-executive relations in trade policy formation. For the most part, with the exception of Schatt-schneider, these authors see trade policy as subordinate to other areas of foreign policy or as an enigma that stands apart from other fields of American politics. Overall, U.S. trade policy has been described as "flexible, disparate, ad hoc, inconsistent, and just plain messy" (Cohen 1988, 143).

Despite this confusion, two conventional models have been used to explain American trade politics. Oddly enough, and perhaps a reflection of this confusion, these models offer diametrically opposed accounts of the political process and differ widely in their policy predictions.

In the first model, private power applied by pressure groups determines public policy. Political institutions are seen as either captives of special interest groups or conduits of social pressures. Schattschneider (1935) argues, for example, that the high tariffs of the 1930s resulted from members of Congress granting protection to politically influential producer interests. Indeed, figure 1.1 shows substantial fluctuations in the tariff over time, including high levels of protection during the recessionary periods in the 1890s and 1930s. These findings support the prediction of the interest group model that the tariff level reflects aggregate economic conditions, rising as imports have a greater effect on domestic producers. Yet something important seems to be missing. Pure pressure group models are unable to predict the shift from protection in 1890 to free trade in 1894 and back to protection in 1896. Did demand for import protection oscillate wildly enough to explain these swings in the tariff pendulum? Moreover, the tariff has declined in the second half of this century. Did demand for protection dissipate after World War II? The first model clearly needs to incorporate the role that political institutions play in policy outcomes.

The second model, which I term a presidential dominance model, is driven by institutional change. It holds that, during this century, a policy of free trade replaced protectionism when Congress passed the 1934 Reciprocal Trade Agreements Act, in which members legislated themselves out of the business of making product-specific trade laws (Destler 1986a). This model asserts that over time, a series of congressional delegations of authority have given the president a predominant role in trade policy making. By shifting the basic authority and responsibility onto the president and executive agencies, legislators insulate themselves from protectionist pressures. The president, having a national constituency and being less susceptible to particularistic concerns, therefore implements less protectionist trade measures than does Congress.

Proponents of the presidential dominance model correctly recognize that the 1934 shift in authority from Congress to the president is associated with a decline in the tariff. However, this decline has not been steady. Indeed, the tariff actually increased immediately after World War II and in the beginning of the 1980s. Nor can proponents of this view account for the fact that it took presidents over forty years to return to the 1913 tariff level, when Congress set duties item by item. Furthermore, it is far from clear that protectionism has declined to the extent that figure 1.1 indicates. Although accurate data are scarce, nontariff barriers appear to have risen in the past quarter century to more than offset gains from tariff reduction.[4]

4. Hufbauer, Berliner, and Elliott (1986, table 1.4), examining thirty-one selected industries, report that in 1984, 21 percent of total imports were covered by special protection, with an average tariff rate of 20 percent. For a discussion of this trend toward nontariff barriers see Ray 1987.

1.2. The New Economics of Organizations and American Trade Policy

The historical trends outlined above indicate that interest group and presidential dominance hypotheses each capture an important part of the total story but are incomplete in and of themselves. We need a broader approach: one that can integrate both the role of interest groups and the influence of institutions in shaping trade policy. Recent advances in regulatory theory, known as the New Economics of Organizations (NEO), suggest one possible integrating approach. NEO provides important insights into how American trade policy is made, many of which run directly counter to traditional scholarship in the discipline.

I argue that Congress and congressional politics, not pressure groups or the president, determine trade policy. The organization of Congress, the institutional details of the House and Senate, and the procedural arrangements designed by Congress to implement legislation shape policy. The argument is based on the premises that legislators are motivated by electoral incentives, that they adopt procedural arrangements to help win reelection, and that through these procedures they affect policy. In my approach, parties and voters play a greater role in policy choice than generally acknowledged by pressure group models. Further, in contrast to the models of presidential dominance, I argue that congressional delegations of authority in this century have not implied that Congress has lost control over trade policy. Rather, Congress meticulously designs procedures to ensure that the actions taken by the president are in line with legislators' preferences.

To disentangle the relation between interests, institutions, and policy outcomes, I begin with three basic questions:

1. Who has the authority to make decisions?
2. Where do preferences come from?
3. And how do individuals organize to make collective decisions?

The Constitution grants Congress the authority to regulate foreign commerce. Thus, the starting point of my analysis must be the individual legislator. Interestingly, both the interest group and the presidential dominance models for the most part ignore Congress. Legislators are either held captive by interest groups from below or are dominated by the president from above. In neither case do Congress and legislative organizations have an independent role in the decision-making process.

Consistent with the interest group model, I assume that legislators' preferences derive from electoral considerations. Given that the nature of trade policy grants concentrated benefits and imposes diffuse costs, the preferences of legislators are distributive.[5] This does not mean, however, that outcomes will necessarily reflect interest group demands. One of the basic findings of NEO is that knowing the preferences of political actors reveals little about the final outcome unless the institutional arrangements that aggregate these preferences are also known.

This leads to the third question: what does collective decision making look like when legislators have distributive preferences? In enacting trade policy, legislators face a series of collective action problems. They could be unable to pass legislation altogether, or policy-making could result in legislative logrolls and inefficiently high levels of protectionism. Yet Congress can also design institutions to avoid these collective dilemmas. As widely recognized by proponents of the presidential dominance hypothesis, Congress has delegated authority to the president. But presidential dominance models begin with the fact of delegation. Thus, they are unable to predict variations in the scope and nature of that delegation over time. Since my analysis derives the option of delegation, I am better able to predict when Congress will delegate authority, what constraints it will place on the use of this authority, and how policy outcomes will be affected.

Three propositions concerning trade policy follow from this approach. The first has to do with the role of parties in determining trade policy. NEO recognizes that preferences do not necessarily translate directly into outcomes. Without denying the importance of interest groups, I argue that if electoral preferences are aggregated through strong parties, then the party that controls national government will have an independent effect on policy outcomes. If parties adopt distinct platforms on certain issues and can commit themselves to enacting these policies, then economic preferences alone do not determine policy.

The second prediction follows from the basic premise that structure determines policy. The most obvious predictions thus concern how legislators structure trade institutions and how these institutions will change over time. In accordance with the literature on principal-agent relationships, I argue that when Congress delegates power to the president it does not abdicate its authority. Instead, legislators establish procedures that constrain executive

5. See the Lowi-Wilson matrix for a classification of distributive issues. It should be noted that this book takes a distributive politics approach to the study of trade policy (see Lowi 1964; Mayhew 1974; Wilson 1980). This approach is distinct from other models of congressional decision making that focus on informational asymmetries and the gains to be made by delegating authority. I recognize that some informational concerns are relevant to the topic I discuss. Fast track procedures have especially strong informational components built into them. By concentrating on distributive issues, however, I am able to capture most of what I believe is important in Congress's designing trade policy over the past century. However, I do not rule out the possibility that in some places my discussion could be fruitfully supplemented by nondistributive concerns. For an excellent overview of this literature, see Krehbiel 1991.

actions. The history of American trade legislation is rich with examples of Congress delegating authority to the president to negotiate with foreign countries for decreased tariffs, for bilateral trade agreements, and, more recently, for complex multilateral trade agreements. This authority, however, has always been subject to constraints. For the most part, instead of Congress legislating itself out of the business of making commodity-specific trade laws (Destler 1986a), it has gone into the business of regulating what the executive can and cannot do, thereby indirectly maintaining control over outcomes.

All presidential power regarding trade policy, except for treaty negotiations, is delegated by Congress.[6] One would expect the extent of this delegation to be more limited as the conflict between the executive and legislative branches over the preferred policy increases. Further, if party affiliation can be used as a proxy for preference, we might predict that more authority will be given to a president of the same party as Congress than to one of the opposing party. My second prediction then is that presidents will be more constrained under divided than unified partisan control of government, and the less authority delegated to the president, the higher the levels of protection, because a constrained president is forced to accommodate more congressional demands for protection than an unconstrained one.

My third prediction focuses on the relation between trade restrictions and policy outcomes. The influence of institutions on policy, though profound, is not always straightforward. Under certain conditions, the president will be forced to accommodate congressional demands. Consider the case where Congress retains a veto over trade proposals. Even though the president may exercise a degree of power, he must in some instances accommodate congressional preferences to obtain his desired policy. In other cases, the ability of the president to set the agenda might mean that he can obtain his preferred outcomes without making any concessions to legislators. Congressional approval requirements may or may not constrain the president's actions. The only difference between the two cases lies in the ex ante preferences of the actors relative to the status quo policy.

1.3. Evidence and Design

The aim of this book is to examine the politics of U.S. trade policy and explain trends in protectionism over time. The analysis centers on the design of institutions and the effect these institutions have on policy outcomes. Although I focus on trade policy, my conclusions should be of interest to other

---

6. Of course, proposals submitted under the treaty process require two-thirds consent of the Senate, which historically has proved rather difficult for presidents to achieve. For example, President Carter was unable to secure support for the 1979 United States–Canada East Coast Fishing Agreement.

students of American politics. Trade policy provides a wonderful testing ground for theories of interest group behavior, the effect of political parties on policy, and the impact of legislative organization. Clearly, each of these elements has an influence on policy. The question becomes how to combine them into a unified approach, derive propositions, and then empirically test these predictions.

This book also offers a new theoretical perspective on many long-standing controversies concerning American trade policy. My intention is not to refute all prior arguments, but to suggest that they are incomplete and provide a framework with which to integrate these views. To clarify the exposition, I adopt a series of spatial models and derive predictions concerning trade policy. To empirically test these propositions, I use time series econometric analysis, a close study of the development of American trade institutions, and additional support from case studies. Even though some scholars may disagree with my conclusions, I hope this framework will help structure future debate.

The book is organized as follows. In the next chapter, I review the literature on trade policy-making. A dichotomy has arisen in this literature between explanations centered on interest group demands and those that focus on the institutional arrangements by which power is delegated to the president. After reviewing the strengths and weaknesses of each approach, I present some empirical evidence that suggests that Congress plays a larger role in trade policy-making than either the presidential dominance or interest group models purport.

What is needed, then, is a theory that is able to combine the strengths of both approaches. In chapter 3, I review the literature that falls under the rubric of the NEO, which recognizes the importance of both constituency pressures and institutional arrangements in explaining policy outcomes. I discuss the central assumptions of this approach and the hypotheses that have been associated with it. I then derive the three propositions detailed above concerning the aggregation of interests and delegations of authority and relate the implications of my analysis to trade policy.

Chapter 4 examines the relation between partisan control of national government and tariff policy in the period after Reconstruction until 1934. There are three central findings. First, even after controlling for interest group demands, partisan control of government has a significant effect on the tariff. Second, tariff increases and decreases are more pronounced when there is unified partisan control than when there is not. And third, political parties differ significantly in the tariff policies they enact, and they benefit certain producer groups at the expense of others.

Given that institutions play an important role in determining policy, chapter 5 examines the congressional design of trade institutions from 1890, when Congress first delegated power to the president, through modern times. Two themes dominate the discussion. First, delegation is flexible; sometimes Congress grants the president large blocks of authority, whereas at other times the president's authority is severely curtailed. Second, delegation of authority responds to economic and political conditions, especially partisan conflict between Congress and the president. I show that as the interests of Congress and the president diverge, delegation declines monotonically. This chapter then provides empirical evidence to show that less power was delegated under divided than unified government and that protectionism was higher when less authority was delegated to the president.

To further disentangle the relation between procedures and outcomes, chapter 6 examines the current method for implementing international trade agreements, "fast track." After discussing the details of fast track, I examine the implementation of the U.S.–Canada Free Trade Agreement and show how Congress used fast track to force the president to accommodate protectionist demands. I then discuss these findings in light of the proposed North American Free Trade Agreement. In the final chapter, I present my conclusions and the implications of this analysis for the study of American politics.

CHAPTER 2

The Debate: Giants vs. Windmills

Too often, literature reviews are boring to author and reader alike. But if the reviewer does more than write a series of brief summaries, [she] can make a real contribution. Moreover, if one is willing to show a bit of contentiousness, critical reviews can be downright exciting.
—Morris P. Fiorina, *Representatives, Roll Calls, and Constituencies*

In recent decades a large and seemingly diverse literature has examined the rate and incidence of protectionism. These studies differ both in the focus of their analysis and in their methodological approach. Some use statistical techniques to examine the determinants of protectionism over time or across industries. Others provide more detailed case studies of the particular institutional arrangements that give rise to protectionism or free trade. For the most part, however, these explanations can be divided into two competing views. The central difference between these models is their conceptualization of the decision-making process. As in Cervantes's *Don Quixote*, one sees giants where the other sees windmills.

The first model has been elaborated mainly by economists, who emphasize the influence of particular industries in policy outcomes. Termed the interest group model, this view asserts that variations in the level of protection are explained by the pressures that firms, industries, and workers apply to bureaucrats and politicians. This model links general economic conditions and interest group demands to trade policy outcomes. In times of economic distress, for instance, demands for import relief will increase; in turn, politicians respond to these demands by raising the level of protectionism.

Political scientists, on the other hand, emphasize the institutional arrangements that insulate executive decision making from parochial concerns. The presidential dominance model, as it is called, focuses on the role of state institutions in determining trade policy. According to this view, Congress delegates authority over trade policy to the president; thus, the president dominates this area as he does other areas of foreign relations. Since the president has a national constituency, he prefers freer trade than Congress.

11

Although the president may make some concessions to legislators or narrow special interests, in general he acts autonomously in pursuing his free trade objectives. The institutions that shift trade policy-making authority to the president, especially the 1934 Reciprocal Trade Agreements Act (RTAA), therefore explain the trend toward trade liberalization shown in figure 1.1.

The purpose of this chapter is to review the assumptions, logic, and predictions of these seemingly diverse views. I argue that each model captures important elements of the decision-making process. I then suggest how these views can be integrated into a unified approach, which is developed more fully in the following chapter.

2.1. Interest Group Models

Pressure group models originate from economic theories of regulation, which focus on why the political process favors specific groups or industries over others. According to these models, industries petition politicians and bureaucrats for regulation that is designed and operated primarily for their benefit. Elected officials are seen as being responsive to these pressures. In the case of perfect responsiveness, they are said to be *captured* by politically influential industries.[1]

The classic Stiglerian (1971) pressure group model is constructed as follows. Suppose all individuals belong to a group—defined by occupation, industry, income, or geography—and maximize their incomes by spending some resources on political pressure. The optimal amount of lobbying is determined both by the productivity of their expenditures and by the behavior of other groups (Stigler 1988, 222). Legislators in this model are motivated by the desire to be reelected; they maximize votes. Maximization implies that the votes gained from supplying industry benefits are balanced, at the margin, by those lost. In equilibrium, then, interest groups balance the marginal costs and benefits of demanding protection, and politicians balance the costs and benefits of supplying it.

In the original article, Stigler analyzes some of the determinants of economic actors' incentives to demand regulation. To obtain their desired policy, a group must expend resources to inform its members of the implications of the policy and organize support for the politician who will implement it. A group will organize and incur these costs only if they are offset by prospective gains. The effectiveness of a group in support of some policy, then, will depend on group size in two offsetting ways. A larger group provides a broader base for support, but it also dilutes the net gain per member and hence lowers the incentives for any one member to contribute. In general,

---

1. For an overview of this literature, see Joskow and Noll 1981.

interest group models predict that the most effective groups are small in size and have significant economic interests at stake.[2]

Peltzman (1976) formalizes Stigler's model and investigates the factors that influence the political supply of regulation. He argues that the political process limits not only the size of the dominant group but also its gains because the decision-making process automatically admits "powerful outsiders" into the decision calculus. These outsiders, such as consumer groups, would not otherwise be able to overcome their costs of organization and enter the process. Thus, a "rational regulator"—that is, one who will distribute costs and benefits to maximize his own political returns—will be forced to take into account these outside interests, and therefore the gains to the dominant group will be less than otherwise.[3]

Becker (1983) further expands this model. He argues that the optimal policy depends not only on group size but also on the dead-weight loss that a policy generates. In Becker's model, equilibrium is achieved when the ratio of the marginal dead-weight costs from subsidizing or taxing groups equals the ratio of their marginal political effectiveness. The distortions created by the dead-weight loss of taxes and subsidies stimulate efforts by taxed groups to lower taxes and discourage subsidies. This process also creates a natural limit to the gains that interest groups can extract.

In sum, pressure group models predict that powerful, well-organized interests will receive benefits from the political process at the expense of more diffuse interests. There may be a limit to the influence of interest groups in the decision-making process, but since in general politicians are motivated solely by the desire to balance the demands made upon them, they will respond to better-organized interests.

The relevance of the pressure group model to tariff policy is straightforward. Because capital is relatively immobile among industries and higher domestic prices yield income gains, import-competing industries want the government to restrict imports. Since the industries that would benefit from protection have more concentrated resources than the consumers that are hurt by protectionism, they will organize more effectively and have greater influence on the political process.

---

2. In a similar vein, Olson (1965) argues that small groups more readily overcome the free-rider problem. For example, taxpayers are a large latent group because the benefits to political pressure are dispersed among many members. The recipients of subsidies, on the other hand, are a small, privileged group because the benefits to political pressure are concentrated. According to the model, subsidized groups more readily invest in the costs of political influence than do taxed groups because the costs to the individual of losing subsidies exceeds a small increase in taxes. This argument is supported by the empirical finding that industry interests are weighted more heavily than consumer interests in determining the structure of protection.

3. This argument is similar to Truman's (1951) assertion that politics is driven by both actual and latent interest groups.

In fact, many authors have applied the pressure group model to explain tariff policy. As discussed in the previous chapter, Schattschneider (1935) views elected officials as directly accountable to producers' demands. He argues that the committee system is devised to ensure that domestic producers are well represented in the policy-making process and claims that this over-representation led to the highly protectionist 1930 Smoot-Hawley Tariff Act. Pincus (1975; 1977), Caves (1976), Coughlin (1985), and W. Hansen (1990) similarly focus on how constituents (producers and workers) lobby bureaucrats and politicians for policies that limit imports. Other scholars view tariff levels as a reflection of political bargains made by dominant economic sectors in response to international economic crises (Gourevitch 1986), shifting comparative advantages (Rogowski 1987), import penetration (Bhagwati 1988) or market characteristics (Ray 1981a; 1981b; 1987; Baack and Ray 1983).

In each of these models, elected officials are merely intermediaries carrying out the wishes of groups or sectors. Indeed, many models do not explicitly consider the role of politicians in making trade policy. Those that do mention the political process implicitly assume that if politicians fail to carry out the wishes of their constituents, voters replace them with others who will. More veritable models incorporate the costs that producers incur in petitioning politicians. As mentioned above, free-rider problems may limit the effectiveness of industry lobbying. These models can be divided into two groups: cross-sectional studies of industry organization and business cycle theories.

Pressure group models assume that import-competing industries favor protection because the resulting higher prices bring income gains. However, although all import-competing industries would like the government to restrict imports, they differ in their ability to effectively lobby politicians. A number of cross-sectional studies have examined the industry characteristics that raise or lower the costs of lobbying and thus their ability to secure benefits. These characteristics include labor intensity (Vaccara 1960; Travis 1964; Basevi 1966; Cheh 1976; Baldwin 1985), capital intensity (Ray 1981b), industry size (Pincus 1975; Caves 1976), geographical concentration (Caves 1976; W. Hansen 1990), unionization (Ray 1981a), and market competitiveness (Caves 1976; Ray 1981b).[4]

A related model argues that whether an industry receives protection is the result of offsetting pressures. This model looks at the influence consumers, or producers that use these goods as input, have in resisting tariffs. In this respect, the offsetting pressure group model is more subtle than those that assume that only producer interests are organized to influence policy. For example, O'Halloran and Noll (1991) recognize that upstream producers have

---

4. For an overview of this literature see Lavergne 1983, Baldwin 1985, Nelson 1988, Magee, Brock, and Young 1989, and Marks and McArthur 1990.

a strong incentive to push for lower tariffs on imports used in their production process. The offsetting pressures model predicts that protectionism occurs most in sectors menaced by foreign competition and lacking strong international ties (Destler and Odell 1987; Milner 1988). Empirical tests of this hypothesis find that commodities higher in the processing chain (that is, final goods sold directly to consumers) receive higher levels of protection than primary or intermediary goods (Stern 1973; Finger and Laird 1987; Laird and Yeats 1990).

In addition to varying cross-sectionally among industries, levels of protection also vary over time. Most economists agree that pressures for protectionist trade policies are related to cyclical changes in the domestic economy. Business cycle models take this into account by relating aggregate economic conditions to levels of protection.[5] Because of the organization and information costs associated with obtaining import relief (e.g., costs of lobbying, campaign contributions, etc.), industries have a limited ability to secure political benefits. It follows, then, that industries will demand higher levels of protection as income gains increase and the costs of lobbying decrease. During times of economic downturns, these models predict that industries will expend more resources to petition politicians for higher tariffs and that during times of economic prosperity they will invest fewer resources because income gains are relatively low. The tariff level thereby moves counter-cyclically to the business cycle (see McKeown 1984; Gallarotti 1985; Cassing, McKeown, and Ochs 1986; Wallerstein 1987).[6]

Takacs (1981) provides one of the first empirical tests of this hypothesis. Using the number of import injury cases before the International Trade Commission (ITC) as a measure for protective pressures, she finds that cyclical movements in aggregate economic activity, as captured either by the unemployment rate or capacity utilization, is a significant determinant of the demands for protectionism. Feigenbaum, Ortiz, and Willett (1985) find further empirical support for Takacs's conclusion that the well-being of the domestic economy is a significant determinant of protectionist pressures, but they assert that the strength of this relationship may be less than originally supposed.

One comprehensive time series study is by Magee, Brock, and Young

---

5. For a general statement of the effects of this model on policy see Kramer 1971, Nordhaus 1975, and Alesina and Sachs 1988.

6. Other scholars reach similar conclusions by a slightly different line of reasoning. The tariff cycle argument can also be motivated by industry and worker entry and exit. Since rates of entry into a sector are positively related to its growth rate, entry will be less during a depression than during prosperity. Pressures for protection then increase and decrease with the ease with which benefits can be captured during a depression as well as profitability of exiting a troubled sector. Thus, the attractiveness of exit in prosperous times undercuts the benefits to lobbying for protection, while the lack of an exit option in times of economic distress increases the benefits to political action.

(1989), who examine U.S. tariff policy from 1900 to 1988. They expand the interest group model by postulating that economic pressures are channeled through the party of the president. Their model assumes that Democrats represent labor, which is used more intensively in import-competing industries that benefit from protective tariffs. Republicans represent capital, which is used more intensively in export-oriented industries that favor free trade. Thus, Republican presidents enact higher tariffs than their Democratic counterparts.[7]

According to Magee, Brock, and Young's analysis, political parties cater solely to the interests of lobbying groups, with one party representing protectionism and the other free trade. Thus, political parties serve as a conduit for interest group demands and have no independent effect on policy: lobbying interests are monolithic and the parties serve one group consistently over time. Although their analysis is an important first step toward placing parties in the tariff debate, their treatment of the political process does not explicitly consider the possibility of coalition building within parties and fluctuations in these coalitions from election to election. In essence, then, Magee, Brock, and Young's conclusions are similar to those of the economic models, where policy is determined only by interest group demands.

The economic models are useful in that they provide a theoretical basis for the link between constituents' interests and policy outcomes. Yet these models tend to speak interchangeably of interests and voters, without clearly distinguishing between the resources pressure groups have (money) and those that voters have (votes). Moreover, by focusing only on constituency preferences, pressure group models overlook the political institutions that allow certain groups access to the decision-making process at the expense of others and shape the way in which these interests become policy.

2.2. Delegation Models

Whereas economic models focus on pressures exerted by interest groups, the political models focus on the institutional arrangements that give rise to protectionism or free trade. Termed presidential dominance (Moe 1984) or perhaps more accurately delegation models, these theories hold that members of Congress and the political interests that they represent play only a minor role in policy formation and predict that trade policy is strongly colored by the preferences of the president. The most extreme view of this model assumes that the president has appropriated power, while others cast the president's power in the context of *delegation* from Congress.

The strong version of a presidential dominance model, what Schlesinger

---

7. For an overview of this literature see Nelson 1988.

(1973, 403) calls the Imperial President, asserts that the executive dominates the decision-making process. Proponents of this version, such as Robinson (1967), Schlesinger (1973), and Margolis (1986), assume that the president can take actions independent of Congress. Margolis (1986, 47) states that

> presidents do use executive agreements to avoid having to get a treaty passed by a two-thirds majority in the Senate. Executive agreements have become the tool by which our government conducts foreign policy. . . . Hence, the treaty process, the Constitution's main safeguard against presidential excess in foreign policy, is no longer much of a restraint.

Margolis further argues, along with Neustadt (1960) and Sundquist (1981), that the other main control Congress has over executive actions, the power of the purse, has weakened. Thus, in pursuing foreign policy objectives, the president is both willing and able to subvert the wishes of Congress. This claim that the president has appropriated power over trade policy is examined more thoroughly in chapter 5.

A more sophisticated version of the presidential dominance model recognizes that Congress retains some control over trade policy (Pastor 1980; Finger, Hall, and Nelson 1982; Destler 1986a; Goldstein 1986; 1988; Haggard 1988). Similar to the economic models, this line of reasoning holds that Congress is strongly influenced by the protectionist pressures of special interest groups. But unlike the economic models, they realize that Congress has incentives to delegate authority to the president to circumvent these pressures.

To avoid disastrous political logrolls like that of the 1930 Smoot-Hawley Tariff Act, legislators granted the president authority over trade policy-making and thereby insulated themselves from protectionist demands. Destler (1986a), for instance, argues that Congress legislated itself out of the business of making product-specific trade laws when it passed the 1934 Reciprocal Trade Agreements Act (RTAA). Instead of setting tariffs item by item, members protected themselves from interest group demands by delegating authority to the executive. According to this view, the president, who has a national constituency, is less susceptible to the kind of particularism (product-specific protectionism) to which Congress is notoriously prone and thus implements fewer protectionist trade measures than does Congress. This argument is consistent with figure 1.1, which shows that U.S. protectionism peaked in the early twentieth century when Congress set tariffs individually and declined precipitously after the mid-1930s when Congress delegated its trade policy-making authority to the president.

By delegating authority to the president and executive agencies, legislators can shirk the blame for damaging administrative decisions while retaining their right to criticize foreign countries and the administration on behalf of disaffected constituents (Bauer, Pool, and Dexter 1963, 456). According to this logic, trade policy-making is characterized as a "cry-sigh cycle" (Pastor 1980). First, there is the cry of protectionism when legislators introduce restrictive trade bills or amendments. But then a sigh of relief follows with the passage of a liberal trade law, which originates from the president and benefits the economy overall. Pastor (1983) argues that such delegation has worked to the advantage of the United States because congressional committees and individual legislators are more interested in sending signals than in making policy. This decision-making process allows the United States to pursue liberal trade policies without holding members of Congress directly accountable to constituents injured by import competition. Legislators can thereby "claim credit" as a champion of the disaffected without having to deliver on their threats (Mayhew 1974).

Delegation models recognize that Congress does retain some power to make trade policy legislation, but they argue that legislators have very little desire to use it. Destler (1986b, 97) asserts that Congress is the very opposite of "the power-hungry force racing to protect particular industries, and that its members typically have wanted more executive branch aggressiveness on trade than have successive chief executives." Overall, Congress is seen as being relatively far removed from actual decision making: legislators serve only to constrain or act as public critics of executive action. But they cannot alter the policy outcomes, and "can only occasionally succeed in forcing the Executive's attention to the need for a change in policy, and hardly ever in developing and securing the adoption of an alternative policy on its own" (Hilsman 1958, 729).

Presidential dominance scholars agree with the pressure group model that legislators are influenced by protectionist demands. They are also more realistic than the economic models in their treatment of the political process, correctly recognizing that Congress has incentives to delegate authority. However, they see the 1934 RTAA as a watershed, whereby Congress was able to free itself from unwanted interest group pressures. For example, Destler (1986a, 19) focuses on the United States Trade Representative as a broker among interests that uses his or her leeway to promote liberal trade policies. Goldstein (1988) asserts that the delegation of authority from Congress to the executive branch limits direct congressional involvement in the decision-making process and thereby allows agencies such as the ITC to pursue free trade despite rising demands for protectionism. Haggard (1988) similarly argues that in passing the RTAA, Congress created a "strong state," which allowed the executive branch to pursue aggressive free trade policies.

Though the presidential dominance scholars are astute in their analysis of executive decision making, to understand trade policy one must first understand how much authority the executive branch has vis-à-vis Congress. I argue that while Congress has delegated considerable authority to the president, it retains much power over trade policy. Whereas presidential dominance scholars are likely to take institutions of delegation as a given, I regard them as an object of continual choice. Over the years Congress has at times expanded and at other times contracted the degree of delegation to the executive branch. The question then becomes under what conditions Congress delegates authority, when it constrains the use of this authority, and how this delegation affects policy outcomes.

2.3. Toward a More General Theory of Interests and Institutions

Interest group models clearly capture an important aspect of trade policy formation, but they are unable to explain the secular decline in the tariff described in figure 1.1. Unless business faces more impediments to organizing now than it did in the pre–World War II era, it is difficult for pure pressure group models to explain the decline in tariffs in the last half century. Presidential dominance models are, however, able to explain this downward trend in the tariff through their emphasis on shifting institutional structures. Without question, the 1934 RTAA marked a shift in power between Congress and the president regarding trade policy, and this shift coincided with lower tariffs. But it is unclear that this delegation implies complete congressional acquiescence to the executive branch. There are indications that Congress still exercises significant authority over trade policy.

Table 2.1 shows that, far from being disinterested observers, members of Congress continue to introduce and enact numerous trade bills. In the Ninety-fourth Congress, for example, members of the House of Representatives introduced 388 trade bills, reported 20 out of committee, and enacted 10 public laws. The bottom row of table 2.1 indicates that trade bills reported out of committee have about a 42 percent chance of becoming law, as compared to the 50 percent chance of any bill being enacted. These numbers suggest that trade legislation is treated like any other policy area on the House floor. In addition, as will be discussed in chapter 5, nearly 85 percent of all international agreements and 72 percent of trade agreements are enacted through statutory authority delegated by Congress to the president. Thus, at the least, Congress has some say in the enactment of almost all international trade agreements.

Furthermore, if legislators delegate authority to the president to absolve themselves of their constitutional responsibility to enact trade laws, then one would expect Congress to pay little attention to the institutions by which trade policy is made. The history of American trade legislation reveals, however,

TABLE 2.1. Congressional Activity on Trade Bills, 1967–88

Congress	Total Trade Bills[a]		Total Trade Bills Reported[d]		Trade Bills That Became Law		All Bills Reported That Became Law	
	Number[b]	Percent[c]	Number	Percent	Number	Percent	Number	Percent
90 (1967–68)	1063	5.16	26	2.44	13	50.00	1002	50.5
92 (1971–72)	386	2.24	18	4.66	7	38.89	768	46.9
94 (1975–76)	388	2.45	20	5.15	10	50.00	729	40.7
96 (1979–80)	255	3.01	31	12.16	10	32.25	736	47.0
98 (1983–84)	309	4.79	19	6.15	6	31.57	677	56.5
100 (1987–88)	457	8.18	17	3.72	9	52.94	761	67.0
Average	476.3	4.68	21.8	4.58	9.17	42.06	778.8	50.2

Source: Coded from the United States House of Representatives, *Calendars of the United States House of Representatives and History of Legislation* for the 90th–100th Congresses.

[a] I define trade bills as only those bills that directly affect the flow of imports and exports. The statistic does not include domestic legislation that indirectly affects imports, such as labeling requirements.

[b] The total number of bills includes all pieces of trade legislation. Some of these bills may be identical, similar, or a companion bill to another. But because there is no systematic method of eliminating possible redundancy, I include all pieces of trade legislation introduced.

[c] The percent of all trade bills introduced is the ratio of trade bills over the total number of bills introduced in the House of Representatives. The total number of bills introduced also includes similar, identical, and companion bills.

[d] All trade bills reported from the House committee for consideration by the committee of the whole.

that Congress invests an enormous amount of time and energy in defining the rules that govern executive actions. These rules include setting limits on tariff-cutting authority, retaining the right to veto presidential trade proposals, and, as the 1988 Omnibus Trade and Competitiveness Act shows, transferring authority away from presidents when they fail to respond to congressional demands (O'Halloran 1993).

Moreover, both the interest group and standard delegation models ignore the role of partisanship. U.S. tariff policy in the late nineteenth and early twentieth centuries is acknowledged to have been highly partisan (O'Halloran 1992). On the other hand, Destler (1986a; 1991, 255) and Baldwin (1988) argue that there is little impact of party divisions on trade policy in the postwar era. One reason why trade policy is often identified as a nonpartisan issue is the emergence of institutional arrangements that appear to isolate legislators from the free trade or protectionist demands of partisan constituencies. Nonetheless, there do seem to be consistent partisan effects in the shaping of trade legislation. For example, table 2.2 shows that, on average, from the Ninetieth to One-hundredth Congresses over 80 percent of all trade bills that became public law in the House of Representatives were introduced by a member of the majority party (the Democrats). Congressional voting on trade bills has also shown markedly partisan voting patterns over time. The 1988 Omnibus Trade and Competitiveness Act was adopted by a vote of 312 to 107, with only 2 Democrats voting against the bill. In the Senate the act was adopted by a vote of 63 to 36, with all but 1 Democrat voting in favor. The 1991 House resolution to disapprove the extension of fast track authority to the North American Free Trade Agreement was denied by a vote of 192 to 231, with only 21 Republicans voting in its favor. It would thus appear that congressional politics creates some partisan effects over the introduction and passage of trade legislation.

At the very least, the above evidence suggests that a number of behavioral patterns are inconsistent with the view that Congress has legislated itself out of the business of making trade policy. Although Congress delegates some authority to the president, it continues to monitor the use of this authority closely and to play an active role in shaping legislation. What is needed, then, is a theory of the political control of policy through, not in spite of, delegation.

My approach to understanding trade policy centers on the role that Congress plays in determining outcomes. It examines the institutional setting within which policy is made and, further, the constituent demands that lead legislators to design these institutions. It differs from the interest group model in that trade policy is not simply a register of pressures; rather, demand is mediated through political parties and other political institutions. My approach differs from the presidential dominance model in that I do not view

TABLE 2.2. Partisan Control of Trade Legislation, 1967–88

Congress	Majority Party	Trade Bills Reported[a]	Trade Bills Reported Introduced by Majority Party[b]	Trade Bills That Became Law	Trade Laws Introduced by Majority Party	Percentage of Trade Laws Introduced by Majority Party
90 (1967-68)	Dem	26	23	13	11	84.60
92 (1971-72)	Dem	18	13	7	6	85.71
94 (1975-76)	Dem	20	13	10	5	50.00
96 (1979-80)	Dem	31	26	10	9	90.00
98 (1983-84)	Dem	19	19	6	6	100.00
100 (1987-88)	Dem	17	14	9	9	100.00

Source: Coded from the United States House of Representatives, *Calendars of the United States House of Representatives and History of Legislation* for the 90th-100th Congresses.
[a] Total trade bills reported from a House committee for consideration by the committee of the whole.
[b] All trade bills reported out of committee whose primary sponsor was a member of the majority party. The bill could have multiple sponsors. Cosponsors are not necessarily from the same party as the primary sponsor.

institutional arrangements as a given. Instead, they are malleable, shaped in part by constituent demands, and designed by legislators to achieve political ends. Nor do I emphasize the autonomy of the executive branch, but rather the specific institutions that constrain executive decision making. By focusing on the incentives of elected officials, the fundamental role of constituencies, and the importance of institutional features, I hope to construct a realistic, Congress-based approach to trade policy-making.

CHAPTER 3

American Politics and Trade Policy

The distance which separates the ideal from the real is . . . a rough measure of the influence of the process of making law on the policy. It follows that legislation cannot be understood apart from the manner in which it is made.

—E. E. Schattschneider, *Politics, Pressure, and the Tariff*

This chapter introduces some of the basic concepts of the New Economics of Organizations (NEO) and applies them to the study of trade policy. NEO defines institutions in terms of collective choices made by rational actors and analyzes the effect these institutions have in shaping policy outcomes. Although NEO in itself cannot necessarily produce a unique set of predictions, it can help clarify complex relations and integrate disparate viewpoints into a coherent framework.

My purpose in this chapter is twofold. First, I show how the apparently conflicting theories detailed in the previous chapter may be accommodated in a single unifying approach. Second, employing a series of spatial models, I derive propositions about U.S. trade policy-making that I test in subsequent chapters.

In section 3.1, I review the basic concepts used in NEO analysis. The second section examines the relation among constituency interests, political parties, and policy outcomes. The third section details the type of collective dilemmas that can arise among reelection-oriented legislators and explains why Congress would delegate its authority to solve these problems. Section 3.4 discusses how Congress designs the procedural arrangements that govern the delegation of authority, and then it explores the effect these procedures have on trade policy outcomes. The last section summarizes my conclusions.

3.1. New Economics of Organizations: An Overview

NEO emphasizes the importance of institutions and procedures in determining policy outcomes. Two questions arise repeatedly throughout the analysis:

1. What motivates legislators to design institutions?
2. How do these institutions shape policy outcomes?

To analyze the relationship among actors, institutions, and outcomes, many NEO proponents employ formal mathematical models complete with theorems and proofs of their propositions. Other NEO analysis is presented less rigorously, but with more scope for detail. In either case, the object is to lay bare the essential dynamics of policy-making and the role of rational individuals in designing institutions and acting within them. The result of this analysis should be a series of testable propositions that can be confirmed or refuted by empirical evidence.

NEO begins with the assumption that political actors have policy preferences and take actions or choose strategies that allow them to achieve their preferred outcome. Often the range of possible policy alternatives is represented as points on a one-dimensional line or in a multidimensional space. In this case, we assume that actors' preferences can be derived from a unique point in that space that they prefer to all others. This is referred to as their "bliss" point or "ideal" point. Knowing the preferences of all actors, however, reveals little about the policies they enact, unless the process by which policy is made is also known. The setting in which these interactions occur is called an institution. In politics, typical institutions are the House of Representatives, an election, or the Supreme Court. Thus, an emphasis on structure and process is one of the distinguishing features of NEO analysis.

In some cases, the policy-making process is imposed from the outside; for instance, the Constitution provides a basic set of rules for decision making within the government.[1] But sometimes the structure of decision making is itself an object of choice. In these cases, the analysis must go one step deeper to explain why rational actors would design such an institution. For example, each chamber of Congress chooses the committees' jurisdictions, the structure of party leadership, and its own rules of parliamentary procedure. Some procedures are not codified as official rules, and most of those that are codified can be changed by a majority vote.

Recent insightful investigations into legislative organization have focused on these questions of institutional choice. Whether their emphasis is informational (Krehbiel 1991) or distributive (Kiewiet and McCubbins 1991), these authors agree that procedures arise to solve some specific inefficiency in the legislative process. In an informational setting, legislators delegate authority to committees with specialized knowledge to reduce uncertainty in policy outcomes. In a distributive setting, legislators delegate authority to committees to facilitate the division of benefits among members. Both lines of research emphasize that legislators carefully consider the terms of delegation

---

1. Of course, the Constitution itself can be changed; however, extraordinary majorities are necessary to do so. For many analyses then it makes sense to take certain rules as given, although there is a valid point that no institution is ever set in stone.

and that these arrangements may change over time. For example, as the complexity in the policy-making environment increases, informational theories predict that Congress delegates more authority to committees (Krehbiel 1991).

Thus, one of the central tenets of NEO is that institutions matter: the process by which policy is made affects outcomes. The relation between institutions and outcomes can be subtle, however, for procedures may have a profound effect even if they are never invoked. For example, even though Congress has never voted to reject a trade proposal submitted under fast track implementing procedures, the threat of a veto may still constrain the president's actions. To avoid a possible veto, a rational president will accommodate congressional demands rather than risk Congress's rejecting an agreement altogether. This phenomenon raises a typical problem of *observational equivalence*. The lack of congressional activity may signify congressional acquiescence, or it may signify that the president has been forced to compromise in order to avert congressional action. Therefore, to understand the impact that institutions have on outcomes, we must examine the reasons for their design and closely analyze their effect on the course of policy-making.

The strength of NEO lies in its ability to disentangle and clarify the effects of procedures on policy outcomes. I adopt this approach because I contend that the procedures that shape trade policy have been inadequately analyzed. Although the more prominent procedural innovations, such as fast track and the Reciprocal Trade Agreements Act, have been given some attention, these delegations of authority are usually seen as evidence that Congress has relinquished its control over trade policy to the president. By using an NEO approach, I hope to show that matters are not so simple. If procedures have a significant effect on outcomes, and if these procedures are ultimately designed by Congress, one must first carefully consider why Congress chooses these institutions, under what conditions Congress will change the terms of delegation, and to what extent these institutions will influence policy.

3.2. Preferences and Policy Outcomes

What motivates legislators to take the actions they do? Following a tradition that dates back to Mayhew (1974), I assume that the origins are electoral. Since being reelected is a prerequisite to enjoying the advantages of office, so the argument goes, incumbents logically make this their primary goal. Further, each congressman has, in the language of Weingast and Marshall (1988), a "politically relevant" portion of their constituency. These are the constituents or interests that make significant campaign contributions, lobby for specific policies, and vote consistently and often. Congressmen can increase their chances of reelection by designing policies to benefit these constituents. This

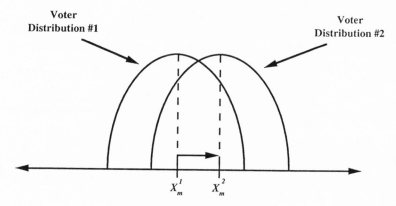

Fig. 3.1. Median voter model

assumption of electoral motivations thus serves as a basis for deriving legislators' preferences over policy outcomes (Fenno 1978).

The argument above implies that constituent demands play a key role in the formation of legislators' preferences. As I discussed in the previous chapter, this assumption is the cornerstone of the pressure group model. Whether the relevant constituency is interest groups or voters, pressure group models predict that changes in the median constituent's preferences[2] translate directly into changes in policy, as illustrated in figure 3.1. Suppose there is a change in constituency preferences represented by a move from voter distribution 1 to voter distribution 2. This change in preferences shifts the ideal point of the median voter from X_m^1 to X_m^2. Consequently, the interest group model predicts that policy shifts from X_m^1 to X_m^2.

Much of the discussion in this book centers on congressional responses to pressure group demands. In my approach, interest groups do play a central role. But one of the central tenets of NEO is that institutions as well as preferences influence policy outcomes. It is erroneous simply to assume then that interest group demands will necessarily be codified directly into law, even if their representatives are eager to cater to these interests. One of the key insights of early social choice theory is that preferences are not immediately translated into policy; outcomes also reflect the method by which these interests are aggregated.[3]

---

2. Whenever decisions are made by majority rule, the median voter casts the decisive vote in determining policy outcomes. Thus, most NEO studies of voting behavior are usually framed in terms of the actions of the median voter.

3. The whole question of preference aggregation is the province of social choice theory. For classic references see Arrow 1951; Plott 1967; McKelvey 1976; and Schofield 1978.

For instance, interest group pressures may be channeled through political parties. If the parties take distinct positions on an issue and enact these platforms when elected to office, then certainly the party that controls government will have an important influence on policy, as in figure 3.2. Again, suppose there is a change in voter preferences from voter distribution 1 to voter distribution 2, shifting the median voter's ideal point from X_m^1 to X_m^2. But notice that this change in the median voter's ideal policy crosses the midpoint between the two parties, $(P_1 + P_2)/2$. Assuming that constituents vote for the party whose platform is closest to their ideal point, a new majority party is elected, Party 2. Accordingly, policy outcomes now change from the platform of the first party, P_1, to the platform of the second, P_2.[4] This policy change is more dramatic than that in figure 3.1, even though the same change in preferences motivated it.[5]

Figure 3.2 shows that policy may respond to shifts in partisan control as well as constituency demands. When strong parties take divergent positions on an issue, a change in the majority party will magnify changes in constituent preferences. This can be summarized by:

PROPOSITION 1: *Changes in the preferences of the median voter that result in a new party taking office will lead to changes in policy outcomes above and beyond that explained by changes in the median voter alone.*

In chapter 4, I argue that tariff policy in the era after Reconstruction until 1934 had these characteristics. The Democrats consistently advocated free trade while the Republicans were protectionist, and each shift in partisan control of national government was followed by a revision of the tariff schedule. Thus, even though the median of all voters determined which party would hold office, tariff rates may not have exactly reflected the interests of the

---

4. Formally, if X_m^1 moves a distance greater than $[(P_1 + P_2)/2 - X_m^1]$, then policy in period 2 is P_2; otherwise, it is P_1.

5. Note that if the median voter's preferences had *not* crossed the midpoint, then no policy change would have resulted despite the shift in voter preferences. See O'Halloran 1992 for a more detailed discussion of this model. The astute reader may have noticed that this model is predicated on the two parties taking different positions on an issue. Baron (1991a) also examines this process of choosing platforms and concludes that parties will take different positions on those issues with particularistic benefits; that is, those characterized by distributive politics. Baron's model is formulated in the context of two candidates and a single policy issue, but it can be easily extended to the case of two parties competing along multiple dimensions. In equilibrium, party platforms represent tradeoffs between votes and contributions, and platforms will diverge most on issues with highly mobilized and affluent interest groups. One implication of the model is that an increase in interest group contributions will cause the parties to adopt more extreme positions. (See Baron and Mo 1991 for another model in which politicians take separate positions on issues in order to attract contributions.)

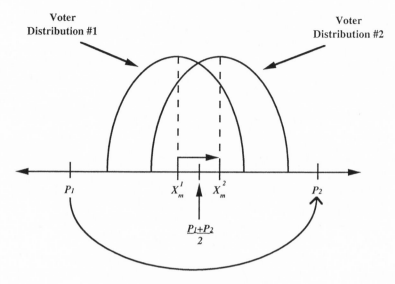

Fig. 3.2. Party model

median voter.[6] If the theory outlined above is correct, changes in the tariff in this period should respond to changes in partisan control of government as well as changes in constituent demands.

The discussion above motivates an appreciation for the role of political institutions, particularly those that aggregate preferences, in determining outcomes. To acknowledge that constituent demands shape legislators' preferences does not imply that congressmen are simply held captive to special interests. Indeed, legislators sometimes design institutions specifically to avoid the problems generated by excessive interest group pressures: the topic to which we now turn.

3.3. Distributive Politics, Collective Dilemmas, and Delegation

Legislators are motivated by their desire to satisfy their politically relevant constituents. If benefiting one legislator's constituents necessarily entails depriving other districts of some benefits, then we call this distributive politics. Legislative decision making in a distributive setting, however, may lead to inefficiencies. This section investigates the origins of these inefficiencies and one possible solution to them widely discussed in the NEO literature, the delegation of authority to some outside agent.

---

6. This is one point of Brady's (1988) analysis of critical elections.

3.3.1. Collective Dilemmas

One of NEO's central insights is that, in certain situations, individually rational actions can lead to a collectively irrational outcomes. Known generally as collective dilemmas, this class of problems includes the tragedy of the commons (e.g., G. Hardin 1968), the prisoner's dilemma (e.g., Taylor 1987), and the free-rider problem (e.g., R. Hardin 1971). It also covers problems associated with distributive politics, which I discuss below.

To develop some intuition for the logic of collective dilemmas, consider the tragedy of the commons, which is constructed as follows. Imagine a common on which the village herdsmen keep animals. Each herdsman is assumed to act rationally to maximize his own gain. As long as the total number of animals is below the "carrying capacity" of the common, a herdsman can add an animal to his herd without affecting the amount of grazing of any of the other animals. But beyond this point, the tragedy of the commons takes over as the common begins to be overgrazed. Each herdsman is now confronted with the decision as to whether he should add another animal to his herd. This decision entails both potential gains and losses. A herdsman obtains the benefit from adding an additional animal to his herd, but because there is now overgrazing, his gain from each animal is reduced. The benefit received from the additional animal is concentrated; all profits go to the herdsman. On the other hand, the cost of overgrazing is shared by all; each herdsman suffers a slight loss. Thus, the benefit to the individual herdsman is greater than his loss, and he therefore adds the animal to the common. Following the same reasoning, each herdsman continues to add to his herd until the ability of the common to support livestock collapses entirely.[7]

The legislative equivalent to the tragedy of the commons is pork barrel politics on distributive issues. In this setting, a large bill is constructed in which every legislator gets to benefit his constituency. Naturally, each legislator is eager to get his share of the proverbial pie. Collectively, however, each member is made worse off. The process works as follows. Each member has a set of constituents that could benefit from a particularistic policy. Since enacting this policy would hurt other districts (i.e., through increased taxes), the legislator cannot persuade others to support his individual proposal. Each legislator, having similar preferences, also prefers to benefit his own district at the expense of everyone else. Thus, each legislator acting individually is unable to pass his proposal, as a majority is required. This situation creates a potential for gains from trade if legislators can cooperate with one another by constructing a bill with many projects in it—one for each district. The political science literature has identified a number of mechanisms that facilitate this

---

7. A more technical presentation of these arguments is provided in appendix 3.1.

trade: for example, norms of reciprocity (Fiorina 1981), deference (Shepsle and Weingast 1987a), and universalism (Weingast 1979) all enable members to cooperate.[8]

In solving one dilemma, however, legislators may create another. Policymaking characterized by logrolling can be inefficient; too many proposals can be included in the final bill, to the detriment of all constituencies. This logic of runaway logrolls has been applied to the study of public works projects (Ferejohn 1974) and the inability of Congress to control overspending (Shepsle and Weingast 1984). Thus, similar to the tragedy of the commons, reelection-minded legislators can collectively produce policies that are inefficient for the country as a whole.

The relevance of this theory to trade policy is readily apparent. Each member of Congress prefers less restrictive overall trade policy, except, of course, on those articles whose imports adversely affect his constituents. Given the distributive nature of trade policy, however, no one legislator can individually achieve these outcomes. One natural solution is a logroll. But, as in other areas of distributive politics, the dangers of unrestrained universalism can be disastrous. The prime example is the 1930 Smoot-Hawley Tariff Bill, in which Congress revised tariffs on 3,221 items, leading to the highest tariff rates of the twentieth century. Although every member of Congress was able to protect some interest in his district or state, the overall result was to deepen the Great Depression. In response to this episode of democracy running amok, Congress delegated tariff negotiating authority to the president in the 1934 Reciprocal Trade Agreements Act.

3.3.2. Delegation as a Solution to Collective Dilemmas

One solution to the negative consequences that commonly arise when Congress passes distributive policies is to delegate policy-making authority to someone without strongly distributive preferences. In trade policy, the natural choice is the president, who, having a national constituency, is in a better position to weigh the overall costs and benefits of protectionism. In the language of economics, when authority is delegated from one actor to another, we call the actor delegating power the principal and the actor receiving power the agent. Thus, congressional delegation of authority to the executive is one example of a principal-agent relationship. If the incentives of principals and agents are perfectly aligned, then the agent will enact the principal's most preferred policy, and the problem is solved. In practice, however, no perfect agent may exist. For example, whenever Congress delegates authority to the

---

8. Baron (1991b) is able to motivate super-majoritarian logrolls in a noncooperative setting.

executive branch, the preferences of the president will often diverge to some extent from those of Congress.

The problem of structuring principal-agent relations when there is a conflict of interests is subtle and complex. The difficulty is that information costs and conflicting interests create the potential for "agency losses" through a combination of hidden action and hidden information. Hidden action (shirking) occurs when a principal is unable to observe an agent's actual behavior after the contract has been entered into. Hidden information (slippage) occurs when a principal is unable to observe the information, beliefs, and values on which an agent bases a decision. The problem the principal faces, then, is how to design procedures, or create incentives, that constrain the actions of the agent in the least costly manner available to ensure that the actions taken by the agent yield, as close as possible, the desired outcome. Given its emphasis on procedure, principal-agent theory fits neatly into the overall views of NEO.

The design of principal-agent contracts is currently one of the most active areas of economic theory. Holmström (1979) explores the optimal sanctions to be levied against an uncooperative agent. Alchian and Demsetz (1972) examine the motivations behind hiring a single manager to oversee a firm and discuss the problems associated with monitoring the manager. Tirole (1986) looks at a multilevel hierarchy of principals and agents and derives conditions under which lower levels in the hierarchy might collude against the upper levels. Demski and Sappington (1987) investigate the optimal amount of information a principal should require of an agent when there are transaction costs involved in communication. And Kanodia (1987) derives optimal surprise inspection schedules to keep agents in line.[9]

The application of formal principal-agent models to the study of politics dates back to Niskanen (1971). He argues that the delegation of authority leads to "runaway bureaucracy." In the absence of effective oversight, bureaucratic agents are likely to pursue personal goals derived from private political values, career objectives, or maximization of agency budgets, instead of those preferred by Congress. Fiorina (1982) takes a similarly pessimistic view of delegation, noting that when Congress delegates authority to the bureaucracy, it retains a veto over bureaucratic decisions. Legislators can thereby enhance their reelection chances by shifting the blame for unpopular decisions to the bureaucracy and claiming credit for fixing bureaucratic miscues.

In recent years, studies of bureaucratic decision making have examined the Federal Trade Commission (Weingast and Moran 1983), the Environmental Protection Agency (McCubbins, Noll, and Weingast 1989), and the appro-

---

9. For an excellent overview of the diverse literature that addresses agency problems and their solutions see Fudenberg and Tirole 1991.

priations process (Kiewiet and McCubbins 1991), to name but a few. They investigate congressional delegations to the bureaucracy and the various tools Congress uses to limit agency losses. The most extreme position is articulated in the "congressional dominance" hypothesis advocated by Weingast (1979) and Weingast and Moran (1983). This model focuses on constitutional (structural) features, such as the powers of the purse and impeachment, that give Congress a veto over executive actions. Proponents of this model also place importance on the more subtle means by which Congress influences the decision-making process. Congress creates safeguards, defined in administrative procedures, such as reporting requirements and public hearings, to ensure that the actions taken by the agent reflect its members' electoral considerations (McCubbins and Schwartz 1984). As a result, congressional dominance theorists assert that executive agents are perfectly constrained and policy looks as if Congress itself had made it.

There is a large literature within political science, less extreme than the congressional dominance approach, that also examines the relation between distributive politics and delegation, especially delegation to congressional committees (Mayhew 1974; Weingast and Marshall 1988; Shepsle and Weingast 1987a; 1987b). By assigning each committee a policy jurisdiction, and allowing committee members freedom to set policy within their issue area, Congress can institutionalize logrolls without falling prey to the dangers of unrestrained universalism discussed above. The point of most of this literature, then, is to motivate absolute delegation to committees, thereby ensuring that cooperative outcomes can be supported within an institutional framework.

In contrast, I argue that when dealing with the executive branch, Congress delegates limited authority in order to solve the problems created by legislative logrolls, and this insight helps explain trade policy in the modern era. My approach assumes that the mechanisms by which authority is delegated are a constant object of congressional concern. In some cases Congress will extend the degree of delegated authority and in others it will decrease this authority, but delegation is never absolute. In this respect, my approach has much in common with legislative informational theorists, who emphasize partial delegation and argue that the median floor voter is better off when committees have some degree of procedural control over the bills they consider (Gilligan and Krehbiel 1987; 1989; Epstein 1992).

At the least, these arguments suggest that the decision to delegate is not the final word. Indeed, it is only the first of many decisions about how the delegation will be structured: what types of constraints and monitoring will be associated with it, and what types of procedural checks will Congress have on policy outcomes? Congress has to perform a delicate balancing act; it wants to delegate in order to overcome its own collective action problems, but it does not want to abdicate power completely to an agent whose preferences differ from its own. It is one of the central arguments of this book that trade policy can be best understood as a series of congressional decisions on the scope and nature of the power Congress delegates to the executive branch. I do not go as far as congressional dominance theorists in insisting that Congress always gets its way; after all, one central reason for delegating authority is to make policy different from what Congress would have passed on its own. But I do recognize that Congress has the constitutional authority to regulate commerce, and therefore any executive authority in this area is delegated authority and should be analyzed as such.

3.3.3. Delegation and the Design of Institutions

I now apply the logic of the New Economics of Organizations to study the design of trade institutions in more detail. As mentioned above, if a principal could find a perfectly representative agent, she could obtain her ideal outcome by delegating completely to the agent. One corollary to this observation is that the greater the difference in preferences between the principal and agent, the less authority will be delegated.

If we take partisanship as a proxy for preferences, then the implications for trade policy are clear. Congress will delegate more power to a president of the same party than to a president of the opposing party, and when there is split partisan control of Congress, the degree of delegation will be somewhere in between.[10] This leads to the following proposition:

PROPOSITION 2A: *Congress will delegate more authority, the closer are the preferences of the president to those of its members.*

This proposition is stated in terms of the amount of authority Congress is willing to delegate to the president in a certain issue area. The flip side of this proposition is the corollary that the more power Congress delegates to the president, the more constraints it will place on the use of that delegated authority.[11] The difference between the two points of view lies in their conceptualization of the delegation process. The first starts with no presidential power and asks how much authority Congress is willing to cede him. The second assumes that some power will be delegated and asks in which ways Congress will limit the president so as not to give him complete authority. Either way, presidents with preferences that diverge from those of Congress have less impact on final policy outcomes than those with more similar preferences.

---

10. See Lohmann and O'Halloran 1994 for a model that explicitly motivates partial delegation as a means to avoid the inefficiencies that arise from distributive politics.

11. This is the view adopted in McCubbins 1985.

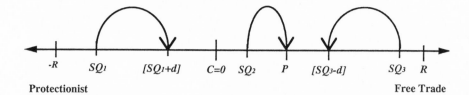

Range	Outcomes	Example
$SQ \leq P\text{-}d$	$SQ + d$	SQ_1
$P\text{-}d \leq SQ \leq P\text{+}d$	P	SQ_2
$P\text{+}d \leq SQ$	$SQ - d$	SQ_3

Fig. 3.3. Discretionary authority and policy outcomes

I argued above that in the area of trade policy, Congress delegates author-ity to the president in order to overcome unrestrained logrolling. The presi-dent is assumed to be less protectionist than Congress simply because he has a national constituency and is less susceptible to particularistic demands. Over-all, then, the chain of reasoning is as follows. The greater the divergence of preferences between the president and Congress, the less authority will be delegated. The less authority that is delegated, the closer outcomes will be to the congressional norm of protectionism. This implies:

PROPOSITION 2B: *Protectionism will be higher the less discretionary authority delegated to the president.*

A simple model motivating Propositions 2A and 2B is shown in figure 3.3. The line drawn represents trade policies measured from highly protec-tionist (left) to free trade (right). The president's ideal point is labeled P, and Congress's ideal point, C, is set to zero. Notice that P is to the right of C, indicating that the president prefers freer trade than does Congress. Suppose that the order of moves is as follows. Congress delegates to the president the power to change policy by some fixed amount d; then the degree of delegation is measured by the magnitude of d.[12] The case where $d = 0$ corresponds to no

---

12. For instance, if Congress prefers not to make policy on a case-by-case basis, it may delegate to the president the power to change tariffs by up to some fixed amount. This arrange-ment is basically the one adopted by the RTAA.

delegation, and setting $d = \infty$ corresponds to congressional abdication. After this decision is made, the state of the world, SQ, is revealed. I term this the "status quo," because it is the policy that would result if the president took no action or if Congress delegated no authority. I assume that there is some uncertainty about SQ at the time of congressional delegation; SQ is uniformly distributed in the range $-R$ to R. After learning the true state of the world, the president can move policy up to a distance d from SQ.

For instance, assume Congress has delegated power d to the president. If the status quo is extremely protectionist, like SQ_1 in figure 3.3, then the president will use the full extent of his authority to promote freer trade. If the status quo involves more free trade than the president would like (SQ_3), then the president will make policy more protectionist. In either of these cases, both Congress and the president profit.[13] However, there is a range of status quo policies, such as SQ_2, for which the president will use his authority to Congress's detriment, moving policy closer to his ideal point and further from that of Congress. This range narrows as congressional and presidential preferences become more similar, and it disappears altogether when they overlap. Thus, Congress faces a tradeoff when deciding how much discretionary authority to delegate to the executive. Legislators want to give the president enough authority to correct for extremely high or low levels of protection, but not so much authority that he dominates policy-making. It can be shown that Congress solves this optimization problem by giving the president more authority over trade policy the more nearly their preferences coincide; and greater authority leads to less protectionism. (See appendix 3.2 for mathematical details.)

The implication of this analysis for trade policy-making is clear. Congress will delegate some power to the executive, but it will abdicate its authority only if its preferences overlap perfectly with those of the president. Although Congress may not always be able to get its ideal point, it will design procedures to limit the president's actions. And as the preferences of the president diverge from those of legislators (i.e., during times of divided government), Congress delegates less authority. Chapter 5 examines the history of delegation in trade policy both through case studies and econometric analysis. Consistent with Propositions 2A and 2B, it shows that Congress carefully structures its delegations of authority and that the amount of delegation decreases as partisan conflict between Congress and the president increases.

---

13. Interestingly, in the case represented by SQ_3, both Congress and the president would be made better off if the president enacted his ideal point. However, because legislators have committed to the delegation rule d, the president is constrained to implementing $[SQ_3 - d]$.

3.4. Procedural Constraints and Policy Outcomes

One of the central arguments of my analysis is that political actors design procedures to affect outcomes. Sometimes the effect of these institutions is obvious; for instance, the ability to negotiate tariff levels or veto trade proposals may have direct effects on policy. In other cases, the effect of procedures is not so obvious, such as the role of public hearings or incorporating interest groups into the decision-making process. Using the framework outlined above, we can identify the conditions under which institutions do or do not constrain the actions of the president, even when direct observation of these influences is difficult. In general, the impact of particular procedures depends on the relative preferences of the actors and the initial status quo policies. Many authors observe qualitatively different outcomes, such as the president dictating the terms of an international agreement in one period or Congress constraining the president in the next, and take this as evidence that a major shift has occurred in trade policy-making. I argue that such changes may be the manifestation of a single institution under differing initial conditions.

One specific procedural constraint imposed on executive authority is the right of Congress to reject presidential proposals, otherwise known as an ex post veto. Since it is one of the key elements in current fast track procedures for negotiating and implementing trade agreements, it merits closer examination. Under this rule, Congress cannot always obtain its preferred policy, but in certain circumstances it can force the president to accommodate congressional demands. This leads to:

PROPOSITION 3: *Procedural constraints (i.e., an ex post veto) imposed by Congress may limit the president's discretionary authority and force him to accommodate congressional demands.*

Figure 3.4 represents the same situation as figure 3.3. Congress's ideal point is C, and the president's ideal point is P. If we again set Congress's ideal point to zero, then the point $-P$ represents the mirror image of the president's preferred outcome. Further, suppose that while Congress has given the president authority to negotiate trade agreements, it has nonetheless constrained the president by an ex post veto. That is, presidential proposals require the support of a majority of Congress. The discussion that follows replicates Romer and Rosenthal's (1978) analysis of committee power under a closed rule, adapted to the context of trade policy.

To examine the effect of procedures on policy outcomes, figure 3.4 reports the results of a comparative statics exercise, whereby the status quo moves from extreme to intermediate values. If the status quo takes on extreme

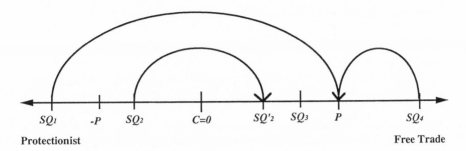

Range	Outcomes	Example
$SQ \leq -P$	P	SQ_1
$-P \leq SQ \leq C$	$C + (C\text{-}SQ) = -SQ$	SQ_2
$C \leq SQ \leq P$	SQ	SQ_3
$P \leq SQ$	P	SQ_4

Fig. 3.4. Ex post vetoes and policy outcomes

values, for example, SQ_1 or SQ_4 in the figure, then the president can get his preferred outcome. Since Congress prefers the president's ideal point to the status quo, it will not reject the president's proposal of P. The ability to make a take-it-or-leave-it offer here allows the president to implement his preferred policy. Under these conditions, it appears as if the president dominates the decision-making process.

If the status quo takes on intermediate values, however, then the president's discretionary authority is limited. This constraint can appear in two ways. First, if the status quo is between $-P$ and C, as represented by SQ_2, then the president can obtain outcomes closer to his ideal point, but will be forced to accommodate congressional preferences to some extent. The president proposes a policy equal to SQ'_2, so that Congress becomes indifferent between accepting his proposal and the status quo. Here the president is able to obtain outcomes closer to his ideal point but is forced to make some concessions to Congress. Second, the president's authority is constrained when the status quo is between C and P, like SQ_3 in the figure. Here the president is unable to change policy at all because Congress will not accept any movement away from its ideal point. This is the case of legislative stalemate, where it appears that the president is completely frustrated by an opposing Congress.

This comparative statics exercise shows that under some conditions the president seems to dominate the decision-making process, in some cases Congress partially constrains the president's authority, and in other cases the president is unable to effect any policy change due to congressional opposition. Thus, the same delegation regime can take on very different appearances depending on the location of the status quo relative to the players' preferences.

One of the implications of this analysis is that one cannot easily infer back from policy outcomes to the relative influence of Congress vis-à-vis the president in the policy-making process. The analysis shows that under some conditions Congress is able to thwart the actions of the president. In other instances, the president is able to implement his ideal policy with little congressional interference, as suggested by the presidential dominance hypothesis. Neither case alone proves anything. What the analysis does show is that to explain complex relations between political actors, one must clearly understand the procedural arrangements that govern policy-making and their effect on outcomes. In chapter 6, I examine fast track procedures and show how the structure of the decision-making process influenced the negotiation and implementation of the U.S.-Canada and the North American Free Trade Agreements.

3.5. Conclusion

Most of the literature on trade policy argues that Congress is a vehicle for special interests or subservient to an all-powerful executive. I assume that legislators' preferences are shaped by the interests that they represent but that policy outcomes are the result of a complex interaction between preferences and the institutions that aggregate them. In the chapters to come, I show that in the post–World War II era Congress delegated a significant amount of authority to the president. But Congress, always vigilantly observing how this power is used, has been willing to diminish the president's authority, at times, as well as increase it. In sum, my approach acknowledges that both the interest group and presidential dominance schools capture important aspects of the truth. By integrating these theories into a broader framework, though, I show that trade policy is more difficult, more obscure, and at the same time more interesting than either of these simpler models suggest.

This chapter outlined an NEO approach to understanding the relation between political parties, Congress, the president, and trade policy. The rest of the book provides empirical support for the propositions advanced above. Chapter 4 explicitly tests the argument that early tariff policy was determined by pressure group demands. I show that interest group pressure clearly affected policy, but the political parties that aggregate preferences also played a significant role. Chapter 5 demonstrates that when Congress delegates authority over trade policy to the president, it designs procedures to constrain the use of this authority. Further, I show that the president is more constrained under divided government than under unified government and that these constraints have a significant effect on trade policy. Chapter 6 investigates how one particular procedural innovation, fast track authority, influences policy. It details fast track procedures and examines their effect on recent free trade agreements.

APPENDIX 3.1

The tragedy of the commons can be formally represented as follows. Suppose there are N individuals. Each individual has the choice of contributing or not contributing to the production of a collective good, and every unit contributed produces an amount of the public good with benefit r. The total benefits produced are divided evenly among all individuals. Further suppose that it costs one unit of effort to contribute.

If m other individuals contribute, an individual gains utility mr/N if he does not contribute, and

$$\frac{(m + 1)r}{N} - 1$$

if he does. A rational individual will contribute to providing the collective good when the gains from contributing exceed the gains from not contributing. This implies that:

$$\frac{(m + 1)r}{N} - 1 > \frac{mr}{N};$$

$$\frac{(m + 1)r}{N} - \frac{mr}{N} > 1;$$

$$\frac{mr}{N} + \frac{r}{N} - \frac{mr}{N} > 1;$$

$$\frac{r}{N} > 1.$$

Thus, an individual is better off contributing *if and only if* his individual gain (r/N) exceeds his individual cost (1). When

$$\frac{r}{N} < 1,$$

therefore, independent of the value of m, an individual's dominant strategy is not to cooperate. Since all individuals reason in the identical manner, no one contributes at all. Each individual prefers that the rest of society pay the cost of providing the collective good, while he reaps the benefits.

Appendix 3.2

This is a formal presentation of the model outlined in Propositions 2A and 2B. Assume there are N issue areas, each one-dimensional, and that Congress's ideal point in each issue area is $C_i = 0$, for $i = 1, \ldots, N$. Further, assume that ex ante the status quo SQ_i in each issue is unknown, and that Congress's priors over SQ_i are uniform in the $[-R, R]$ interval.

The president has an ideal point $P_i > 0$ in each dimension, and positive outcomes are associated with greater degrees of free trade. The assumption that $P_i > 0$ for all i can be motivated by the president's having a national constituency and thus less protectionist preferences than does Congress. Both the Congress and president have quadratic preferences[14] over outcomes:

$$U_C(x) = -(C - x)^2 = -x^2;$$

$$U_P(x) = -(P - x)^2.$$

The game is played as follows. First, Congress gives the president the authority to move outcomes up to an amount d in each dimension. Next, nature reveals the status quo policies SQ_i. The president then chooses final outcomes according to the powers given to him by Congress. He is thus constrained to implementing a policy p such that $|SQ - p| < d$.[15] It is immediately apparent that the president will choose final outcomes according to the rule:

$$x = \begin{cases} SQ + d & \text{if } SQ \leq P - d; \\ P & \text{if } P - d \leq SQ \leq P + d; \\ SQ - d & \text{if } P + d \leq SQ. \end{cases}$$

In choosing d, Congress maximizes its expected utility across dimensions, which is equivalent to solving

$$\max_d EU_C = -\int_{-R}^{P-d} (SQ + d)^2 \frac{1}{2R} dSQ - \int_{P-d}^{P+d} P^2 \frac{1}{2R} dSQ - \int_{P+d}^{R} (SQ - d)^2 \frac{1}{2R} dSQ$$

$$= \frac{-R^3 - 3P^2d + 3R^2d - 3Rd^2 + d^3}{3R}.$$

14. Although quadratic preferences display risk aversion, the results derived below are identical to those where risk neutral preferences are employed.

15. Alternatively, the model could be formulated as follows. Suppose there is a status quo (ω), which is unknown when the game begins. The president may implement any policy p such that $|p| < d$. Then outcomes are given by $x = p + \omega$, the standard setting for games with incomplete information.

To find the optimal amount of discretion d that Congress gives the president, we solve

$$\frac{\partial EU_C}{\partial d} = 0$$

$$\frac{(P + R - d)\,(P - R + d)}{R} = 0.$$

This equation has two solutions: $d = R - P$ and $d = R + P$. Given our assumption that $P > 0$, $d^* = R - P$ is the appropriate choice. Since $\partial d^*/\partial P < 0$, as the president's ideal point diverges from Congress's ideal point he will be given less authority to set policy. At the extremes, when $P = R$, the president has no authority ($d^* = 0$), and when $P = C$, the president has complete authority ($d^* = R$). Furthermore, expected outcomes are

$$E(x) = \int_{-R}^{P-d} (SQ + d)\,\frac{1}{2R}\,dSQ + \int_{P-d}^{P+d} P\,\frac{1}{2R}\,dSQ + \int_{P+d}^{R} (SQ - d)\,\frac{1}{2R}\,dSQ$$

$$= \frac{Pd}{R}\,.$$

Since this expression rises with d, outcomes move toward freer trade as the president is given more authority.

CHAPTER 4

Preferences, Parties, and Tariff Policy

American tariff history is the account of an unsuccessful attempt to set up a beneficently discriminating set of privileges, resulting in legislation so indiscriminately broad as to destroy the logic and sense of the policy. The very tendencies that have made the legislation bad have, however, made it politically invincible.

—E. E. Schattschneider, *Politics, Pressure, and the Tariff*

Schattschneider characterizes the view of most scholars examining pre-1934 tariff policy. Sundquist (1981) argues, for example, that the tariff, more than any other single topic, engrossed congressional energies, that American tariff policy was a paradise for pressure groups, and that protectionism and high tariffs were the rule, not the exception. According to this argument, prior to the mid-1930s policymakers were held captive by politically influential pressure groups whose influence peaked in a notoriously disastrous political logroll, the 1930 Smoot-Hawley Tariff Act. As discussed in chapter 2, this reasoning derives from the pressure group theory of public policy. As the constituency preferences of the median member become more or less protectionist, so too do policy outcomes.

As argued in the previous chapter, however, by focusing on constituency preferences, interest group models minimize the impact of the institutions, such as political parties, that aggregate group demands. The purpose of this chapter is to test Proposition 1, which states that changes in the preferences of the median voter that result in a new party taking office will lead to changes in policy outcomes above and beyond that explained by changes in the median voter alone. Thus, in a competitive political system with strong parties, a shift in partisan control may bring a dramatic change in policy (see fig. 3.2).

The chapter first briefly reviews the history of tariff legislation from the beginning of the Republic through 1934. According to Proposition 1, partisan effects should be most easily discernible when the parties take strong opposing stances on the tariff. Historically, preferences regarding the tariff have been geographically determined. Thus, partisan effects should be most apparent when electoral support for the parties is also sectionally divided. The

45

following historical overview shows that at first the tariff served mainly as a source of revenue and was not a major point of contention between the parties. In the period leading up to the Civil War, the tariff became more of a partisan issue. But because the electoral support for the Whigs and Democrats crossed geographic regions, swings in the tariff did not correlate strongly with control of national government. After the Civil War, however, the parties arrayed themselves for the first time along sectional lines. These divisions corresponded with sentiments on the tariff, and consequently clear partisan effects were visible. The Democrats favored low tariffs, the Republicans favored high protective tariffs, and whenever a new party controlled national government, a major overhaul of tariff schedules followed.

I next present an econometric test of the proposition that partisan control of government is a significant determinant of the tariff. To test this prediction, I examine U.S. tariff policy in the period after Reconstruction to 1934, a time when the tariff was a central distributive issue in American politics. I detail the data and estimation techniques used in the analysis and then present my empirical findings. My results concur with the economic model's prediction that policy responds to interest group demands, but I also show that even when Congress is most susceptible to these pressures, political parties none-theless have a significant independent effect on the tariff. The final section summarizes my conclusions.

4.1. History of Tariff Legislation: Revenue Raising vs. Protection

The debate over regulating foreign trade dates from the beginning of the republic. The delegates to the Constitutional Convention argued fiercely over how Congress would regulate commerce and navigation. Southerners feared that the North would try to prohibit the importation of slaves. This led Mr. Charles Pinkney of South Carolina to propose that "no act of the Legislature for the purpose of regulating the commerce of the United States with foreign powers, or among the several states shall pass without the assent of two-thirds of the members of each House" (Farrand 1911, 449). Given the division of interests between the North and South, Mr. Pinkney argued, "these different interests [will] be a source of oppressive regulation if no check to a bare majority should be provided" (Farrand 1911, 449). Although eight of the twelve states supported the two-thirds rule, Mr. James Madison of Virginia argued that "the power of foreign nations to obstruct our retaliating measures on them . . . would be less if a majority should be made competent than if two-thirds of each House should be required to legislate acts in this case" (Farrand 1911, 452). The northern and southern states eventually resolved the issue by a compromise. The North agreed to the temporary importation of slaves; the South conceded, in return, that navigation and commercial laws would pass by a majority; and treaties required the consent of two-thirds of the Senate. Thus ended the first of many political compromises surrounding the tariff.

4.1.1. The Tariff as Revenue

In the first years of the new Republic, the tariff was the main source of government revenues. Indeed, the first law enacted was the tariff act of July 4, 1789, introduced by Madison for the purpose of raising revenues and protecting industry. From 1821 to the beginning of the Civil War, nearly 85 percent of total government receipts were from custom revenues alone (see fig. 4.1). The other 15 percent were mostly from excise taxes on alcohol, tobacco, and stamps.

Early in the nineteenth century a protectionist movement reflecting strong regional concerns took root, leading to the passage of the tariff acts of 1824, 1828, and 1832. For example, the 1824 tariff act raised about 30 percent of the duties specified in earlier acts and added about 70 new ones (Pincus 1977). The stronghold of the protectionist movement at this time lay in the middle and western states: New York, New Jersey, Pennsylvania, Ohio, and Kentucky. They were the agricultural states, and the ones directly concerned with the development of a domestic market for their products. The New England states mostly opposed these protectionist demands. The mainstay of the New England economy at the time comprised importers, shipping merchants, and vesselers, who naturally rejected any measure that reduced the volume of foreign trade. Some support for the protective tariff, however, was found in New England among the nascent manufacturing interests that developed during the War of 1812. The southern states strongly opposed the protective system. Because manufactured goods were imported from Europe, a protective tariff would make these goods dearer. Moreover, the South had just begun to export cotton on a large scale, and it was feared that England, in retaliation for high duties on English goods, might tax or exclude American cotton.

During this period congressional voting on the protective tariff reflected these regional interests, with the western and middle states in support, the South in opposition, and New England divided (Stanwood 1903; Taussig 1931). Also during this time, the parties of John Quincy Adams and Andrew Jackson crystallized into the Whigs and Democrats. Adams and the Whigs favored the protective tariff; Jackson and the Democrats, representing a North-South coalition, had no settled policy on the tariff. There was thus no clear partisan division between protectionists and so-called free traders; consequently, the vote on the tariff ignored party lines insofar as they existed at the time (Pincus 1977).

Between 1832 and 1860 partisan competition began to affect tariff policy as the parties became more regionally based. The Whigs, predominantly from

**Fig. 4.1. Custom revenues as a percent of total federal receipts, 1821–
1960**

the northern and western states, passed the tariff act of 1832, a distinctly
protectionist measure. Congress levied high duties on cotton and woolen
goods, iron, and other articles that competed directly with American industries. On articles not produced in the United States, either low duties were
imposed, such as on silks, or no duties at all, as on tea and coffee. The debate
over the tariff reached a fever pitch during this time, with South Carolina
claiming the right to nullify federal acts, and threatening secession if the tariff
acts of 1828 and 1832 were not abolished.[1] Thompson (1888, 299) writes that
"the Union . . . was seriously threatened by the sectionalism incited by the
cotton-growers of South Carolina and . . . their inflammatory threats to se-
cede from the Union and destroy it."

---

1. For a discussion, see Schlesinger 1945.

An accommodation was finally reached when Senators Clay of Kentucky and Calhoun of South Carolina, the leaders of the protectionists and free traders, agreed to the Compromise Tariff Act of 1833. The act retained a considerable degree of protection for nearly nine years, and thereafter mandated a rapid reduction to a uniform 20 percent rate (Taussig 1931). This famous compromise masked the growing sectional differences over the tariff, but it could not remove the underlying tensions.

As it happened, the 20 percent duty remained in force for only two months, until Congress enacted the highly protectionist 1842 tariff act, which passed by a vote of 104 to 103 in the House.[2] The close margin of victory reflected regional concerns. In the House of Representatives, those Whigs who voted against the bill represented agricultural interests in western and southern states, while those Democrats who supported the protective tariff represented iron producing regions in Pennsylvania and New York. President Tyler finally signed the protectionist bill, but it did not reflect strong popular feeling as had the 1824, 1828, and 1832 protective measures. As congressional voting on the bill indicates, the farming states had lost enthusiasm for the home-market idea, and support for protection in the manufacturing states came directly from the producers rather than the public at large (Taussig 1931, 113).

In the late 1840s, the political climate began to change. Voting on the tariff switched from reflecting purely sectional interests to more partisan concerns. In 1846, the Democratic Congress led by President James K. Polk repealed the tariff law of 1842. The administration, in keeping with traditional Democratic statements, entered office pledging to lower duties. True to form, a new low-tariff bill passed the Senate by a vote of twenty-eight to twenty-seven. Before that, however, numerous amendments were introduced to raise or lower specific duties. Analyzing voting patterns, Silbey (1985, 36–37) finds that congressional support for the tariff shows a persistent cleavage along national partisan lines, rather than sectional divisions. Eighty percent of the Democratic senators consistently voted together for low tariffs, while 96 percent of the Whig senators similarly voted for high tariffs. In the House, over two-thirds of the Democrats voted in favor of a low tariff, and over 98 percent of the Whig representatives favored a more protective tariff (Silbey 1985, 37). The 1846 act remained in force until 1857, when a further reduction of duties was made.[3]

---

2. In fact, this was the third attempt by congressional Whigs to pass the tariff bill. President Tyler vetoed the previous two proposals because they included a clause regarding the sale of public lands. Unable to muster sufficient support to override the president's veto, the Whigs reintroduced the original bill, minus the offending provisions.

3. Act of July 30, 1846, 29th Cong., 9 Stat. 42. The act of 1846 established several schedules, indicated by letters A, B, C, D, and so on. All the articles in schedule A paid

From 1853 to 1861, the Democrats controlled the White House. The national platform of the Democratic party continued to articulate the position that the tariff should be no higher "than required to defray the necessary expenses of Government."[4] By 1856 the Whig party had nearly disappeared and was replaced by the Republicans, which adopted, for the most part, the Whig's mantel of protectionism. The 1860 Republican platform stated that although the party favored "revenue for the support of the general government by duties upon imports, sound policy requires such an adjustment of these imports as to encourage the development of the industrial interest of the whole country" (Porter 1924, 58).

The Republican party took control of national government in the critical election of 1860. With the collapse of the second party system and the rise of the Republicans, American political parties were for the first time divided on a purely sectional basis. The Morrill Tariff Act of 1861 reflected Republican, and thus Northern, sentiment on the tariff, and it began a trend toward higher duties. The act substituted specific for ad valorem duties. In many cases, the specific duties were considerably above the 1846 rate. The most distinctive change was the increase in wool and iron duties, by which the Republicans hoped to appease the eastern manufacturing regions (Pennsylvania) and some western states.

With the advent of the Civil War, no session passed without some increase in duties. From 1857 to 1867, Congress altered the tariff schedule over twenty-three times, thus increasing the average tariff from 20 to 44 percent of the value of total imports. Congress also increased internal taxes on alcohol, tobacco, manufactures, and stamps (including playing cards). This increase in excise taxes explains the drop in the tariff as a percent of total revenues during the early 1860s, as shown in figure 4.1.

The end of the Civil War brought demands for a reduction in both taxes and tariffs. The Republican Congress repealed or modified many of the internal taxes established during the war, but hesitated to reduce the tariff. Many industries that had benefited from the protective war tariffs depended upon their maintenance. As Taussig (1931, 173) stated, "the pressure from domestic producers was strong; the power of the lobby was great." As a result, Congress only moderately reduced tariffs in 1870 and again in 1872. Republican dominance of national government ensured that duties remained high despite large federal budget surpluses.

---

100 percent, all articles in schedule B paid 40 percent, all in schedule C paid 30 percent, and so on. Also see the Act of March 3, 1857, 35th Cong., 11 Stat. 192, which reduced the tariff levied in the 1846 act on goods classified in schedules A and B to 30 percent and reduced all other categories by 20 percent.

4. See Porter 1924, 5. Reprinted from the *New York Evening Express*, June 3, 1844, 1.

4.1.2. Party Politics and the Swing of the Tariff Pendulum

After the Civil War, the tariff became the litmus test for political affiliation. Grover Cleveland, in his 1887 presidential address, declared the tariff the most important issue of the day. The tariff continued to divide the political parties and defined the political debate for the next fifty years. Each election that brought a change of party also brought a comprehensive revision of tariff schedules. High tariffs were followed by low tariffs, which were succeeded by high tariffs. The acts of 1890, 1894, 1897, 1912, 1922, and 1930 were the direct result of federal elections. Each peak in the tariff rate was associated with Republican control of government and each trough with Democratic control of government.[5]

What is important to note is that in the post-Reconstruction period, sectional interests and partisan affiliation lined up almost one-to-one. Although partisan concerns existed before the Civil War, there was never a close correlation between regional interests and party. Northern and Southern interests were represented, to some extent, by each party. After the war, however, the parties did divide along regional lines. It so happened that these regions had opposing interests on the tariff, and consequently sectional and partisan differences on the tariff were reinforced. These are exactly the conditions under which Proposition 1 suggests that party will have a significant impact on policy.

During this period, changes in congressional procedure made it easier for the majority party to enact its platform once elected to office. The so-called Reed Rules, named after House Speaker Thomas Brackett Reed (R-Maine), made it impossible for minorities in the House to prevent a quorum from being established simply by not voting. Reed declared that minority members could be counted as "present but not voting," thus contributing to a quorum even if they cast no votes.[6] This and other procedural innovations gave the majority party leadership effective control over the legislative agenda, without which national party platforms could not be translated into policy.[7] The confluence of sectionally based parties and changes in legislative procedures

---

5. Moreover, Brady (1988) identifies the tariff as one of the major issues in the realigning election of 1896. For similar findings see Stewart 1991.

6. He also declared that the Sergeant at Arms could force minority members to be present. See Brady 1973, 24–26, and Galloway 1962, 131–35, for an overview of the Reed Rules and the events surrounding their enactment.

7. Reed was also a pioneer in the strategic use of committee appointments. In 1897 he postponed naming any standing committees until the Dingley Tariff Act was passed. As Hasbrouck (1927, 37) notes, the hope of good committee assignments was, of course, expected to

ensured that whenever a new party took office, tariff rates would change dramatically.

The sectional bases of the parties evident after the war remained remarkably stable throughout the post-Reconstruction period. The Republican party represented eastern manufacturing and some western agricultural regions, while the Democrats represented agrarian interests in the South. The producer interests in the Republican coalition depended upon the federal government for high protective tariffs. The Democrats viewed high tariffs as exploitative of the farmer and worker interests. Brady (1988, 54) argues that "the [Democratic] party's general stand on tariffs was embodied in one sentence: 'We hold that tariff duties should be levied for purposes of revenue, such duties to be so adjusted as to operate equally throughout the country, and not discriminate between class or section.'"

Clearly, there were other important issues during this period, such as coinage, federal pensions, the use of public lands, and prohibition. But even single-issue third parties, such as the Greenbacks and the Prohibitionists, found themselves having to position their issue with regard to the tariff. For example, the 1884 Greenback National Platform asserted that

> the question as to the amount of duties to be levied upon various articles of import has been agitated and quarreled over and has divided communities for nearly a hundred years. . . . While we favor a wise revision of the tariff laws, with a view to raising a revenue from luxuries rather than necessaries, we insist that as an economic question its importance is insignificant as compared with financial issues; for whereas we have suffered our worst panics under low and also high tariff, we have never suffered from a panic nor seen our factories and workshops closed while the volume of money in circulation was adequate to the needs of commerce.[8]

My historical account of this period begins with tariff fluctuations in the decade from 1887 to 1897.[9] In the Fiftieth Congress, the Democratic majority in the House introduced the Mills Bill, which proposed to reduce duties on numerous manufactures and place hemp, flax, lumber, and, most important of all, wool on the duty-free list. All but four Democrats voted for the measure, and the Republicans were unanimous in voting against it. Meanwhile, the Republican majority in the Senate prepared its own bill. The measure raised a

---

keep members "regular." This tactic was repeated in 1909 by Speaker Cannon to ensure the passage of the Payne-Aldrich Tariff bill and in 1913 by Speaker Clark to promote the Underwood Tariff Act.

8. See Porter 1924, 127. Reprinted from the *Chicago Tribune*, May 30, 1884, 6.

9. For an excellent review of partisan politics in this era, see Brady 1973.

considerable number of duties, especially on manufactures, finer cottons, and woolens. On a few articles concessions were made, but in the crucial case of wool, the Senate bill increased the 1883 rates (Taussig 1931, 254–55). In the end, the House and Senate reached a stalemate and no tariff bill was passed that session.

In the 1888 election, the Republicans once again opposed the policy of lower tariffs. The Republican platform of 1888 denounced the Mills Bill as "destructive to the general business, the labor and the farming interest of the country," and heartily endorsed "the consistent and patriotic action of the Republican Representatives in Congress in opposing its passage" (Porter 1924, 147).

On returning to power, with Harrison as president and a majority in both the House and the Senate, the Republicans enacted the protectionist 1890 McKinley Tariff Act, which set a maximum and minimum value for duties. The Republicans used every means at their command to protect domestic industries. For instance, at that time, the tariff schedules recognized three grades of wool. The lowest class of wool received only minimal tariffs because it was not produced domestically. United States producers of high-grade wool, fearful that cheap imports might be substituted for their products, convinced Congress to reclassify articles so that almost all woolens were categorized as high grade and received the maximum rate of duty. Tariffs on agricultural items were raised similarly. The act did, however, allow for the duty-free importation of sugar, molasses, coffee, tea, and hides.

The Republican defeat in the 1892 election led the Democrats to pass the 1894 Wilson "Free Trade" Act. Congress moderately reduced the tariff on most commodities, but removed the duty on wool altogether. The return of the Republicans to power in 1896 was followed by the highly protectionist tariff act of 1897 and higher protective duties. The 1909 Payne-Aldrich Tariff Act moderately revised duties downward and created the first Tariff Board to recommend tariff adjustments to the president (see chap. 5 for more details). Continued Republican control over national government throughout this period, however, assured that tariffs would remain high.

The Democratic presidential victory of 1912 ended fourteen years of consecutive Republican control. With President Wilson in the White House, the Democratic majority in the House and Senate dramatically reduced tariff rates by enacting the Underwood Tariff Act of 1913.[10] Every Democrat in the

---

10. The Democratic victory in the 1912 election was in part the result of the revolt of the Stalwart Republicans against the Speaker "Uncle" Joe Cannon (see Brady, Brody, and Epstein 1989). This break sheds some important insights into the politics of the tariff. At this time, the political parties shifted fundamentally their policies on key issues, such as taxes and federal pensions. There are several reasons why this shift may be important for tariffs. First, it coincides roughly with the outbreak of World War I. During this time, domestic industry faced little or no

House supported the measure except the four representatives from Louisiana. The Republicans were equally unanimous in opposing the move toward free trade: only six House Republicans supported the measure.

In the 1920 presidential campaign, the Republican party under Warren Harding reaffirmed its belief in protective principles and pledged itself to a revision of the tariff (Porter 1924, 460). After regaining control of both Congress and the presidency, the Republicans held true to their pledge and enacted the 1922 Fordney-McCumber Act (Taussig 1931, 489). One of the major factors influencing the 1922 tariff legislation was the attitude of western agricultural regions. In 1909 the agricultural interests were a moderating force in the Republican party's push for the protective tariff. However, the severe decline in agricultural prices after World War I led to strong protectionist demands. Representatives of the agricultural states also committed themselves to a high tariff, and in the end the protective system had been carried further than ever before. The Democrats declared the act to be "the most unjust, unscientific and dishonest tariff tax measure ever enacted in our history."[11] The Democrats soon had cause to revise this statement.

In 1930 Congress faced yet another debate over whether to increase or decrease the tariff. The Republicans controlled both houses of Congress and the presidency. Upholding his campaign pledge, President Hoover called a special session of the Seventy-first Congress to consider an agricultural relief program and modest tariff increases for depressed industries. By the time the Smoot-Hawley Tariff Bill reached the president's desk, tariffs on 3,221 items, affecting more than 25,000 imported commodities, had been revised. Interestingly, Congress raised duties on many goods, but only minimally, so that the composition of protection was not altered. Congress imposed new duties on manufactured goods, such as cotton, silk, and chinaware. On imported articles that competed directly with domestic industries, Congress had already carried the protective system so far that no further displacement of imports was expected (Schattschneider 1935, 16).

Clearly, the tariff issue had become alluring and, if played right, promised enormous political benefits. Republican dominance of national politics between the Civil War and 1932 can be attributed largely to the successful exploitation of the protective tariff. The Republican party attached itself to a formidable array of interests, including agriculture and industry, dependent upon the protective system and intent on keeping it (Schattschneider 1935, 29). But the tariff issue also condemned Congress to truly Sisyphean labor, endlessly repetitious and futile.

---

foreign competition. Second, and related to the prior point, western agriculture, instead of industry, became the thrust behind the protectionist movement. And third, Congress in 1916 passed the Internal Revenue Act. Thus, the tariff no longer served as the primary source of federal income.

11. Porter 1924, 479. Reprinted from the *Des Moines Register*, June 29, 1924, 1.

4.1.3. Summary

What are the lessons of the 1930 Smoot-Hawley Tariff Act? Schattschneider argues that Smoot-Hawley represents democracy run amiss. Under an electoral system of single member districts, legislators are highly susceptible to political pressures. Elected officials could resist these pressures if they were forced to, but they had little reason to take any risks. For Schattschneider (1935, 292), "party majorities in Congress are, therefore, like armies in which each captain is given full discretion to take all measures necessary to ensure the safety of his company." The Republicans had little choice but to succumb to protectionist pressures.

Constituents' demands undoubtedly influenced the behavior of elected officials. The foregoing historical discussion suggests, however, that more than interest group pressures alone drove the tariff. Political parties also seem to have played a pivotal role: after the Civil War each party took a distinct position on the tariff issue and enacted its platform when elected to office. If Proposition 1 holds true, then we should observe the tariff during this period responding not only to changes in aggregate economic conditions, but also to the party in control of national government. I now turn to an empirical test of this proposition.

4.2. Econometric Analysis

It appears that tariff legislation strongly reflected the influence of partisan affiliation in postbellum politics. Stanwood (1903, 389) argues, for example, that "all tariff acts have been to a large degree political measures, chiefly designed by their promoters to further the ends of party." Yet oddly enough, in most empirical studies of the tariff, party as an explanatory variable is ignored or found to be insignificant. Since economic models of the tariff assume that the party in office is either rewarded or punished for its overall economic performance, the pressure group approach asserts that all policy changes reflect constituency demands. Thus, the fact that a new tariff law ensued every time a new party took office could simply reflect changes in voters' preferences working through the party system. If so, political parties serve merely as a proxy for economic interests. Conybeare (1991), for instance, argues that once constituency interests are taken into account, party affiliation has no effect on tariff levels. Furthermore, Baack and Ray (1983) find little evidence that political parties had any influence on the tariff during the postbellum period and argue that production and market characteristics were the predominant determinants. Eichengreen (1989) asserts that the Smoot-Hawley Act resulted more from an unusual coalition of interest groups than from party politics. And McKeown (1984) even omits party entirely from his analysis of tariff levels from 1857 to 1914.

Although assertions that the tariff responds solely to economic conditions may seem convincing, there is a potential flaw in the analysis. The data used in most of these studies are cross-sectional; consequently, they are unable to systematically test the impact of party on tariff levels over time. The question of why some industries or regions receive more protection than others at a given point in time is different from the question of what impact changes in partisan control of government have on tariff rates from one period to the next.

This section provides empirical support for the hypothesis that partisan control of government is a significant determinant of the tariff exceeding that explained by interest group demands. Since Proposition 1 states that tariffs will respond to changes in party control over time, this section is based on time series analysis of economic conditions, political conditions, and tariff rates.

4.2.1. Data

The heyday of pressure group dominance over tariff policy occurred from 1877 to 1934. By all accounts, elected officials were highly susceptible to interest groups' demands for higher or lower tariffs during this period. The tariff figured prominently in national political debate and Congress set tariff schedules item by item.

For this period, I examine three estimates of the tariff, which are described in table 4.1 and shown in figure 1.1. The first measure is the average duty levied on dutiable imports (AVGDUTY), defined as the ratio of the duties collected to the total value of dutiable imports. As a general measure of protectionism, however, the average duty is insensitive to the possibility that a few articles may have received a very high tariff, while all others entered duty free.[12] A second measure of the level of protection is found by looking at the average duty levied on total imports (AVGTOTAL), defined as the ratio of duties collected to the total value of imports (dutiable and free).

The first measure shows, on average, how heavily dutiable imports are taxed. The second measure shows how heavily total imports are taxed. Thus, neither ratio alone indicates the degree of product-specific protectionism. But the *difference* between these ratios [AVGDUTY − AVGTOTAL], which I label AVGDIFF, does provide a useful measure. When a few products receive a very high tariff, the difference is large. When tariffs are more evenly distributed among commodities, the difference is small. In effect, AVGDIFF measures the degree to which the tariff burden is concentrated in a few imports.

---

12. In the late 1800s Congress taxed certain goods heavily. For example, in 1895 cotton manufactures received an ad valorem duty of 45 percent, wool manufactures received a rate of 57 percent, and metal manufactures received a rate of 45 percent. But coffee, tea, and sugar were imported duty-free. See U.S. Department of Commerce, *Statistical Abstract* 1912, table no. 257.

This variable thus indicates if the tariff is being used for revenue or protection. If the purpose of a tariff is to raise revenue, then all goods should be taxed until their marginal rates of return equate. According to this scheme, the tariff rate imposed on a specific commodity depends on its elasticity of demand. The more inelastic the demand for a good, the higher the tax. If the tariff burden is concentrated in a few goods, noted by a large difference

TABLE 4.1. Descriptive Statistics of Aggregate Trade Data, 1877–1934

Variable Name	Description	Mean	S.D.
AVGDUTY	Duties collected as a percent of the value of dutiable imports.	42.2%	7.9%
AVGTOTAL	Duties collected as a percent of the value of total imports.	21.3%	7.5%
AVGDIFF	The difference between the average duty on dutiable imports and the average duty on total imports, [AVGDUTY–AVGTOTAL].	20.9%	5.8%
GNP	Gross National Product in billions of 1982 dollars.	354.3	175.3
REPUBLICAN	Dummy variable equal to 1 if the Republicans control both a majority in Congress and the presidency; 0 otherwise.	0.48	0.50
DEMOCRAT	Dummy variable equal to 1 if the Democrats control both a majority in Congress and the presidency; 0 otherwise.	0.18	0.38
DIVIDED	Dummy variable equal to 1 if neither party controls a majority in Congress and the presidency; 0 otherwise.	0.34	0.48
REPGNP	The cross-product of REPUBLICAN and GNP.	192.9	235.6
DEMGNP	The cross-product of DEMOCRAT and GNP.	72.0	166.7

Sources: Tariff Data—U.S. Bureau of the Census (1975), *Historical Statistics of the United States,* Series U 207–12; and U.S. Bureau of the Census, *Statistical Abstract* (1876–1964). Political Data—U.S. Bureau of the Census (1975), Series Y 204–10. Economic Data—Balke and Gordon (1989) and Kuznets (1946).

between the average duty on dutiable imports and the average duty on total imports, then tariffs serve purposes other than revenue raising.[13]

Several weaknesses of these statistics should be noted. First, a full measure of protection would also include the value of imports discouraged by the tariff rate and the duties foregone because of lost imports—that is, the price elasticity of demand. For example, if tariffs are so protective that imports are forestalled totally, then no duties are collected, but neither are any dutiable imports sold. Second, the average duty on dutiable and total imports, as well as their difference, is affected by changes in duties collected and by changes in national income. Thus, there are two ways for the ratios to decrease: when the demand for dutiable imports decreases *relative* to the demand for nondutiable or free imports, and when the actual tariff rate decreases.

To avoid the problem of separating changes in demand and changes in the tariff ratios, I disaggregate the data and calculate the average duty levied on sixteen commodity-specific groupings. These commodities comprise the principal classes of imported dutiable merchandise used for consumption during the sample period. Table 4.2 describes these variables.

If the pressure group or business cycle models are correct, then slowdowns in economic growth cause producers to increase their demands for protection from foreign imports, to which politicians respond by enacting higher tariffs. One proxy for constituent demands is the real Gross National Product (GNP).[14] These models predict that changes in national income are negatively correlated with demands for tariffs.

The model presented in chapter 3 suggests that partisan control of government also plays a central role in policy formation. To capture this effect, I introduce two party control variables. DEMOCRAT indicates that the Democrats control both a majority in Congress and the presidency. REPUBLICAN indicates that the Republicans control both a majority in Congress and the presidency.[15]

The sample period contains twenty-eight Republican and ten Democratic governments. The effects of the party control variables are measured against twenty observations of divided government. The average duty levied on dutiable imports is 39 percent when the Democrats control government as opposed to 43 percent when the Republicans control government. These statistics

---

13. This assumes that the differences in elasticity of demand are not sufficiently large to account for the differences in tariff rates. See J. Hansen 1990 and Baack and Ray 1985 for a discussion of the tariff as tax policy.

14. See appendix 4.1 for a discussion of this variable.

15. Usually, Congress requires at least a year to pass and enact legislation. Because of the delay between when a new Congress takes office and when a policy takes effect, I lagged the party control variables by two years. For instance, the Republicans gained control of Congress in 1888 and passed the McKinley Tariff Act in October, 1890.

concur with the preceding historical discussion and reinforce the expectation
that, on average, Republicans increase and the Democrats decrease the tariff.

4.2.2. Estimation

I next present three equations that define the relation among economic conditions, political parties, and policy outcomes. These equations are estimated by

TABLE 4.2. Descriptive Statistics of Commodity-Specific Trade Data, 1877–1934

Variable Name	Description	Mean	S.D.
AGRI[a]	Agricultural products and provisions	27.3%	7.9%
CHEM	Chemicals, oils, and paints	29.2	6.2
CHINA	Earths, earthenware, and glassware	46.9	7.5
COTTON	Cotton manufactures	40.5	8.8
FLAX[b]	Unmanufactured and manufactures of flax, hemp, and jute	33.4	9.6
METAL	Metals and metal manufactures	35.4	8.0
PAPER	Pulp, paper, and books	22.7	3.2
SILKS	Silks and silk goods	52.0	5.5
SPIRITS	Spirits, wines, and other beverages	65.6	16.6
SUGAR	Sugar, molasses, and sugar manufactures	59.7	29.8
SUNDRY	Luxury articles like lace, embroideries, etc.	29.3	6.3
TOBACCO	Tobacco and tobacco manufactures	83.8	20.3
WOOD	Wood and wood manufactures	18.3	3.7
WOOL[c]	Wool and wool manufactures	59.1	14.0
RAWWOOL	Wool (unprocessed)	42.0	6.3
MANWOOL	Manufactures of wool	78.1	14.4

Source: U.S. Bureau of the Census, *Statistical Abstract* (1876–1964).
[a]For 1877 to 1889, the tariff rate was calculated from a weighted average of bread-stuffs and fruits.
[b]For 1877 to 1889, the tariff rate was calculated from a weighted average of manufactured and unmanufactured imports of flax.
[c]For 1877 to 1889, the tariff rate was calculated from a weighted average of manufactured and unmanufactured imports of wool.

least squares, correcting for both heteroskedasticity and autocorrelation. As the series tests positive for a unit root, the equations are estimated in first difference form.[16] (See appendix 4.2 for details.) These three equations are estimated for each of the three dependent variables, making nine estimations in all.

The first equation characterizes the business cycle or pressure group model. It estimates the change in the tariff by a constant term and the change in GNP:

$$\Delta Y_t = \alpha + \beta_1 \Delta GNP_t + \epsilon_t. \tag{4.1}$$

In this simple regression equation, β represents the estimated coefficient, α the constant, and ϵ_t the error term associated with each year.

The second equation tests the proposition that partisan control of government has a significant effect on the tariff in addition to changes in national income. Equation 4.2 introduces into the standard economic model the political control variables, REPUBLICAN and DEMOCRAT:

$$\Delta Y_t = \alpha + \beta_1 \Delta GNP_t + \beta_2 \Delta REPUBLICAN_t$$

$$+ \beta_3 \Delta DEMOCRAT_t + \epsilon_t. \tag{4.2}$$

Equation 4.2 presumes that the mean level of protection depends on changes in GNP and partisan control of government. The equation further assumes that parties tend to raise or lower tariffs at the same rate regardless of economic conditions (that is, the slope of the tariff equation does not vary with GNP). If Proposition 1 is correct, the coefficients of the political variables should be significantly different from zero.

Another way to distinguish partisan effects is to examine not only how much the mean level of protection changes (the intercept), but also how responsive tariff levels are to changes in GNP (the slope) when there is unified partisan control. A third equation that explains changes in aggregate tariff levels, then, includes an interaction between party control and changes in national income:

$$\Delta Y_t = \alpha + \beta_1 \Delta GNP_t + \beta_2 \Delta REPUBLICAN_t + \beta_3 \Delta DEMOCRAT_t$$

$$+ \beta_4 \Delta REPGNP_t + \beta_5 \Delta DEMGNP_t + \epsilon_t. \tag{4.3}$$

Equation 4.3 introduces two new variables, REPGNP and DEMGNP, which are simply the cross-products of changes in national income and the party variables. These variables can be interpreted as follows. What is the

---

16. This functional form is similar to that used by Gardner and Kimbrough (1989).

effect of a one unit change in GNP on the tariff level when the Republicans control government? I label this effect REPGNP. The variable DEMGNP holds exactly the same interpretation for Democratic control of national government. In this model, the reference group is DIVIDED. That is, the effect of unified partisan control on the tariff is measured from the baseline of when neither party controls both Congress and the presidency.

4.2.3. Results

Tables 4.3 through 4.5 show the results of estimating the tariff measures by

TABLE 4.3. **Partisan Effects on AVGDUTY**

Dependent Variable: Average Duty as a Percentage of Dutiable Imports

Independent Variables	Model 1	Model 2	Model 3
Constant	0.40	0.39	0.38
	(0.83)	(0.99)	(1.04)
ΔGNP	-0.048	-0.045	-0.047
	(-2.83)**	(-2.83)**	(-2.89)**
ΔREPUBLICAN		1.10	-1.28
		(1.19)	(-0.88)
ΔDEMOCRAT		-6.47	-1.18
		(-3.59)**	(-0.39)
ΔREPGNP			0.0087
			(2.12)**
ΔDEMGNP			-0.016
			(-1.73)**
No. Observations	58	58	58
R^2	0.12	0.36	0.41
D.W. Statistic	1.36	1.68	1.87
Wald Test ~χ^2		14.29**	27.41**
REP-DEM		3.74**	

Note: t-statistics in parentheses. Standard errors are White heteroskedastic-consistent estimates.
* $\alpha < .10$. ** $\alpha < .05$.

equations 4.1, 4.2, and 4.3. The findings reported in column 1 of each table indicate that GNP is negatively and significantly correlated with changes in AVGDUTY, AVGTOTAL, and AVGDIFF at the 5 percent significance level. Column 1 in the tables shows that a one unit increase in GNP decreases the tariff rate from about 0.015 to 0.05 percent, depending on the measure. These findings support the economic model's hypothesis that policy responds in a predictable way to interest groups' demands. That is, as economic activity declines, the level of protection increases.

TABLE 4.4. Partisan Effects on AVGTOTAL

Dependent Variable: Average Duty as a Percentage of Total Imports

	Model 1	Model 2	Model 3
Independent Variables			
Constant	-0.11	-0.049	-0.065
	(-0.42)	(-0.21)	(-0.28)
ΔGNP	-0.015	-0.019	-0.018
	(-1.75)**	(-2.16)**	(-1.93)**
ΔREPUBLICAN		1.69	2.14
		(3.00)**	(2.01)**
ΔDEMOCRAT		-1.51	-2.23
		(-2.16)**	(-1.19)
ΔREPGNP			-0.0016
			(-0.47)
ΔDEMGNP			0.0020
			(0.45)
No. Observations	58	58	58
R^2	0.05	0.21	0.21
D.W. Statistic	1.51	1.73	1.67
Wald Test ~ χ^2		13.91**	14.68**
REP-DEM		7.75**	

Note: *t*-statistics in parentheses. Standard errors are White heteroskedastic-consistent estimates.

* $\alpha < .10$. ** $\alpha < .05$.

Equation 4.2 tests the hypothesis that partisan control influences the aggregate tariff rate *above* the effect of changes in national income. Column 2 of tables 4.3 through 4.5 shows the results. The Democrats lower all measures of protection. For example, a switch from divided to Democratic control decreases the average duty on dutiable imports by about 6.5 percent. On the other hand, the only significant coefficient for the Republicans occurs when

TABLE 4.5. Partisan Effects on AVGDIFF

Dependent Variable: Difference between Average Duty on Dutiable Imports and Average Duty on Total Imports

Independent Variables	Model 1	Model 2	Model 3
Constant	0.50	0.51	0.51
	(1.35)*	(1.56)*	(1.62)*
ΔGNP	-0.033	-0.031	-0.034
	(-2.95)**	(-2.96)**	(-3.07)**
ΔREPUBLICAN		1.04	-0.83
		(1.10)	(-0.58)
ΔDEMOCRAT		-4.40	-2.51
		(-2.93)**	(-0.65)
ΔREPGNP			0.0069
			(1.43)*
ΔDEMGNP			-0.0055
			(-0.61)
No. Observations	58	58	58
R^2	0.10	0.28	0.31
D.W. Statistic	1.63	1.62	1.77
Wald Test ~ χ^2		9.87**	15.36**
REP-DEM		3.08**	

Note: *t*-statistics in parentheses. Standard errors are White heteroskedastic-consistent estimates.
* $\alpha < .10$. ** $\alpha < .05$.

the tariff is measured by the duties collected over total imports. Republican governments increased AVGTOTAL by about 1.7 percent. Tables 4.3 and 4.5 also show that Republican governments are positively correlated with changes in the average duty on dutiable imports and with AVGDIFF, but the coefficients are insignificant at the 5 percent level.

These results indicate that Republicans increased the scope of goods subject to import duties, whereas the Democrats significantly decreased both the scope of goods subject to duties as well as the tariff rate on dutiable goods. The case of wool is typical. In 1894 the Democrats lowered tariff rates generally and removed woolens from the dutiable list altogether. When the Republicans regained control in 1896, they reintroduced the tariff on woolen imports and only moderately raised protective tariff rates. This example illustrates why the average duty on both dutiable and total imports are necessary to fully capture the effects of tariff policy.

One possible reason why the estimates do not identify Republican responsiveness to changes in economic activity is that the relation between changes in GNP and political control is not additive, but multiplicative. To test this hypothesis, I estimate the tariff measures by equation 4.3. Column 3 in table 4.3 and shows that both DEMGNP and REPGNP are significant for explaining changes in the tariff placed on dutiable goods. When there is unified control by either party, levels of protection are highly responsive and significantly related to changes in national income. Further, table 4.5 indicates that REPGNP is significant at the 10 percent level for explaining changes in AVGDIFF. The interactive variable between Democratic control and economic activity, DEMGNP, is not significant, but it has the predicted sign. Thus, Republican tendencies toward product-specific protectionism, as measured by AVGDUTY and AVGDIFF, increase with changes in GNP.

The implication of this result is straightforward. The tariff is more sensitive to changes in national income when there is unified partisan control than when there is divided government. When the same party controls both Congress and the presidency, members can agree on a policy (i.e., to raise or lower tariffs). But when political control is divided between the parties, members are less likely to agree, and therefore the tariff rate is less responsive to changes in national income.

As discussed above, one argument advanced by those who favor the pressure group model is that political parties have no significant effect on the tariff after interest group demands have been taken into account. To determine whether the political models in columns 2 and 3 of each table do indeed outperform the economic model, I conduct a linear restrictions test. In effect, this procedure nests the economic model in each of the alternative models and estimates the additional impact of each new variable on the tariff. In this case, the F-test is inappropriate because the underlying error structure is heteroskedastic. The Wald test is preferable because it relaxes the normality assumption and can be calculated using only the unrestricted coefficient estimates. The null hypothesis for this test with respect to equation 4.2 is $\beta_2 = \beta_3 = 0$. For equation 4.3, the null hypothesis is $\beta_2 = \beta_3 = \beta_4 = \beta_5 = 0$. The test statistic, which has a chi-squared distribution, is calculated as

$$W = \hat{g}' \Sigma_g^{-1} \hat{g} \sim \chi_m^2,$$

where $\hat{g}' = g(\hat{\beta}_1, \hat{\beta}_2, \ldots, \hat{\beta}_k)'$ is the vector of restrictions evaluated at the unrestricted coefficient estimates,

$$\Sigma_g^{-1} = \left(\frac{\partial \hat{g}}{\partial \hat{\beta}} \right)' \hat{\sigma}^2 (X'X)^{-1} \left(\frac{\partial \hat{g}}{\partial \hat{\beta}} \right) \qquad (4.4)$$

is the estimated variance-covariance matrix of $\hat{g}$, m is the number of restrictions, and $\hat{\sigma}^2$ is the estimated variance.[17]

The Wald statistic, reported at the bottom of each table, indicates that in all cases inclusion of the political variables significantly improves the explanatory power of the pressure group model. For instance, the Wald statistic at the bottom of column 2 in table 4.4, 13.91, exceeds the critical value of χ^2 (2), 5.99, and the Wald statistic at the bottom of column 3, 14.68, exceeds the critical value of χ^2 (4), 9.49, all at the 5 percent level.

Another test of my hypothesis investigates whether, once in office, Republicans and Democrats act differently from one another with regard to the tariff. That is, after controlling for changes in economic conditions, do Republicans and Democrats enact significantly different tariff policies? If Republicans are more protectionist than Democrats, then the quantity

$$\frac{\beta_R - \beta_D}{\sqrt{\sigma_R^2 + \sigma_D^2 - 2\mathrm{Cov}(\beta_R \beta_D)}} \sim t_{n-k-1}$$

will be significantly greater than 0. Similar to calculating a normal t-ratio, β_R and β_D are the estimated coefficients of the Republicans and Democrats, respectively. The denominator is the adjusted standard error, calculated as σ_R^2 plus σ_D^2 (the estimated variances of the political control variables) minus twice their covariance. The row labeled [REP-DEM] in column 2 of tables 4.3 through 4.5 reports the results of this difference of means test. The estimated t-statistics are 3.74, 7.75, and 3.08 for AVGDUTY, AVGTOTAL, and AVGDIFF, respectively. Thus, I reject the hypothesis that $\beta_R - \beta_D = 0$ at the 5 percent level. The Republicans were indeed significantly more protectionist than the Democrats in their treatment of the tariff.

There remains the puzzle of why two out of the three measures do not

---

17. For a discussion of linear restriction tests, see Johnston 1984 or Kmenta 1986.

pick up a significant increase in tariffs under Republican control. One possibility is that the Republican party's rhetoric did not match its members' actions. Another possibility is that there are some items on which both parties raise tariffs and some on which they decrease tariffs. A decrease in the average duty on noncontroversial goods could offset the Republicans' increasing tariffs on politically sensitive items. For instance, the 1890 McKinley Tariff Act

TABLE 4.6. Commodity-Specific Data Estimated by Equation 4.2, 1877–1934

Dep Var	Constant	ΔGNP	ΔREP	ΔDEM	REP-DEM
ΔAGRI	0.61	-0.043	1.72	-3.86	
	(1.10)	(-1.81)**	(2.20)**	(-2.74)**	3.50**
ΔCHEM	0.40	-0.027	0.80	-3.14	
	(1.06)	(-1.70)**	(0.93)	(-2.00)**	2.17**
ΔCHINA	0.17	0.0082	-0.38	-5.85	
	(0.33)	(0.51)	(-0.31)	(-1.96)**	1.71**
ΔCOTTON	0.15	-0.0041	1.82	-3.30	
	(0.27)	(-0.18)	(1.70)**	(-1.93)**	2.58**
ΔFLAX	0.19	-0.034	2.12	-2.52	
	(0.46)	(-2.41)**	(1.41)*	(-2.55)**	2.62**
ΔMETAL	-0.047	0.017	-0.72	-4.55	
	(-0.086)	(0.90)	(-0.60)	(-1.62)**	1.25
ΔPAPER	-0.10	-0.0084	1.43	-1.10	
	(-0.30)	(-1.17)	(2.76)**	(-3.75)**	4.26**
ΔSILKS	-0.13	0.018	1.04	-2.77	
	(-0.45)	(1.49)*	(1.57)*	(-2.51)**	2.93**
ΔSPIRITS	0.014	-0.0090	-4.39	-3.34	
	(0.014)	(-0.35)	(-0.94)	(-1.55)*	-0.203
ΔSUGAR	2.05	-0.24	0.86	-3.46	
	(0.98)	(-2.58)**	(0.22)	(-0.34)	0.400
ΔSUNDRY	0.48	-0.030	2.47	-1.14	
	(1.27)	(-2.14)**	(2.33)**	(-0.86)	2.12**
ΔTOBACCO	0.23	-0.0080	-3.11	-3.57	
	(0.26)	(-0.25)	(-1.66)**	(-1.41)*	0.148
ΔWOOD	-0.047	0.0082	0.57	2.24	
	(-0.18)	(0.55)	(1.07)	(1.42)*	-1.01
ΔWOOL	0.77	-0.056	0.65	-9.35	
	(0.76)	(-1.47)*	(0.48)	(-1.56)*	1.63**
ΔRAWWOOL	-0.38	0.054	0.066	-2.87	
	(-0.54)	(1.07)	(0.066)	(-3.05)**	2.43**
ΔMANWOOL	1.35	-0.099	4.77	-19.27	
	(0.98)	(-1.05)	(1.55)*	(-1.34)*	1.63**

Note: t-statistics in parentheses. Standard errors are White heteroskedastic-consistent estimates. * α < .10. ** α < .05.

raised duties on many goods, but also eliminated duties on coffee and tea. The important finding, however, is that there is a consistent and significant difference between the political parties with regard to the tariff. My analysis shows that in no case can I exclude the party variables from the tariff equation.

To further investigate the effect that political parties have on the tariff, I estimate the sixteen commodity-specific groupings by equation 4.2. According to a simple pressure group model, if we assume that economic sectors are equally disadvantaged and face similar costs in entering the political process, a downturn in economic activity should lead to roughly similar levels of protection for special interests no matter whether the Democrats or the Republicans control government.

In contrast to this prediction, table 4.6 suggests that Republicans raise duties on agricultural products, cotton, flax (used for rope and twine), paper, silks, sundries,[18] and wool manufactures. On the other hand, the Democrats alone lowered tariffs on agricultural products, chemicals, china, cotton, flax, metal products, paper, silks, spirits (liquors and wines), raw wool, and wool manufactures. Surprisingly, both the Republicans and the Democrats lowered duties on tobacco, and the Democrats raised duties on wood. As discussed above, the Republicans created a separate category that distinguished manufactured woolen articles from other wool products. Accordingly, although the Republicans had no effect on wool imports in general, they did raise tariffs on wool manufactures. Moreover, the difference of means tests reported in the last column of table 4.6 shows that except for metal, spirits, sugar, tobacco, and wood products, the political parties differed significantly in how they treated various commodity groupings, with the Republicans enacting higher tariffs in every case.

These commodity-specific data shed further light on why the two aggregate measures did not identify the effects of Republican control. Table 4.6 shows that there were a few items on which the Republicans focused their protective efforts. On the majority of goods, however, they either lowered tariffs moderately or left them unchanged. On the other hand, the Democrats significantly lowered tariffs on all goods except for sundries, wood items, and sugar. Consistent with the party model, these findings suggest that there is a constituency base for partisan preferences for high or low tariffs and that the relation between interest group demands and tariff levels depends on which party controls national government.

4.3. Conclusion

During the first century and a half of the republic, the parties gradually developed sectoral bases of support. Electoral shifts from one party to another

---

18. This category includes mostly luxury items, such as lace and embroideries.

were driven in part by changes in aggregate demands for or against protectionism. The ensuing oscillations in the tariff, however, also depended heavily on which party controlled national government. This is the point of Proposition 1: partisan competition has an independent effect on policy.

My empirical findings support Proposition 1. Even after accounting for changes in constituency demands, party significantly influences the tariff. Furthermore, changes in the tariff are more responsive to changes in business conditions when there is unified partisan control as compared to divided government. The commodity-specific data show similar partisan effects. Political parties enact significantly different tariff policies from one another that benefit certain producer groups at the expense of others.

Although interest group demands are an important determinant of the tariff, the institutions that aggregate preferences for or against protectionism also influence policy, suggesting that legislators are not necessarily held captive by producer interests as Schattschneider so eloquently opined more than a half century ago. If institutions shape policy outcomes, and political actors can design institutions to further their political ends, then at times procedures will be developed to circumvent protectionist pressures. The next two chapters investigate the institutions that have governed trade policy-making from 1890 to the present, the rationale for their design, and their effects on policy.

Appendix 4.1

A note regarding some of the aggregate estimates used in the analysis may be in order. As discussed in the text, three measures of the tariff are used to estimate the level of protectionism. All of these measures are sensitive to changes in the duty rate and in the actual volume of sales. It is therefore difficult to precisely disentangle the various factors influencing tariff fluctuations.

The commodity-specific tariff data cover various import groupings used throughout the period. Many of these goods are clearly no longer important in terms of volume sales, such as flax and hemp. For the period in question, however, they were the leading categories.

Early GNP estimates are dubious at best.[19] Until the 1921 Budget Act, there was no systematic method to obtain accurate figures for GNP and its components. These estimates were constructed from available input-output data. The first figures were reported by Kuznets (1946) and were later revised by Kendrick (1961), Gallman (1966), and Berry (1988). Recently, Romer (1989) and Balke and Gordon (1989) published new estimates. The central difference between these studies concerns the volatility and the amplitude of the business cycles. The variance of these estimates

---

19. Unfortunately, other reliable measures for aggregate economic activity, such as unemployment and inflation, are not available for my sample period. In chapter 5, where I examine more recent tariff trends, I include these measures in the analysis.

hinges on the elasticity assumption and on the accuracy of the underlying commodity output estimates.

In my analysis, I use the estimates reported by Balke and Gordon (1989) for two reasons. First, Romer (1989, 14) replaces Kuznet's assumption that deviations from the trend of GNP and commodity output move together one-to-one with estimates of the percent deviations from the trend of GNP and commodity output for which there exists accurate data. By definition, if the rate at which GNP responds to a one unit change in output decreases, then cyclical peaks and troughs will be moderated. Predictably, this is Romer's central finding. Second, Balke and Gordon (1989) include railroad and construction data, sectors of the economy that are highly responsive to economic conditions, whereas Romer does not.

APPENDIX 4.2

A common problem of time series analysis is that the error terms covary systematically over time. Generally, economic variables (customs, duties, GNP, etc.) are nonrandom phenomena, so that variances or excluded variables tend to be correlated, and thus the moments exhibit autocorrelation. This effect does not create biased estimators, but inefficient ones. To explore these possibilities, I first conducted ordinary least squares estimation of equation 4.2 for each of the three tariff series. The Durbin-Watson statistic showed that my model was first degree autoregressive in all cases. I then included a first order lagged dependent variable and again tested for serial correlation. The Durbin h-test now indicated that I could not reject the null hypothesis of no autocorrelation.

The next step is to ensure that the tariff measures are indeed stationary processes. To determine if the process generating the tariff series has a unit root, a simple first order autoregressive equation

$$Y_t = \rho Y_{t-1} + \epsilon_t \qquad\qquad (4.5)$$

was estimated using the annual data of each of the three tariff measures for the period 1877–1934. The null hypothesis $\rho = 1$ is tested against the alternative that $\rho \neq 1$ at the 5 percent significance level. The estimated t-statistics are -0.24, -1.28, and 0.15 for AVGDUTY, AVGTOTAL, and AVGDIFF, respectively. Using the tables provided by Fuller (1976), the critical value is -1.95. Thus, we cannot reject the null hypothesis that $\rho = 1$ at the 5 percent level.

To determine the level of differencing for each tariff measure, I reestimated equation 4.5 in first differences. The estimated t-statistics are now -5.32, -5.73, and -6.21. This time, I am able to reject the hypothesis that the differenced tariff series have a unit root.

Second, I tested the null hypothesis of *no co-integration* by a Dickey-Fuller test for a unit root in the residuals. The t-statistics are -1.86, -1.99, and -2.39 for AVGDUTY, AVGTOTAL, and AVGDIFF respectively. Using the tables provided in MacKinnon (1991), the critical value is -4.43. Thus, I am unable to reject the hypothesis that the tariff series are not co-integrated at the 5 percent significance level. This indicates that there is no equilibrium relationship between the series and that the analysis should therefore be undertaken in differences.

Furthermore, a White test supports the hypothesis that the tariff series is hetero-skedastic. To correct for the inefficient estimates, the reported variances and standard errors are White heteroskedastic-consistent estimates.

A final test conducted was for autoregressive conditional heteroskedasticity (ARCH), which determines if the error terms correlate with previous error terms. I estimated the square of the equation's error terms by the first and second order lagged error terms, and found that in neither case were the lagged error terms a significant explanatory variable. I therefore rejected the hypothesis that the model was ARCH.

CHAPTER 5

Delegation and the Design of Trade Institutions

Beginning in the mid-1930s, Congress . . . no longer [gave] priority to protecting American industry. Instead, its members would give priority to protecting themselves: from the direct, one sided pressure from producer interests that had led them to make bad trade law. They would channel that pressure elsewhere, pushing product-specific trade decisions out of the committees of Congress and off the House and Senate floors to other governmental institutions.

— I. M. Destler, *American Trade Politics*

Chapter 4 argues that trade policy does not merely respond to interest group demands, but that the legislative institutions that structure policy-making play an integral role in mediating these pressures. This chapter investigates the institutions that have governed trade policy in the past century. Congress has a long history of delegating authority to the president and executive agencies. But it has always limited this delegation by designing procedures that give interest groups a voice in the decision-making process, that compensate industries injured by increased import competition, and that allow legislators to modify or reject executive decisions. Furthermore, I show that these procedures have had a profound effect on the course of American trade policy in the post–World War II era.

Most scholars examining trade policy after 1934 agree that institutions matter. But, as suggested by the quotation above, their institutional analysis is straightforward: legislators voluntarily abdicated their control over trade policy to the executive branch in the 1934 Reciprocal Trade Agreements Act (RTAA). By fashioning a system that insulated them from protectionist demands and delegating responsibility to the executive branch, legislators thereby paved the way for presidents to tilt trade policy in a liberal, market-expanding direction. Though Destler acknowledges that Congress sometimes sets limits and general guidelines on the president's discretion, his analysis suggests that legislators are unable or unwilling to oversee effectively the executive's actions, and therefore it is the president (or executive broker) who dominates the decision-making process.

Other scholars in the presidential dominance camp contend that in recent years presidents have increasingly used executive agreements, proclamations, and other unilateral instruments to circumvent congressional influence altogether in making foreign policy (Robinson 1967; Schlesinger 1973; and Margolis 1986). To support their claim, they cite the rising number of international accords enacted by executive agreement as compared to treaties. As indicated by figure 5.1, from 1934 to 1988, 88 percent of all international agreements were enacted by executive proclamation. Of these agreements, 37 percent were classified as economic, 14 percent were military, and the remainder were procedural.[1]

There are thus two hypotheses about why the president controls trade policy. The stronger one asserts that the president has wrenched authority from Congress. The other claim, typified by Destler, asserts that Congress has voluntarily relinquished control to the executive branch. The crucial difference between these approaches is that the latter still allows the possibility of a congressional role in decision making. If the first claim is true and the president circumvents the legislative branch, then we have nothing more to say about Congress with respect to trade policy and need only look to the executive branch. If the second claim is true, and the president has not seized power, but rather Congress has willingly delegated authority, then two cases are again possible: delegation may be absolute and final, or partial and constantly changing. If the delegation of authority is indeed final and cast in stone, then again we need only examine executive branch politics to explain trade policy. But if delegation is incomplete or partial and monitored constantly, as I argue here, then Congress will retain an important and at times decisive role in shaping trade policy.

First, I investigate the claim that the executive branch has seized control over trade policy. The data from figure 5.1 confirm that today most international accords are enacted by executive agreement, many of which affect foreign commerce. But more careful analysis shows that the president was empowered to negotiate these agreements by Congress, and only rarely were agreements entered into by the constitutional authority of the president alone. Table 5.1 indicates that 85 percent of all international agreements were enacted pursuant to authority delegated by Congress to the president. Further, a sample of trade agreements from 1925 to 1975 suggests that 72 percent were enacted either by prior or by subsequent statutory authority (see table 5.2). In fact, all substantive (economic and military) agreements resulted from delegated authority.[2] This evidence suggests that the president does not unilaterally set trade policy without prior congressional authority.

---

1. For a more detailed breakdown of these data, see Johnson 1984, King and Ragsdale 1988, and O'Halloran 1990.

2. I define trade agreements as those that directly affect the flow of goods across national borders. I classify international agreements by their legal authority, of which there are three main

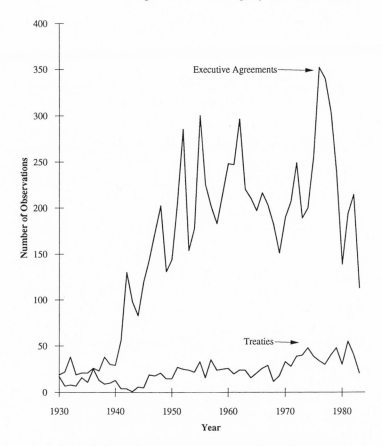

Fig. 5.1. Executive agreements and treaties, 1930–88

The strong form of presidential dominance does not seem to capture the dynamics of policy-making, so Congress and congressional delegation may still have an important effect on policy. A question still remains as to whether delegations of authority are malleable and shaped by current political pressures, or permanent and impervious to such concerns. The review of the history of delegation in the area of trade policy below shows that in the past century Congress has periodically decided to extend, expand, and at times even revoke the president's negotiating authority. The extensions of the RTAA throughout the postwar era have been accompanied by times when Congress denied the president negotiating authority or imposed restrictions on the use of

types: international agreements entered into force pursuant to statutory authority; international agreements entered into force pursuant to prior treaty authority; and international agreements entered into force by the constitutional authority of the president. See Appendix 5.1 for more details.

TABLE 5.1. International Agreements Classified by Legal Authority[a]

Year	Prior Legislation	Subsequent Legislation	Legislation and Treaty	Legislation, Treaty	Treaty and Constitutional	Constitutional Authority
1946-55	1632	12	79	12	178	23
1956-65	2127	16	109	10	120	11
1966-77	2395	11	115	18	244	64
Total	6154	39	303	40	542	98
Percentage	85.76	0.54	4.22	0.65	7.55	1.36

Source: Department of State, *International Agreements Other Than Treaties, 1946–78: A List with Citation of their Legal Basis.*
[a] Agreements are classified by the authority by which they became effective. See appendix 5.1 for more details.

TABLE 5.2. International Trade Agreements Classified by Legal Authority[a]

Year	Prior Legislation	Subsequent Legislation	Legislation and Treaty	Treaty	Legislation, Treaty, and Constitutional	Constitutional Authority
1925	0	0	0	0	8	1
1935	10	0	0	0	1	0
1945	6	0	0	0	2	0
1955	5	0	0	10	0	0
1965	17	1	0	2	0	1
1975	39	0	0	1	3	0
Total	77	1	0	13	14	2
Percentage	71.96	0.93	0	12.14	13.08	1.87

Source: Department of State, International Agreements Other than Treaties, 1946–78: A List with Citation of their Legal Basis. Agreements prior to 1946 coded from Department of State, United States Treaties and other International Agreements, 1776–1949. See appendix 5.1 for more details.
[a] Agreements are classified by the authority by which they became effective.

this authority. For example, from 1967 to 1973 Congress voted down the president's request for tariff-cutting authority and was unwilling to abide by the Kennedy round of multilateral GATT negotiations that would have repealed the American Selling Price provision. Furthermore, as exemplified by the 1988 Omnibus Trade and Competitiveness Act, Congress can force the president's hand in many circumstances, either to retaliate against the pervasive and unfair trade practices of foreign countries or to grant relief to industries adversely affected by import competition.

Thus, even though Congress no longer writes individual tariff schedules, it remains active in the legislative process by taking a flexible approach to the institutions that govern trade policy. Sometimes Congress will legislate blanket grants of authority to the president with few guidelines on its use. Other times, Congress will impose restrictions that force the president to accommodate congressional demands. In either case, Congress is anything but a passive observer in setting national trade policy: the debate has simply shifted from the setting of specific tariff rates to defining the criteria by which the executive can exercise delegated authority.

In elaborating these points, I first examine the history of congressional delegation in trade policy, beginning in the 1890s and continuing though the present. This overview broadly supports the notion that delegation is flexible and reflects changing economic and political conditions. Two key features appear throughout the analysis: Congress delegates less power to a president of the opposing party than to a president of the same party, and it designs institutions in response to industry-specific demands for protection. I then present empirical evidence to support Propositions 2A and 2B detailed in chapter 3. I find that unified government is associated with Congress delegating greater discretionary authority to the president and divided government is associated with less delegation. Moreover, the less authority delegated to the president, the closer will be the policy outcome to the congressional norm of high tariffs. The last section summarizes my conclusions.

5.1. A Century of Congressional Delegation

Appendix 5.2 summarizes the major procedural innovations in trade legislation during the last century. For clarity of exposition, I define four dimensions by which Congress either expands or restricts the president's authority: the discretionary authority delegated to the president, restraints on the use of this authority, provisions to retaliate against unfair trade practices, and special protection for industries injured by imports. The following historical overview details the evolution of trade institutions along these four dimensions and examines the congressional politics surrounding their enactment. Four broad patterns emerge from this wealth of detail:

1. Congress designs intricate administrative procedures that limit the scope of the president's authority, both directly by ex post vetoes and indirectly by enfranchising interest groups into the decision-making process.
2. Over time, these procedures have become more complex as Congress has delegated a broader scope of authority to the president.
3. As the authority to set tariffs moved from the congressional to the executive arena, the focus of legislative debate and interest group pressure shifted from individual tariff rates to the criteria by which industries receive protection.
4. Finally, limits on discretionary authority reflect partisan differences between Congress and the president; legislators are more willing to delegate authority to presidents of the same party.

5.1.1. Early Reciprocal Trade Provisions

I am mistaken if any men, bodies of men or Countries, will enter into any compact or treaty, if one of the three is to have a negative controul over the other two. . . . There must be reciprocity or no Union, which of the two is preferable, will not become a question in the mind of any true patriot.
—*George Washington, 1787*

The basic premise of American trade policy has always been reciprocity. Since the earliest commerce and navigation acts, Congress delegated authority to the president to retaliate against unfair trade practices and to grant trading partners equivalent and reciprocal concessions. In the commercial acts of 1799, 1806, 1807, 1809, and 1810, for example, Congress delegated considerable reciprocal negotiating authority to the president. The 1810 act provided that if either Great Britain or France should cease to violate the neutral commerce of the United States, the president was empowered to open American ports to their goods. The constitutionality of the 1810 act was challenged in *Brig Aurora v. the United States*.[3] It was contended that Congress could not transfer legislative powers to the president. Nevertheless, the Supreme Court upheld the constitutionality of the act.[4] Throughout the history of American trade legislation, Congress continued to delegate limited authority to the president to negotiate reciprocal agreements or retaliate against unfair trading practices.

---

3. *Brig Aurora v. U.S.*, 11 U.S. 382 (1813).
4. See House Ways and Means Committee, *Amend Tariff Act of 1930: Reciprocal Trade Agreements*, 73d Cong., 2d sess., H. Rept. 1000, 8.

The McKinley Tariff Act

Substantive delegations of trade authority to the president began with the 1890 McKinley Tariff Act. Congress included a reciprocity clause, which provided that sugar, molasses, tea, coffee, and hides could be admitted into the United States duty free, but the president could retaliate against any country that "imposes duties or other exactions upon the agricultural or other products of the United States which in view of the free introduction of such sugar, molasses, tea, coffee, and hides in to the United States he may deem to be reciprocally unequal or unreasonable."[5] McKinley used this authority to negotiate reciprocal trade agreements that greatly favored the United States. These agreements promoted the sale of surplus U.S. products in other countries in exchange for low tariffs on imported goods that the United States did not produce. From 1891 until 1892, Secretary of State James G. Blaine and later John W. Foster negotiated ten commercial agreements and suspended the duty-free admission of the specified goods four times under the reciprocal trade clause.[6]

The Wilson-Gorman Tariff Act

The Democrat's national platform in 1892 condemned the McKinley Tariff Act as a "culminating atrocity." The results of the 1890 and 1892 elections assured the Democrats full control of both branches of the federal government. With Cleveland back in the White House and majorities in both houses of Congress, the Democrats prepared to fulfill their promise to dramatically revise tariff legislation. While the Democrats controlled a decisive majority in the House (197 to 118), the Democrats controlled the Senate by only a slim margin (44 to 38). Congress considered the tariff bill for over eight months, at which time the House finally conceded to protectionist sentiments in the Senate. As a result, the 1894 tariff act only moderately reduced tariffs. The Democrats did manage, however, to repeal the 1890 reciprocal trade clause

---

5. Act of October 1, 1890, §3, 26 Stat. 612. The constitutionality of this act was attacked in the case of *Field v. Clark*, 143 U.S. 649 (1892) on the ground that the Congress had delegated to the president both legislative and treaty-making powers. The Supreme Court upheld the constitutionality of the act, simply stating that the provision was not liable to the objection that it transfers legislative and treaty-making power to the president. See House Ways and Means Committee, *Amend Tariff Act of 1930: Reciprocal Trade Agreements*, 73d Cong., 2d sess., H. Rept. 1000, 9. This was an important early precedent in the development of U.S. administrative law in which it was established that certain constitutional powers of Congress could be delegated to the executive branch.

6. The commercial agreements were concluded with Brazil, Dominican Republic, Spain, Great Britain, the German Empire, Nicaragua, Honduras, Guatemala, Austria-Hungary, and El Salvador. Duty-free suspensions were imposed on El Salvador, Columbia, Haiti, and Venezuela. Coded from the Joint Committee on Printing, *Tariff Acts Passed by the Congress of the United States from 1789 to 1909*, 61st Cong., 2d sess., H. Doc. 671. Also see United States Tariff Commission, *Summary of the Report on Reciprocity and Commercial Treaties* (1919).

and nullify the commercial agreements made under the 1890 provision.[7] Disappointed by the slight tariff reductions, Cleveland permitted the Wilson-Gorman tariff to become law without his signature.

Manufacturers blamed the Democrats' tariff legislation for the ensuing depression, declining prices, and business failures. Among many other things, the Wilson-Gorman tariff discontinued the reciprocity features of the McKinley Act, thereby alienating many large producers and farmers who hoped the reciprocity clause would expand their export markets. The victory of the Republican party and President McKinley in the 1896 elections reflected this discontent.

The Dingley Tariff Act

The Dingley Tariff Act of 1897 promised producers a secure domestic market by raising tariffs to unprecedented levels and increasing exports through the renewal of the reciprocity provision. Congress reauthorized the president to enter into commercial agreements on specified articles to secure reciprocal and equivalent concessions.[8] From 1897 to 1909, when the act was repealed, consecutive Republican administrations negotiated some ten commercial agreements under the reciprocity clause.[9]

The Republican-controlled Congress also empowered the president, within limits, to enter into treaties of up to five years that reduced duties set in statute. Congress restricted tariff cuts to 20 percent and prohibited transfers from the dutiable to the free list. To protect domestic producers, legislators also introduced the first countervailing duties. The secretary of the treasury could offset any export bounty imposed by another country by levying countervailing duties equal to the net amount of the subsidy.[10]

The Payne-Aldrich Tariff Act

In the early twentieth century, Congress delegated authority subject to seemingly "objective" rules, such as equalization of the costs of production and the competitive tariff. Of course, these rules had different effects on the tariff schedules. When the Republicans proposed the "equalization of the costs of production," they meant that duties should be high enough to protect domestic

---

7. See the Tariff Act of August 27, 1894, §71, 28 Stat. 569.

8. Eligible articles included argols, crude tartar, wine lees, brandies, other spirits manufactured or distilled from grain or other materials, champagne and all other sparkling wines, still wines, and vermouth, and paintings and statuary. See act of July 24, 1897, §4, 30 Stat. 204. For a discussion of the act, see Kenkel 1983, 36.

9. These agreements were concluded with Switzerland, Germany, Italy, Spain, Bulgaria, Portugal, Great Britain, France, and the Netherlands. Coded from Joint Committee on Printing, *Tariff Acts Passed by the Congress of the United States from 1789 to 1909*, 61st Cong., 2d sess., H. Doc. 671.

10. Act of July 24, 1897, §5, 30 Stat. 205.

producers. When the Democrats proposed the "competitive tariff," they meant that duties should be below the point of prohibition.

In the 1908 election, for example, President Taft promised to revise the tariff along the lines of the Republican party's national platform, which asserted that "in all tariff legislation the true principle of protection is best maintained by the imposition of such duties as will equal the difference between the cost of production at home and abroad."[11] The platform further called for the establishment of maximum and minimum rates to be administered by the president under limitations fixed in law.

True to their campaign pledge, the Republicans enacted the 1909 Payne-Aldrich Tariff Act, which set up a system of maximum and minimum tariffs.[12] The act specified the minimum tariff rates, and the maximum tariff was the rate set by statute plus 25 percent ad valorem of the imported product. Unless the president was satisfied that a country did not "unduly discriminate" against American commerce, the maximum tariff applied. Countries that accorded "reciprocal and equivalent" treatment to the United States received the minimum rates. In determining the application of minimum and maximum rates, the act allowed President Taft to create the Tariff Board. In addition to imposing the appropriate tariff rate, the board served as a fact-finding agency regarding domestic and foreign costs of production. The Republican-controlled Congress also eliminated the 1897 reciprocal trade clause and renewed the countervailing duty provision.[13]

In contrast to previous years, the Republican party in 1909 did not uniformly support a protective tariff. Western agricultural states vigorously protested high tariffs on manufactures. This split in the Republican ranks and the formation of the new Progressive party undoubtedly contributed to the crashing defeat of the Republicans in the 1910 congressional and the 1912 presidential elections.

The Underwood Tariff Act
In the ensuing 1913 Underwood Tariff Act, the Democrats dramatically reduced general tariff rates and dropped the provisions for the maximum and minimum tariff. In its place, they introduced the "competitive tariff," whereby rates would be just high enough so that domestic producers could compete with foreign imports. Those articles not produced domestically received little or no protection. Congress empowered President Woodrow Wilson to negotiate comprehensive trade agreements,

---

11. See Porter 1924, 301.

12. Act of August 5, 1909, Pub. L. No. 61-5, §2, 36 Stat. 82.

13. The Tariff Commission's report on *Reciprocity and Commercial Agreements* (1919, 270) asserted that the 1909 act "marked an important reversal of practice by the U.S. in regard to tariff bargaining: the policy of giving concessions for concessions was abandoned for that of penalizing countries which made discriminations unfavorable to the United States."

wherein mutual concessions are made looking toward freer trade relations and further reciprocal expansion of trade and commerce: *Provided, however,* That said trade agreements before becoming operative shall be submitted to the Congress of the United States for ratification or rejection.[14]

Unlike the 1890 and 1897 reciprocal trade clauses, the 1913 act did not limit the president to only a few specified goods. But while Congress delegated this broad authority to the executive branch to negotiate international trade agreements, it also retained a veto over presidential actions. At the same time, the Tariff Board expired quietly through the failure of the House Democrats to extend appropriations (Taussig 1931, 424). In addition, Congress extended the countervailing duties clause.[15]

In the period from 1890 to 1913, as detailed in the previous chapter, Congress set tariff schedules according to partisan preferences: Republicans enacted high tariffs, Democrats reduced tariffs. At the same time, however, both parties established the precedent of delegating authority to the president to negotiate reciprocal concessions or to adjust tariff levels along the lines of an "objective" criterion. This trend continued even after the tariff no longer served as the federal government's primary source of income.

The 1916 Anti-Dumping Act

The 1916 Revenue Act created the nation's first permanent income tax system, thereby establishing that a more stable revenue base would replace tariffs as the main source of financing government expenditures. As shown in figure 4.1, during this period there was a dramatic decline in custom revenues as a percent of total receipts. In the first decades of the twentieth century, duties still accounted for nearly 60 percent of total receipts. Afterward, custom revenues never exceeded 20 percent of total federal revenues.

As part of the revenue act, the Democrat-controlled Congress enacted the first anti-dumping provisions and reincarnated the Tariff Board as the Tariff Commission, an executive agency with broad investigative powers. The anti-dumping clause was enacted primarily in response to the protests of domestic industries facing steep competition from cheap European imports that were flooding the U.S. market after World War I. The provision granted individuals the right to sue for triple damages if any merchandise was imported into the United States at a price systematically below market value. In addition, the Democrats created the Tariff Commission to handle tariff adjustments and investigate unfair trade acts. Unlike its predecessor the Tariff Board, the commission was bipartisan, had large powers of investigation, and enjoyed

---

14. Act of October 3, 1913, Pub. L. No. 63-16, §4, 38 Stat. 192.
15. Act of October 3, 1913, Pub. L. No. 63-16, §4(e), 38 Stat. 193.

considerable appropriations. Congress authorized the commission to investigate the administrative, fiscal, and industrial effects of the customs laws and to report these findings to Congress.[16]

Proponents of the commission hoped that it would eventually fix tariff rates and remove the tariff question from the legislative sphere—"taking the tariff out of politics" (Taussig 1931, 482). The Tariff Commission's findings could also serve as evidence in anti-dumping cases and other unfair trade practice investigations.[17] For example, Congress authorized the secretary of the treasury to use the evidence provided by the commission to determine if an article was imported into the United States under trade restrictions and to retaliate against such practices by imposing a double duty.[18] The use of such procedural devices as anti-dumping measures to offset the complaints of domestic industries about "unfair competition" are seen throughout the twentieth century.

The Fordney-McCumber Tariff Act

After the Republicans won an overwhelming victory in the 1920 congressional elections, Taussig (1931, 488) writes,

> The session began with hot enthusiasm for a new tariff. Between the feeling of exultation in the dominant party from their overwhelming victory at the polls and their eager search for a remedy to meet the industrial depression of 1921, the protectionist feeling was more fervid than ever before.

The Republicans immediately set out to grant farmers relief from falling prices, which had declined dramatically after World War I.[19]

The 1922 Fordney-McCumber Tariff Act delegated further authority from Congress to the executive branch. The Republican Congress broadened the definitions of anti-dumping and unfair competition to make it easier for injured industries to receive import protection. President Harding was authorized to declare by proclamation countervailing duties to offset discriminatory actions against the commerce of the United States, not to exceed 50 percent ad valorem or its equivalent. The Tariff Commission was to ascertain

---

16. Specifically, the Commission was to provide information to the president and the Ways and Means and Finance Committees whenever requested. Revenue Act of September 8, 1916, Pub. L. No. 64-271, §702–4, 39 Stat. 796.

17. Revenue Act of September 8, 1916, Pub. L. No. 64-271, §796, 39 Stat. 796.

18. Revenue Act of September 8, 1916, Pub. L. No. 64-271, §800, 39 Stat. 798–99.

19. The Tariff Act of 1921 imposed temporary duties on wheat, corn, meat, wool, and sugar until the final passage of the 1922 act. Emergency Tariff Act of May 27, 1921, Pub. L. 67-10, §1, 42 Stat. 9.

the extent of these discriminations. Furthermore, whenever the secretary of the treasury determined that the purchase price was less than the market value, a special dumping duty was to be imposed in an amount equal to the difference.

The act also gave the president broad discretionary powers.[20] The Republicans enacted the so-called flexible tariff, which provided for the lowering or raising of duties by proclamation of the president, when the Tariff Commission determined that changes in rates fixed in statute were necessary to equalize differences in the costs of production.[21] If the costs of production could not be determined, the commission was to impose an ad valorem rate of duty equal to the American Selling Price.[22] Rates specified in statute could not be decreased or increased by more than 50 percent and no article could be transferred from the dutiable to the free list.

In the 1922 act, Congress had delegated considerable authority to the president and executive agencies: they could alter the tariff schedules fixed in statute and impose safeguards to protect domestic producers. However, the costs-of-production criterion that Congress had also imposed almost inevitably led to an increase in the tariff rate. The 1930 Smoot-Hawley Tariff Act replicated this structure, but with much more dramatic results.

The Smoot-Hawley Tariff Act
As we saw in chapter 4, the Smoot-Hawley Act began as a modest bill to aid the failing agricultural sector and, as amendment after amendment was introduced to protect domestic industries, ended in the highest overall tariffs in the twentieth century. The Smoot-Hawley Act clearly raised many commodity-specific duties, but it left the composition of the protective system largely unaltered. For the most part, only those goods on the dutiable list received an additional tax. By that time, the protective tariff had been extended so far that

----

20. The constitutionality of the act was questioned in *Hampton and Co. v. United States*, 276 US 394 (1928), in *Frischer and Co., Inc., v. Tariff Commission*, 282 US 852 (1930), and in *Frischer and Co., Inc., v. Elting*, 287 US 649 (1932), on the grounds that the act granted too large a delegation of power to the president. The Supreme Court of the United States nonetheless upheld the law arguing that this delegation was no more than an extension of Congress's rate-setting authority. See House Ways and Means Committee, *Amend Tariff Act of 1930: Reciprocal Trade Agreements*, 73d Cong., 2d sess., H. Rept. 1000, 11.

21. For the criteria in ascertaining the differences in the cost of production, see the Act of September 21, 1922, Pub. L. No. 67-318, §315(a), 42 Stat. 941.

22. The American Selling Price of any article manufactured or produced in the United States was defined as the price at which such article is freely offered for sale to all purchasers in the principal market of the United States, in the ordinary course of trade, and in the usual wholesale quantities in such market. Act of September 21, 1922, Pub. L. No. 67-318, §401(f), 42 Stat. 950.

increasing duties on these articles did not have any significant effect in restricting imports. Recall that figure 1.1 illustrates the huge difference between the means of the average duty and the ratio of dutiable imports to total imports during the 1930s. The outcome of the 1930 Smoot-Hawley logroll was that those industries and firms already enfranchised in the protective system received the added perk of a slightly higher import duty, while the rest of the articles were left untaxed (Taussig 1931, 519).

Seldom recognized in most discussions of the 1930 tariff act is that Congress also gave considerable attention to changing the legislative system for considering trade bills by delegating additional tariff adjusting power to the Tariff Commission. Congress intended for a new and improved commission to correct the details of the schedules and modify "inequitable" or "unwarranted" rates. In short, the commission was to save Congress from itself.[23] Indeed, the congressional committee reports indicate that the central debate between the House and Senate regarding the Smoot-Hawley bill centered not so much on individual tariff rates but on the delegation of authority to the president to raise or lower tariffs set in statute based on the Tariff Commission's recommendations. The House, which was less protectionist than the Senate, wanted changes in tariff rates to be enacted by presidential proclamations. The Senate, with a disproportionate representation from the farm states, wanted changes in tariff rates to be enacted only after congressional action. Congress also argued over the criteria upon which to base the Tariff Commission's determinations. The House wanted determinations of unfair trade practices based on comparative business conditions in foreign and domestic markets. The Senate wanted to base determinations on a less rigorous criterion, the costs of production. In the end, the House-Senate conference committee reached a compromise: the 1922 cost difference provision was adopted, but no congressional approval was required for presidential action.[24]

In the new system, the Tariff Commission was to investigate differences in the costs of production for all 3,221 articles specified in the 1930 act.[25] The president would then proclaim a new duty based on the commission's findings. As before, the president could proclaim changes in the rates of up to 50 percent but could not increase rates fixed by statute. Again, articles were not transferable between the dutiable and free lists. If the president judged that the commission's findings were not necessary to equalize cost differences, he

---

23. The constitutionality of congressional delegation of legislative authority was questioned and upheld in the case of *Sears, Roebuck and Co. v. United States*, 290 US 633 (1932).

24. House Conference Committee, *Tariff Bill of 1930*, 71st Cong., 2d sess., H. Rept. 1893, 27.

25. For the criteria governing the commission's determinations see the Tariff Act of June 17, 1930, Pub. L. No. 71-361, §336(e), 46 Stat. 702.

was not required to act. If the president did act, however, he could not modify the commission's recommendation.[26]

As I explained in the previous chapter, the political parties fought over specific tariff rates throughout the nineteenth and early twentieth centuries. The Republicans raised tariffs and the Democrats lowered tariffs. But Congress also established the practice of delegating authority to the president and executive agents to adjust rates along objective criteria: equalizing costs of production or setting tariff rates to ensure that domestic products could compete with foreign imports. Delegations of authority came mostly from a Republican Congress to a Republican president in response to aggregate economic conditions, such as declining agricultural prices or the Great Depression. These early acts also established a number of important precedents, such as antidumping ordinances, countervailing duties, reciprocal trade provisions, and adjusting the tariff rates set in statute along specified criteria.

5.1.2. The 1934 Reciprocal Trade Agreements Act and Its Extensions

In 1932 the Republicans lost control of Congress for the first time since 1918. With President Roosevelt in office and the Democrats holding a majority in both the House and Senate, the Seventy-third Congress enacted the 1934 Reciprocal Trade Agreements Act (RTAA) over the nearly unanimous opposition of the Republicans. To reduce the excessive tariff rates set by the Republicans in the 1930 Smoot-Hawley Tariff Act, the Democrats shifted authority to modify duties and import restrictions away from the Tariff Commission and to the president.[27] At this time, the commission had completed only seventy-four investigations into the differences of the costs of production out of the 3,221 items covered in the 1930 act. To overcome these inefficiencies and expedite the process, Congress provided that the president could enter into reciprocal trade agreements to reduce tariffs by executive proclamation alone.

Legislators thereby changed the way in which tariffs were set. Instead of giving the president limited authority to increase or decrease certain tariffs set by Congress either through reciprocal trade concessions or through objective

---

26. The act directed the Tariff Commission to submit a report to Congress no later than July 1, 1932, which converted the rates imposed by statute (pursuant to the 1930 act) to rates based upon "domestic value." Domestic value was defined as the wholesale selling price in the United States of similar imported merchandise, or an estimated value based on the wholesale selling price in the United States of comparable merchandise. The Tariff Act of June 17, 1930, Pub. L. No. 71-361, §340, 46 Stat. 707. Also see House Conference Committee, *Tariff Bill of 1930*, 71st Cong., 2d sess., H. Rept. 1893, 28–29; and Taussig 1931, 525.

27. Act of June 12, 1934, Pub. L. No. 73-316, 48 Stat. 943, amending 46 Stat. 708.

criteria, the president could now enter into commercial agreements and change any rate by proclamation. However, this did not mean that Congress would refrain from making trade policy altogether. The president's tariff-reducing power was subject to termination if, at the end of three years, Congress failed to extend his authority. In addition, the president was limited to 50 percent reductions, and he could not transfer articles between the dutiable and the free lists.

The House and Senate committee reports provide an interesting illustration of how Congress designs administrative procedures and document the debate over delegating authority to the executive branch. The House Ways and Means Committee, for instance, downplayed the revolutionary aspects of the proposed legislation, arguing that the bill went no further than preceding measures, as Congress imposed limits on the president's discretionary authority.[28] The House report stated that

> the proposed bill nevertheless does not remove from Congress its control of policy which must underlie every tariff adjustment. Although the exigencies of present-day conditions require that more and more of the details be left to Presidential determination, the Congress must and always will declare policy to which the Executive gives effect.[29]

Congress retained control over trade policy not only by setting limits on the president's authority, but also by securing avenues to protect producers' interests. Foreshadowing the 1946 Administrative Procedure Act, Congress required the president to hold public hearings and disclose information before changing rates. For example, the Senate Finance Committee introduced a provision to protect American producers and manufacturers who feared that hasty or ill-considered action would be taken without their knowledge and without a chance to present their views. The Senate amendment imposed ex ante restraints on delegated authority by requiring public hearings and consultation with executive departments prior to entering into an international agreement. The Senate Finance Committee Report stated:

> in order that any interested person may have an opportunity to present his views to the President, or to such agency as the President may designate, under such rules and regulations as the President may prescribe; and before concluding such agreement the President shall seek information and advice with respect thereto from the United States Tariff Commis-

---

28. As discussed above, former enactments delegated to the president the power to fix certain tariff rates and enter into executive agreements.

29. House Ways and Means Committee, *Amend Tariff Act of 1930: Reciprocal Trade Agreements*, 73d Cong., 2d sess., H. Rept. 1000, 14.

sion, the Departments of State, Agriculture, and Commerce, and from such other sources as he may deem appropriate.[30]

To further protect American industry, Congress retained the unfair trade practices provisions. Congress would extend unconditional most-favored-nation treatment (MFN) to all nations, except those that discriminated against American commerce. Both anti-dumping and countervailing duties were legitimate exceptions to the obligations of the most-favored-nation clause. The only restrictive provisions repealed by the 1934 amendments were contingent duties.[31]

The 1934 act established the basic structure of trade legislation for the next quarter century. Congress continued to renew the president's authority to negotiate trade agreements, extend the advisory system to give interested parties input into the decision-making process, create direct and indirect oversight mechanisms, and provide industries and groups injured by foreign competition or unfair trading practices opportunities for exemption, compensation, and delay.

The 1948 and 1949 Extensions of the RTAA
Between 1934 and 1945, under the RTAA, President Roosevelt entered into twenty-eight trade agreements. Congress renewed the president's negotiating authority in 1937, 1940, and 1943 without significant amendments.[32] In 1945 Congress gave the president further authority to lower existing rates by an additional 50 percent. For rates already reduced by the full 50 percent, this change would permit a total reduction of 75 percent from the 1934 rates.

After World War II, tensions between trade liberalization and compensating industries injured by foreign imports intensified. Congress was more reluctant to renew the president's authority to negotiate tariff reductions, and

---

30. Act of June 12, 1934, Pub. L. No. 73-316, §4, 48 Stat. 945. Also see Senate Finance Committee, *Reciprocal Trade Agreements*, 73d Cong., 2d sess., S. Rept. 871, 3.

31. Contingent duties varied with the tariff level placed by another country on U.S. exports. The text of the 1930 act did not name which goods would receive this preferential treatment but explicitly applied these duties to subparagraph d of paragraph 369 (trucks), the last sentence of paragraph 1402 (paper board), the proviso to paragraph 371 (bicycles), paragraph 401 (timber), paragraph 1650 (coal), paragraph 1687 (gunpowder), and paragraph 1803 (wood). See the act of June 12, 1934, Pub. L. No. 73-316, §2(a), 48 Stat. 944. Also, Congress did not remove any power from the Tariff Commission with respect to lowering duties in accordance with the differences in the cost of production. The provision applied, however, only to those articles for which the United States had not entered into an agreement. See the Tariff Act of June 17, 1930, Pub. L. No. 71-361, §336, 46 Stat. 701.

32. The renewals were enacted by joint resolutions of the House and Senate. See Act of March 1, 1937, Public Resolution 75-10, H.J. Res. 96, 75th Cong., 1st sess., 50 Stat. 24; Act of April 12, 1940, Public Resolution 76-61, H.J. Res. 407, 76th Cong., 3d sess., 54 Stat. 107; and Act of June 7, 1943, Public Resolution 78-66, H.J. Res. 111, 78th Cong., 1st sess., 57 Stat. 125.

sometimes extended his tariff-cutting powers for only one year. In 1947, for example, with the election of the Republican-controlled Eightieth Congress, protectionist concerns called for the repeal of the trade agreements program and postponement of the ongoing General Agreements on Tariffs and Trade multilateral negotiations in Geneva. Although the question of changing the trade act was deferred until 1948, GOP pressure forced President Truman to agree to include an "escape clause" in all future trade agreements. The Tariff Commission was directed to investigate complaints of injury arising from U.S. trade concessions. If these concessions were shown to injure domestic industries, the articles would be exempt from the agreement.

In October, 1947, Truman signed the General Agreements on Tariffs and Trade (GATT), which defined the protocol for conducting multilateral negotiations on international commerce. But Congress continued to restrict the president's negotiating authority to bilateral trade agreements and to only those provisions consistent with domestic statutes. As a result of this protectionist sentiment, Truman never submitted the GATT agreement to Congress for formal ratification.[33]

In 1948 Truman asked Congress to extend the trade agreements program for another three years. The Republican majority, with one eye on the presidential election in November, insisted on another one-year extension, contingent on minimum tariff "peril points" being established prior to further tariff negotiations. The peril point provision directed the Tariff Commission to investigate anticipated rate adjustments and determine the rate below which imports would seriously injure domestic industries. After this determination was made, no tariff concessions could be negotiated below the peril point.

President Truman, who had strongly opposed the peril point provision, made it an issue in the 1948 campaign. After unexpectedly reelecting Truman and gaining control of the Eighty-first Congress, the Democrats repealed the Trade Agreements Act of 1948, including the peril point clause, and extended the president's negotiating authority for three years from the original 1948 expiration date.[34] The Republicans strongly opposed the bill but were unable to alter it in any significant way. Representative Richard M. Simpson's (R-Pa.) motion to reintroduce the peril point provision was rejected by a vote of 151 in favor and 241 against. The Democrats voted 7 to 235 against recommitting the bill, and on the other side of the aisle the Republicans voted 144 to 5 in favor.

The Senate Finance Committee, by straight party vote, reported out the

---

33. Indeed, referring to the 1947 Geneva round, the 1949 Annecy round, and 1951 Torquay round of GATT negotiations, the 1951 and 1954 trade acts explicitly stated "this Act shall not be construed to determine or indicate the approval or disapproval by the Congress of the executive agreement known as the General Agreement on Tariff and Trade."

34. Act of June 26, 1948, Pub. L. No. 80-792, 62 Stat. 1053.

bill with no amendments. A substitute amendment, introduced by Senator Eugene Donald Millikin (R-Colo.) on the Senate floor, provided for a two-year extension of the 1948 act, including the peril point provision, but was rejected by a vote of 38 in favor and 43 against. Only three Democrats voted favor of the substitute bill, whereas the Republicans were unanimous in their support.

The conflict over the peril point illustrates the shift in the focus of congressional debate from specific tariff rates to procedural measures. The peril point added by the Republicans to the Trade Agreements Act in 1947 was repealed by the Democrats the following year. This emphasis on the procedures by which industries were eligible for import relief was to become a regular feature of legislative debates over trade policy. After the Republicans made major gains in the 1950 congressional elections, the peril point was once again a central issue of debate.

The 1951 Extension of the RTAA
When Truman's three years of authority were about to expire in 1951, the Democrats were much less favorably disposed toward the administration's liberal trade policies. Democratic opposition was concentrated largely in the textile, oil, and coal producing areas that faced strong competition from abroad. Congressional voting on the extension reflected members' concerns over Truman's unresponsiveness to the problems of those industries (Baldwin 1988). The Republicans were able to enlist enough Democrat defectors to enact several restrictive amendments in the authorizing legislation.

The 1951 Extension of the Reciprocal Trade Agreements Act renewed the president's tariff-cutting authority for two years. At the same time, it reintroduced the peril point and wrote into legislation the escape clause provision, thereby strengthening safeguards for American industry.[35] Before entering into any trade agreement, Congress required that the president submit to the Tariff Commission a list of all articles under negotiation. In turn, the commission's report to the president specified limits on modifications and the minimum increases in duties or import restrictions required to avoid serious injury. In making determinations, the commission was to hold hearings and give reasonable opportunities for interested parties to express their views. The president was not bound by the commission's determination. If the president failed to comply with the commission's report, however, he was required to notify Congress, identify the recommendations not complied with, and state his reasons for the action taken.[36]

---

35. See Act of June 16, 1951, Pub. L. No. 82-50, 65 Stat. 72.

36. Before concluding any international agreement, Congress also required that the president consult with the Departments of State, Agriculture, Commerce, and Defense, and other appropriate sources. Act of June 16, 1951, Pub. L. No. 82-50, §3(a), §3(b), §7, 65 Stat. 72, 74.

Congress also codified Truman's 1947 executive order regarding escape clause actions, which prohibited concessions on imports that injured or threatened to injure domestic industries.[37] Requests for investigations could be made by the president, either house of Congress, by a resolution of the Finance or Ways and Means Committees, by the Tariff Commission, or by any interested party.[38] The act required the Tariff Commission to look into any case of alleged "serious injury" caused by tariff concessions and, if necessary, recommend withdrawal or modification of these concessions. The president could reject the commission's recommendations, but he must explain his actions within sixty days to the Ways and Means and Finance Committees.

The votes on these restrictions show that Truman had lost the solid backing of congressional Democrats. In the House, 42 out of the 247 Democrats along with 183 out of the 187 Republicans voted for the restrictive provisions. After rejecting eleven additional protectionist amendments, the Senate passed the House bill unaltered by a vote of 72 in favor and 2 against. Thus, industry-specific pressures led to one of the rare occasions that a Congress of the same party as the president restricted the executive's discretionary authority.

The 1953, 1954, and 1955 Extensions of the RTAA

In 1953 President Eisenhower agreed to a one-year extension of the RTAA along with the establishment of a bipartisan Commission on Foreign Economic Policy, chaired by Mr. Clarence B. Randall, "to study all existing legislation and procedures relating to American foreign economic relations." When the commission's report was delayed the next year, however, Eisenhower had to request another one-year extension. Thus, in 1955, he found himself facing a Democratic Congress with no negotiating authority.[39]

Eventually, Congress renewed Eisenhower's trade negotiating authority for three years, enabling him to enter a fourth round of GATT tariff negotiations. However, Congress also took the opportunity to introduce new safeguards that constrained the president's use of this delegated authority. First, Congress specified staging requirements. The total decrease of any existing

---

37. Act of June 16, 1951, Pub. L. No. 82-50, §6(a), 65 Stat. 73.

38. Within one year after a petition was filed, Congress required that the Tariff Commission hold public hearings, complete the investigation, and publish and report findings. In arriving at a determination, the Tariff Commission was to take into consideration a downward trend of production, employment, prices, profits, wages in the domestic industry concerned, a decline in sales, an increase in imports, either actual or relative to domestic production, a higher or growing inventory, or a decline in the proportion of the domestic market supplied by domestic producers. Act of June 16, 1951, Pub. L. No. 82-50, §7(b), 65 Stat. 74.

39. See House Ways and Means Committee, *Trade Agreements Extension Act of 1955*, 84th Cong., 2d sess., H. Rept. 50, 6; and "Special Message to Congress on Foreign Economic Policy" (March 30, 1954) in Eisenhower 1954.

duty was not to exceed 15 percent, with an initial decrease of not more than 5 percent in the first year. These staging requirements afforded industries additional time for adjustment to import competition and possible dislocation. The Democrat-controlled House included a provision by which industries "vital to national security" could apply for exemption from tariff reductions.[40] This clause was later invoked to protect the oil and coal industries, both strong Democratic constituencies.

Congress also made it easier for industries to receive import relief. The act amended existing peril point and escape clause provisions to permit the Tariff Commission to recommend action if any segment of an industry (rather than the industry as a whole) was damaged by imports. The act further amended the escape clause provision, shifting the criterion of import relief from imports being the *primary cause* of injury to *contributing substantially to injury*.

In addition, the act included numerous informational requirements regarding the proposed trade agreements and their possible effects on domestic industries. For instance, the Tariff Commission was required to publish its findings and recommendations regarding peril point and escape clause decisions in the *Federal Register* at the same time that these decisions were submitted to the president.[41] Moreover, the president was to publish notices, hold hearings, and disclose information concerning the trade agreements program. Congress explicitly required that the president submit an annual report, to include information about new negotiations, modifications in duties and import restrictions, reciprocal concessions obtained, and changes of existing trade agreements. The Tariff Commission was also to report annually to Congress.[42]

What is apparent in the extensions of the RTAA during the mid-1950s is that Congress often used procedural provisions to restrict the executive's latitude in exercising delegated authority. One of the key elements in the 1955 act was to relax the criteria that industries had to meet in order to be eligible for government relief. These debates over procedural details would be a recurring theme in future legislation, and they contrast with earlier congressional battles over specific tariff rates.

The 1958 Extension of the RTAA

In 1958 Eisenhower requested a five-year extension of the trade agreements program. In an effort to mollify protectionists, the administration asked for authority not only to lower the 1958 tariff rates by 25 percent, but to raise rates up to 50 percent above their 1934 levels if necessary to protect domestic

---

40. Trade Agreements Extension Act, Pub. L. No. 84-86, §§3–7, 69 Stat. 164–66 (1955).

41. Trade Agreements Extension Act, Pub. L. No. 84-86, §5, 69 Stat. 166 (1955).

42. Trade Agreements Extension Act, Pub. L. No. 84-86, §3(e), 69 Stat. 165 (1955).

industry. The administration's proposal nonetheless met with strong opposition from the Democratic Congress.

The House passed a bill extending the president's negotiating authority, but new restrictions on the use of this authority were again imposed. The Ways and Means Committee renewed the peril point provision and increased from 120 days to nine months the time given to the Tariff Commission to complete peril point investigations. With regard to the escape clause, Congress reduced from nine to six months the deadline for commission reports and introduced a congressional veto over the president's decision to disregard the Tariff Commission's recommendation. The House proposed that Congress could override presidential disapproval of escape clause actions if two-thirds of the members of each chamber passed a concurrent resolution. The Senate Finance Committee introduced an even more restrictive provision: the Tariff Commission's recommendation would be final unless a majority in both houses upheld the presidential veto.

In the end, the House and Senate agreed to extend the president's authority for four years, authorizing him to reduce tariff rates in effect on July 1, 1958, by a total of 20 percent (but no more than 10 percent in any twelve-month period). The president could also raise rates up to 50 percent above their 1934 level and impose tariffs of up to 50 percent on duty-free items. In addition, the act incorporated the less stringent House provision regarding congressional override of presidential escape clause decisions.

The 1958 act extended the president's authority through 1962. The period from 1934 through 1962 is usually described as a time when Congress simply renewed the RTAA without question; however, even this relatively placid period was characterized by partisan politics, congressional-executive friction, and constraints on the use of delegated authority.

5.1.3. On-Again Off-Again Delegation: 1962 through 1973

In 1962 the trade agreements program was once again due to expire. The newly elected Kennedy administration requested unprecedented negotiating authority. Kennedy asked for special authority to reduce or even eliminate tariffs on imports in cases where the United States and the European Economic Community (EEC) together accounted for 80 percent or more of the total free world trade. In addition to this "dominant supplier" authority, Kennedy requested power to cut tariffs up to 50 percent of the 1962 levels, to cut or remove tariffs on agricultural products, and to eliminate tariffs on products currently dutiable at the 5 percent level.

In the 1962 Trade Expansion Act, the Democratically controlled Congress empowered the president to negotiate both bilateral and multilateral trade agreements, allowing the president to pursue broad tariff reductions with the EEC. However, Congress coupled this delegation of authority with safeguards against injury to American industry and agriculture. As in previous legislation, the act included the escape clause and national security clause, although these provisions were revised to make proof of injury more difficult. Qualifying for exemptions under these provisions now required that firms and workers prove to the Tariff Commission that growing imports were the major cause of injury. A legislative veto of escape clause determinations, however, was made easier. It required only a majority of both houses by concurrent resolution instead of the previous two-thirds.[43] In addition, the act repealed the peril point provision, instituting instead a much weaker prior notification and advice requirement.[44]

In many ways the 1962 trade bill marks a break from past legislation, which had operated under the premise that trade negotiations should not hurt a domestic industry. The new trade law recognized that certain industries might be injured in order to get the best overall agreement, but these industries would be partially compensated for the damage. The major emphasis of import relief thus shifted from the peril point and escape clause provisions that exempted sensitive industries from trade concessions to trade adjustment assistance (TAA) that would help affected industries adjust to foreign competition. Originally proposed by the Randall Commission, the TAA provision authorized aid to firms in the form of technical assistance, loans, loan guarantees, or tax cuts, and to workers in the form of unemployment compensation, retraining, and relocation allowances.[45]

Besides the expansion of authority and safeguards for firms and workers, there were several procedural innovations that distinguish the 1962 tariff act from previous extensions of authority. Congress shifted the basic responsibilities for negotiating agreements from the State Department to a new executive office, the Special Representative for Trade Negotiations (STR). In addition to the standard restrictions on authority, Congress expanded the

---

43. In effect, this required the approval of the Ways and Means and Finance Committees, since the resolution had to originate in these committees. See *Congressional Quarterly Weekly Report,* October 5, 1962, 1806.

44. In the original peril point provision, the commission would set a level of duty below which an industry would be harmed. In the new clause, the commission would report back to the president as to the probable economic effects tariff modifications would have on U.S. industries producing similar goods. Further, the president was to seek advice from the executive departments (Agriculture, Commerce, Defense, Interior, State, and the Treasury) and hold public hearings. Trade Expansion Act, Pub. L. No. 84-794, §302, 76 Stat. 885 (1962).

45. Upon the Departments of Labor and Commerce's certification, workers and firms could petition for relief. Trade Expansion Act, Pub. L. No. 84-794, §311, 76 Stat. 886 (1962).

prenegotiation advisory system by requiring members of the House Ways and Means and the Senate Finance Committees to actively participate in the negotiation process and by increasing opportunities for private sector input.[46]

In enacting the bill, clear partisan politics were played out on the House and Senate floors. The Democratically controlled House Rules Committee sent the bill to the floor under a closed rule, barring all but committee-approved amendments. The ranking minority member of the Ways and Means Committee, Representative Noah M. Mason (R-Ill.) moved to recommit the bill. The House rejected the motion by a vote of 171 in favor and 253 against; only 44 of the 263 Democrats voted in favor, while only 43 of the 174 Republicans voted against the motion. In the end, the House passed the bill without amendment.

The Senate Republicans also introduced several restrictive amendments. Senator Carl T. Curtis (R-Neb.) proposed an amendment to delete the trade adjustment program. Although defeated by a vote of 23 to 58, over two-thirds of the Republicans supported the amendment, while only five Democrats did. Minority Leader Senator Everett McKinley Dirksen's (R-Ill.) amendment to reduce the president's negotiating authority from 5 to 3 years was defeated by a vote of 28 to 56, with only 5 Democrats voting for the amendment and only 5 Republicans voting against. Senator Prescott Bush (R-Conn.) introduced an amendment to restore the more restrictive provisions of the existing peril point procedure, which carried 39 to 33 before Democratic leaders persuaded enough abstainers to vote nay to defeat it 38 to 40.[47]

To secure final passage of the bill, Kennedy sought and obtained the support of Democratic constituents in the textile industry. He negotiated a five-year agreement to limit textile imports to about 6 percent of the domestic market. He also promised to extend the price supports that protected cotton farmers to protect textile manufacturers as well.[48] In the end, Congress passed Kennedy's original proposal largely unmodified, clearing the way for the first comprehensive multilateral trade negotiations under GATT.

---

46. Trade Expansion Act, Pub. L. No. 84-794, §221, 76 Stat. 874 (1962). The roles of the STR, congressional delegates, and private sector advisory committees in the negotiation, implementation, and administration of trade agreements are discussed further in chapter 6.

47. In the 38 to 40 vote on the Bush amendment, 25 Republicans supported it and none opposed it; 13 Democrats supported it and 40 were opposed. At the end of the first tally for the vote, the Bush amendment had actually carried 39 to 33. Six Democrats from states with strong protectionist pressure who had abstained from voting then cast their votes against the amendment. Although this made the vote 39 to 39, which would have rejected the amendment, Majority Leader Mike Mansfield (D-Mont.) convinced Thomas Dodd (D-Conn.) to withdraw his vote for the amendment and B. Everett Jordan (D-N.C.) who had not voted, to vote against it. *Congressional Quarterly Weekly Report,* September 21, 1962, 1555–56; *Congress and the Nation 1965,* 203.

48. *Congress and the Nation 1965,* 204.

The Battle over the Kennedy Rounds

In 1967 the Johnson administration concluded the Kennedy round GATT negotiations authorized by the 1962 Trade Expansion Act. The accord reduced average duties by about 35 percent on some sixty thousand items. The 1962 authorizing legislation, however, made no mention of other trade restrictions, such as nontariff barriers. The Johnson administration nonetheless sought to include these measures in the multilateral trade agreements negotiated during the Kennedy rounds.

A heated debate broke out between Congress and the administration. Indeed, while the Kennedy round negotiations were still in progress, the Senate passed a concurrent resolution, reasserting that the president had no authority to negotiate provisions not explicitly provided for in the Trade Expansion Act.[49] Congressional approval was thereby required to enact some parts of the agreement, such as the repeal of the American Selling Price (ASP) that calculated duties on certain imports on the basis of higher U.S. product prices. When the administration introduced such a bill that year, however, Congress tacked on numerous protectionist import quotas, partly in response to Johnson's request for the repeal of ASP and partly in response to the tariff reductions enacted by the signing of the Kennedy Round agreement. These quotas included such items as steel, oil, textiles, meat, dairy products, mink skins, strawberries, and baseball gloves.[50] Johnson, in return, threatened to veto any quota bills passed by Congress. In the end, no quotas were enacted, and the ASP provision remained intact. The lines were thus drawn: the Johnson administration refused to accept protectionist bills that would unravel the GATT accord and the Congress refused to adopt the procedural changes necessary to enact the agreement.

Stalemate: 1967–73

Congress subsequently allowed the president's trade negotiating authority to expire. In 1968 the Johnson administration once again attempted to implement the trade package. The administration's proposal was limited to restoring the expired tariff-cutting authority of the Trade Expansion Act and repealing the controversial ASP provision. Again, numerous product-specific quotas were introduced as amendments. The protectionist thrust was led by the steel, chemical, textile, and oil industries, who pushed for a variety of measures to counter the effects of the Kennedy Multilateral Trade Agreement. The bill was never reported out of committee.

In late 1969 President Nixon asked the Democratic Congress to extend his tariff-cutting authority by an additional 20 percent. Instead, in 1970 the

---

49. *Congressional Quarterly Almanac 1967*, 810.

50. *Congressional Quarterly Almanac 1967*, 810.

House passed a protectionist trade bill drafted by the Ways and Means Committee. Besides imposing import quotas, the committee rejected a repeal of the ASP system and wrote into law the oil import quotas established by presidential proclamation in 1959.[51] Growing protectionist concerns were partly a result of the 1962 Trade Expansion Act, which required that an injured firm prove to the Tariff Commission that imports were the major cause of injury. This criterion was so difficult to substantiate that, despite twenty applications from 1962 to 1967, no awards were made.[52]

The bill passed the House but faced stiff opposition in the Senate and the threat of a possible presidential veto. The Senate Finance Committee attached the controversial measure to a popular Social Security bill in an attempt to ensure its passage. When the bill went to the Senate floor, however, a filibuster forced the Democrats to delete the trade section.[53] Thus the standoff continued. Nixon could not convince Congress to extend his trade negotiating authority, and the Democratically controlled Congress was unable to enact industry-specific protectionist measures.

5.1.4. 1974 Trade Reform Act and Beyond

In 1973 Nixon once again asked Congress for the right to adjust tariff and nontariff barriers over a five-year period. After a seven-year hiatus of the president having no authority to enter into such agreements, Congress finally enacted the 1974 Trade Reform Act, and thereby dramatically changed the nature of U.S. trade policy-making. The act revised administrative procedures in four areas: the implementation of trade agreements, reporting requirements, retaliation against unfair trade practices, and import relief to industries harmed by foreign competition. In each area, Congress tempered its delegation by adding procedural safeguards, enfranchising interest groups into the process, and shifting authority away from the president to executive agents more responsive to Congress.

First, Congress extended for five years the president's authority to enter into trade agreements to reduce tariffs by 40 percent and, for the first time, to eliminate nontariff barriers.[54] In addition, the president could extend preferential trade treatment for ten years to developing countries through the duty-free entry of specific items under the Generalized System of Preferences provision (GSP). Delegating such authority to the president without additional constraints, however, would have empowered the executive to not only set tariff

---

51. *Congress and the Nation 1965*, 130.
52. *Congress and the Nation 1969*, 95.
53. *Congress and the Nation 1973*, 124.
54. Trade Act of January 3, 1975, Pub. L. No. 93-618, 88 Stat. 1978.

rates, but also to change existing law.[55] Accordingly, the authority that Congress delegated to the president was under stricter statutory guidelines and limitations than ever before. In past acts, Congress had authorized the president to enter into agreements to reduce tariff rates by proclamation subject to specified conditions and limits. After the 1974 act, international agreements required congressional approval. Congress established elaborate implementing procedures known as the "fast track," which assured presidential trade proposals would be considered by an up-or-down vote.[56] To ensure that delegated authority would not be exercised to the detriment of domestic firms and workers, Congress limited tariff reductions. These limits included staging requirements and reserving certain articles from negotiations.

Second, Congress established prenegotiation procedures for consultation with Congress, domestic producers, and private organizations, and thereby ensured that legislators would have full and complete information on all proposed tariff modifications before they approved any agreement.[57] By creating an institutional framework that increased the participation of the public and various governmental agencies in all international trade agreements, legislators greatly expanded their control over the negotiation process. Private sector advisory groups, which represent labor, industry, agriculture, consumers, and the general public, were to provide policy and technical advice during the negotiations and issue official reports at their conclusion.[58]

Congress further required that the president seek advice from the Tariff Commission (renamed the International Trade Commission [ITC]), various departments, and congressional committees. The act expanded the role of the ITC and, by granting it an independent budget, made the trade agreements program less susceptible to executive influence. Congress also created the Office of the Special Representative for Trade Negotiations, headed by the United States Trade Representative (USTR), which provided a focal point in the executive branch to oversee all international trade negotiations. These elaborate provisions assured that representative elements from the private sector were granted the opportunity to express their views and provided negotiators a formal mechanism through which to seek information and advice.[59]

Third, Congress revised the president's authority to retaliate against un-

---

55. Nontariff barriers include health and safety standards, labeling requirements, "buy American" provisions, government procurement policies, and conservation measures (such as limiting the size of lobster imports) that are written into domestic statutes and have an indirect (and sometimes direct) effect on restricting imports.

56. In chapter 6, I discuss fast track procedures and their effects on international trade agreements in detail.

57. *Congressional Record*, 93d Cong., 1st sess., 1973, 119, pt. 31:40505.

58. *Congressional Record*, 93d Cong., 2d sess., 1974, 120, pt. 28:39509.

59. *Congressional Record*, 93d Cong., 1st sess., 1973, 119, pt. 31:40509.

fair trade practices. The Democratic majority wanted to assure a swift and certain response to foreign import restrictions, export subsidies, price discrimination (dumping), and other unfair trade practices. Section 301 of the trade act authorized the president to unilaterally retaliate against unjustifiable or unreasonable import restrictions (that is, violations of MFN), including restrictions on American services and supplies. Upon petition, the USTR would review complaints, hold pubic hearings, and publish determinations in the *Federal Register*. The USTR was to submit a semiannual report to the House and the Senate summarizing the reviews and hearings conducted. If the secretary of treasury determined that foreign subsidies decreased sales, and the ITC determined that such increased imports substantially injure American industries, then the president could retaliate to deter violations. If the president acted on the ITC's advice, he was required to report to Congress. Presidential actions that differed from the ITC's recommendations were subject to a two-house congressional override.[60]

Congress also strengthened the secretary of treasury's ability to identify and take assertive action against unfair trade practices. Congress required the secretary of the treasury to provide notice of proceedings within thirty days after a complaint.[61] If the secretary concluded that an industry was not being injured by dumped goods, and the ITC concurred with the secretary's determination, then the dumping investigation would terminate, with final determinations subject to judicial review.[62] Similarly, if an imported article benefited directly or indirectly from a subsidy, Congress required the secretary of treasury to impose countervailing duties equal to that subsidy, publish all determinations in the *Federal Register*, and report findings and supporting evidence to Congress. If *either* the Senate or the House adopted a disapproval resolution, Congress could rescind the secretary's determination.[63]

Fourth, Congress made it easier for groups to receive protection from foreign competition by liberalizing eligibility requirements for import relief

---

60. Trade Act of January 3, 1975, Pub. L. No. 93-618, §301, §302(b), 88 Stat. 2041–43.

61. Foreign manufacturers, exporters, domestic importers, as well as domestic manufacturers, producers, and wholesalers of the merchandise, would have an automatic right to a hearing before the secretary of the treasury or the Trade Commission. Within six months (nine months in complicated cases), the secretary was to conduct preliminary injury determinations. Final determinations were to be made three months afterward. Trade Act of January 3, 1975, Pub. L. No. 93-618, §321, 88 Stat. 2045–46.

62. Under the 1962 Trade Expansion Act, importers and foreign producers were entitled to judicial review. In the 1974 Trade Reform Act, Congress authorized judicial review for foreign as well as domestic producers and manufactures in the U.S. Customs Court. Trade Act of January 3, 1975, Pub. L. No. 93-618, §321(f)(1), 88 Stat. 2048.

63. Preliminary determinations were to be made within six months after a petition was filed. Congress requested that the secretary conclude a final determination within twelve months. Trade Act of January 3, 1975, Pub. L. No. 93-618, §331, 88 Stat. 2052.

and trade adjustment assistance, even if imports in no way represented unfair trade practices, and by eliminating the causal link between increased imports and trade agreement concessions.[64] Congress changed the criteria for import relief under the escape clause provision from increased imports being a major part (generally, assumed to mean a cause greater than all other causes combined) to a substantial cause (a cause which is important and not less than any other cause) of injury to the domestic industry. In making its investigation, the commission was to consider relevant economic factors and hold public hearings. Upon an affirmative determination, the commission was to report to the president, make recommendations for remedy, and publish these recommendations in the *Federal Register*.[65] In determining whether to provide assistance, the president was to take into account advice from the Departments of Labor and Commerce, as well as the potential economic impact alternative remedies would have on producers, workers, and consumers.[66] To assist industries, the president could proclaim an increase in, or an imposition of, any duty or quantitative restriction, or negotiate orderly marketing agreements. Presidential determinations that differed from the commission's recommendation were subject to a two-house congressional veto.[67]

Congress also renewed the trade adjustment assistance (TAA) provisions. Firms were eligible for adjustment assistance if increased imports (whether or not the result of concessions) were a substantial cause (rather than being a major factor) of a decline in sales. Similarly, workers in affected industries were eligible for assistance if imports were a substantial cause of unemployment. The secretary of labor and the secretary of commerce determined workers' and firms' eligibility. The ITC investigated the economic impact of increased imports and made recommendations to the president.[68] In deciding whether and in what form to extend assistance, the president was to consider the ability of an industry to adjust to import competition and the

---

64. In 1955 Congress changed the criteria for relief so that increased imports would not have to be the sole cause but contribute substantially toward injury. The 1962 Trade Expansion Act required that increased imports be in major part the result of trade agreement concessions before import relief measures were undertaken. See Trade Expansion Act, Pub. L. No. 84-794, §301(a), 76 Stat. 885 (1962). Also see House Ways and Means Committee, *Trade Reform Act of 1973*, 93d Cong., 1st sess., H. Rept. 571, 8; and the Trade Act of January 3, 1975, Pub. L. No. 93-618, §201, 88 Stat 2012.

65. Trade Act of January 3, 1975, Pub. L. No. 93-618, §201(a), 88 Stat. 2012.

66. Trade Act of January 3, 1975, Pub. L. No. 93-618, §202(c), 88 Stat. 2014.

67. The president could provide relief only in the following order: tariff increase, tariff-rate quotas, quotas, and orderly marketing agreements (the latter two are subject to a congressional veto procedure). Trade Act of January 3, 1975, Pub. L. No. 93-618, §203, 88 Stat. 2016.

68. Trade Act of January 3, 1975, Pub. L. No. 93-618, §231, 88 Stat. 2021. Also see House Ways and Means Committee, *Trade Reform Act of 1973*, 93d Cong., 1st sess., H. Rept. 571, 8.

impact of import relief on communities, workers, consumers, exporters, and other domestic industries.[69] The House Committee on Ways and Means asserted that the act was designed

> to give additional time to permit a seriously injured domestic industry to adjust and to become competitive again under relief measures and, at the same time, to create incentives for the industry to adjust, if possible, to competitive conditions in the absence of long-term import restrictions.[70]

For the most part, the bill passed though the House and Senate with few restrictive amendments added, mostly because of key procedural rules attached to the consideration of the bill. The Ways and Means Committee opposed an open rule, which would have permitted protectionist amendments. As proposed by the House Rules Committee, only three specific amendments could be considered, including the restrictions on trade credits for exports to the Soviet Union, unless the Soviet government eased its emigration policies (the Jackson-Vanik amendment). There was strong pressure by the AFL-CIO to defeat the rule and thereby delay consideration of the bill. After a lengthy debate, the House nonetheless adopted the restrictive rule by a vote of 230 to 147, thereby ensuring the trade bill's passage.[71]

When the Senate took up the trade proposal the following year, protectionist pressures were again mounting. A series of amendments were proposed dealing with natural gas deregulation, income tax changes, and taxation on the foreign operations of multinational corporations. The Senate eased the passage of the bill by an innovative use of the Cloture Rule to prevent unrelated amendments like natural gas deregulation and taxation of multilateral corporations' foreign operations that could have jeopardized the trade bill entirely.[72]

In the end, the legislature gave Nixon almost all of his requested negotiating authority. But his discretionary powers were restricted in several important ways. For the first time since 1913, presidential trade agreements

---

69. Congress imposed stricter time limits on import relief determinations, the duration of import relief, and the phasing out of such relief. Final determinations were to be made within sixty days after a petition had been filed. For the criteria of determinations see the Trade Act of January 3, 1975, Pub. L. No. 93-618, §231, 88 Stat. 2021.

70. House Ways and Means Committee, *Trade Reform Act of 1973*, 93d Cong., 1st sess., H. Rept. 571, 44.

71. In the vote for the closed rule, the Republicans voted 136 in favor and 24 against, while the Democrats voted 94 in favor and 123 against, *Congress and the Nation 1977*, 129.

72. Under the Senate's Standing Rules, nongermane amendments can be ruled out of order after cloture has been invoked. Floor debate is also limited. The procedural measure was passed by a vote of 71 to 19, with 34 Republicans voting in favor and 4 against, and 37 Democrats voting in favor and 15 in opposition. See *Congress and the Nation 1977*, 132.

required congressional approval. The act established procedures requiring that both houses of Congress approve nontariff barrier trade agreements, GATT revisions that changed domestic law, and bilateral trade agreements with Communist countries. In addition, the act established a two-house disapproval procedure over presidential import relief decisions that differed from the recommendations of the ITC, as well as retaliatory actions against unfair trade restrictions under the 301 clause. Furthermore, the act instituted a one-house legislative veto over countervailing duty determinations, bilateral agreements with Communist countries, annual reviews of MFN status, and government credits and guarantees.

The 1974 Trade Reform Act redefined congressional-executive relations in making trade policy. The act set a new standard for both the amount of power delegated and the scope and precision of congressional checks on this authority. This delegated authority was coupled with an amazing set of detailed provisions that afforded industries a means to get around the general system of tariff reductions. In future legislation, Congress would further refine these procedures in response to industry demands for protection and partisan conflict between the legislative and executive branch.

The 1979 Trade Agreements Act
On January 4, 1979, President Carter notified Congress of his intent to enter into the Tokyo round multinational trade agreements. In accordance with the provisions of fast track authority, he signed the agreements ninety days later, and on June 19 he submitted them to the Democratically controlled Ninety-third Congress for approval. The purpose of the 1979 Trade Agreements Act was to implement the Tokyo round GATT negotiations. This was the first time a president enacted a multilateral trade accord through fast track procedures, which accelerate legislative consideration of the agreement and restrict amendments on the House and Senate floors. Congress adopted these special approval procedures to avoid the conflict between the legislative and executive branches that had erupted over the enactment of the Kennedy round.

The 1979 act, in addition to codifying the Tokyo round into law, had three significant aspects. First, it extended the president's negotiating authority for eight more years. The Senate Finance Committee recommended that future negotiations address American service industries, particularly the insurance and banking industry, and the effects of foreign government subsidies on these industries.[73]

Second, Congress explicitly defined fast track procedures for implementing trade agreements. The Senate emphasized that trade agreements are not

---

73. Senate Finance Committee, *Trade Agreements Act of 1979*, 96th Cong., 1st sess., S. Rept. 249, 257.

self-executing and reaffirmed that no change in domestic statute would take effect without congressional approval.[74] Indeed, Congress wrote very detailed procedures describing the exact timing, consulting and reporting requirements, and contents of the implementing bill that the president must submit for Congress to consider any agreement under fast track. In adopting the Tokyo GATT Agreement, the Senate Committee on Finance asserted that

> the provisions of HR 4537 reflect the decisions of the House and Senate committees. . . . The implementing bill was drafted in the offices of the House and Senate Legislative Counsel with the participation of staff members of the committees of jurisdiction in both Houses and representatives of the Administration. The bill reflects the understanding achieved on all issues.[75]

Further, the committees emphasized that only if the president first consulted with Congress and published notice in the *Federal Register* could he negotiate international agreements under fast track proceedings.[76] The act also broadened the mandate of the private sector advisory committees: in addition to economic impact statements, the committees were to give advice on negotiating objectives, bargaining positions, and implementing trade agreements. Congress required the president to consolidate the general policy advisory committees, establish sectoral or functional advisory committees, and add service sector advisory committees. The act further centralized the authority to negotiate international trade agreements in the office of the United States Trade Representative, who was to keep congressional representatives continually informed as to the operation of the trade agreements.[77]

Third, with the support of the Democratic Congress, President Carter obtained legislation making retaliation against unfair trade practices more difficult. Congress enacted the agreement on the *Implementation, Interpretation and Application of Articles VI, XVI and XXIII of the GATT*, which substantially revised American laws pertaining to countervailing and antidumping duties. The criteria for affirmative determinations were changed

---

74. Senate Finance Committee, *Trade Agreements Act of 1979*, 96th Cong., 1st sess., S. Rept. 249, 36.

75. Senate Finance Committee, *Trade Agreements Act of 1979*, 96th Cong., 1st sess., S. Rept. 249, 6.

76. Trade Agreements Act of July 26, 1979, Pub. L. No. 96-39, §3(c), 93 Stat. 149.

77. In fact, the Senate actually delayed consideration of the trade agreement until President Carter submitted his proposal to reorganize the trade bureaucracy. The reorganization plan went into effect after neither the House or Senate approved a resolution to disapprove it. See *Congress and the Nation 1981*, 271.

from a substantial cause to a material injury test.[78] Unlike most nations, the United States did not previously have an injury requirement. Under the GATT rules adopted by Congress, neither anti-dumping nor countervailing duties could be imposed unless the imported product caused or threatened to cause material injury to a domestic industry or materially retarded the establishment of a domestic industry.[79] In addition, the American Selling Price provision, which had caused so much friction a decade before, was finally repealed.

The anti-dumping and countervailing duty provisions were the most controversial parts of the agreement. Many industries feared that injury would prove so difficult to document that no firms would ever qualify for assistance. To counteract the possible adverse effects of the GATT provision on American industries, Congress provided more expedient decisions and more effective relief for domestic industries damaged by subsidized or dumped imports. Congress accelerated the period for decisions on dumping and subsidy complaints.[80] It also expanded the opportunities for judicial review of some provisional and all final rulings by the Treasury Department and the ITC in anti-dumping or countervailing duty cases,[81] thereby offsetting some of the negative consequences of the new GATT agreement by redesigning the procedures by which domestic industries could seek import relief.

Unlike previous trade agreements that emphasized tariff cuts, the Tokyo rounds developed new international rules to address nontariff barriers to trade, such as export subsidies. These nontariff aspects of the multinational trade agreement required congressional approval. The 1974 Trade Reform Act had established expedited rules for considering such agreements that prohibited amendments to the implementing bill once introduced in Congress. But under the legislative process laid out in the 1974 act, congressional committees in consultation with the administration's trade officials would write the legisla-

---

78. The act defined material injury as harm that is not inconsequential, immaterial, or unimportant. For criteria of ITC determinations see the Trade Agreements Act of July 26, 1979, Pub. L. No. 96-39, §771, 93 Stat. 178.

79. Trade Agreements Act of July 26, 1979, Pub. L. No. 96-39, §101, 93 Stat. 150.

80. Determination by the administering authority was to take place within twenty days after petition, forty-five days afterward for preliminary determinations, and the final determination was required within seventy-five days after the preliminary determination.

81. The legislation preserved an interested party's right to challenge final determinations issued by either the administering authority or the ITC in anti-dumping and countervailing duty cases. The act enlarged the opportunities for judicial review of interim decisions made during investigations. The Senate Finance Committee asserted that the provision for interlocutory review of administering authority and ITC determinations in anti-dumping and countervailing duty procedures was intended to obtain faster review of administered determinations and avoid delay. See Senate Finance Committee, 96th Cong., 2d sess., S. Rept. 249, 246–53. Pub. L. No. 96-39, §1001, 93 Stat. 300. Also, see *Congressional Quarterly Weekly Report*, July 7, 1979, 1374.

tion. Most of the controversy surrounding the agreement was eliminated during the drafting phase, when concessions were made to mollify the opposition from such key industries as steel and textiles and from the farm and labor interests. In the end, nearly all major grievances were resolved before the bill was formally submitted to Congress, which then passed the trade agreement overwhelmingly by a vote of 395 to 7 in the House and 90 to 4 in the Senate.

The Trade and Tariff Act of 1984

When Reagan entered office in 1980, the Republicans controlled the Senate for the first time in over a quarter century. The 1984 Trade and Tariff Act was an amalgam of more than 100 measures that contained numerous temporary and permanent changes to the U.S. tariff schedules, ranging from toys to caffeine, and special assistance for the copper, wine, and steel industries. In addition, the Generalized System of Preferences (GSP), which was established by the trade act of 1974 and grants duty-free treatment to certain imports from developing countries, was scheduled to expire. Reagan requested an eight-and-a-half-year extension of the GSP authority, but for the first time Congress tied preferential treatments to whether the target countries opened their markets to U.S. exports. Furthermore, Congress granted the president authority to create a free trade zone between Israel and the United States, but any future agreements were subject to approval by the House Ways and Means and the Senate Finance Committees. Congress also included numerous noncontroversial tariff and trade provisions involving temporary duty reductions and suspensions.

The 1984 act made two central changes to the structure of the legislative process for implementing trade agreements. First, Congress added an additional congressional veto over international trade agreements. Before the president could *begin* trade negotiations under fast track proceedings, he had to provide written notice to the committees on Finance and Ways and Means. If within sixty days either Ways and Means or Finance disapproved the negotiations, fast track implementing procedures would not apply.[82] The president could still negotiate the agreement, but he would have to submit it to the Senate for ratification as a treaty or to the Congress as separate legislation.

The second change concerned the ex post veto legislators held over certain presidential decisions to extend import relief. The ripples of the 1983 *Chadha* decision[83] extended to the legislative vetoes that Congress had included in provisions regulating retaliation against unfair trade practices, waiver extensions for nonmarket countries, and violations of nondiscriminatory (MFN) treatment. In the *Chadha* decision, the Supreme Court declared

---

82. Trade and Tariff Act of October 30, 1984, Pub. L. No. 98-573, §401(b), 98 Stat. 3014.

83. *Immigration and Naturalization Service v. Chadha*, 462 US 919 (1983). For a more extensive discussion, see Craig 1988.

congressional veto provisions unconstitutional on the grounds that they violated the doctrine of separation of powers. The court held that a congressional veto did not involve bicameral approval and presentment to the president. Congress had never before vetoed a negative presidential import-injury decision. The threat of doing so, however, had influenced the president to help industries in ways other than an increase in protection on a most-favored-nation basis (Cooper 1985, 369). To make the disapproval provisions conform to the *Chadha* decision, Congress substituted joint disapproval resolutions, which the president can veto, for the previous concurrent resolutions, which are not subject to presidential veto. This clearly weakened the powers of Congress in relation to those of the president. Only the three provisions mentioned above were affected by the *Chadha* decision, however; other checks on presidential power, such as fast track, did not involve explicit legislative vetoes (Baldwin 1985, 202).

To offset the authority the *Chadha* decision conveyed to the president, Congress shifted the initiation of unfair trade practices cases from the president to the USTR. Under the 1974 Trade Reform Act, the president could initiate investigations upon petition or by proclamation. In the 1984 act, Congress provided that any interested person could file a petition with the USTR requesting the president to take action under unfair trade provisions. The USTR was required to review allegations and, within forty-five days of receiving the petition, determine whether to initiate an investigation. If the USTR decided not to initiate an investigation, it was to publish its reasons in the *Federal Register*.

Congress also broadened the definition of unfair trade practices to include discrimination against services, transfers of information, and foreign direct investment. In addition, the terms "unreasonable," "unjustified," and "discriminatory" included a wider range of practices, acts, and policies.[84] If the USTR initiated an unfair trade practices investigation, it was required to publish such determinations in the *Federal Register*, hold public hearings, and consult with the private sector advisory committees. Once the USTR made an affirmative determination, it was left to the president's discretion whether to respond. Thus the Democratic House and the Republican Senate expanded the USTR's investigative and policy-making powers, but stopped short of mandating presidential retaliation against unfair trade practices.

The 1988 Omnibus Trade and Competitiveness Act
In the 1986 congressional elections, the Democrats regained control of the Senate and subsequently tightened the administrative procedures governing

---

84. For specific definitions see the Trade and Tariff Act of October 30, 1984, Pub. L. No. 98-573, §304, 98 Stat. 3005–6.

delegated authority in the Omnibus Trade and Competitiveness Act of 1988 (OTCA). Congress extended the president's negotiating authority for three years, with the possibility of a further two year extension if the president requested it and neither house passed a disapproval resolution. In addition, the act

1. extended the prenegotiation advisory system and provided for "reverse fast track" procedures, whereby fast track could be rescinded if the USTR did not keep legislators adequately informed;
2. relaxed the eligibility requirements for trade adjustment assistance, making it easier for workers and firms to receive import relief; and
3. shifted the determinations of unfair trading practices and their remedy from the president to the USTR, and created "Super 301" provisions making retaliation against such practices mandatory.

First, the Democrats added an additional veto over the president's use of fast track implementing procedures. There were now three ways in which Congress could repeal the president's fast track negotiating privileges: 1) if both houses of Congress separately agreed to disapproval resolutions within any sixty days (reverse fast track); 2) if the president did not notify Congress of his intent to enter into an international trade agreement; or 3) if the Finance or Ways and Means Committees disapproved of the negotiations within sixty days from when notice was provided.[85] The reverse fast track provision, newly introduced by the OTCA, was largely a response to the Reagan administration's failure to adequately keep legislators informed during the U.S.-Canada Free Trade Agreement negotiations that were being considered simultaneously by the 100th Congress.

Second, Congress renewed trade adjustment assistance for two years. The act extended TAA benefits to secondary workers employed in firms that supply essential goods or services to industries eligible for import relief. In addition, all workers and firms engaged in exploration and drilling in the oil and natural gas industry were entitled to assistance[86]—an obvious payoff to

---

85. A procedural disapproval resolution is a resolution of either house of Congress which states that the president has refused to consult with Congress on trade negotiations and trade agreements in accordance with the provisions of the Omnibus Trade and Competitiveness Act of 1988, and therefore the provisions of section 151 of the trade act of 1974, as amended by the 1984 act. If both houses adopt a resolution within sixty days disapproving consideration of the bill under fast track procedures, then these procedures would not apply to any implementing bill submitted with respect to the trade agreement. The Omnibus Trade and Competitiveness Act, Pub. L. No. 100-418, §1103, 102 Stat. 1131 (1988).

86. The Omnibus Trade and Competitiveness Act, Pub. L. No. 100-418, §1421(a), §1423, 102 Stat. 1242 (1988); see also House Conference Committee, *Omnibus Trade and Competitiveness Act of 1988*, 100th Cong., 2d sess., H. Conf. Rept. 576, 695.

the petroleum industry for potential displacement by cheap Canadian imports that would result from the Free Trade Agreement.

Third, the OTCA emphasized retaliation against unfair competition. Perhaps the most contentious aspects of the act were the action-forcing Super 301 provisions. Legislators had long complained about the president's refusal to retaliate against pervasive unfair trade practices. Amongst those countries labeled as the biggest offenders were Japan, Taiwan, and Brazil. The OTCA included changes in agency control, limits on agency discretion, and transfers of authority away from the president to the USTR. These procedural changes offered groups injured by import competition more opportunities for protection.

The 301 provision of the 1974 trade act had assigned basic responsibilities for retaliation against unfair trading practices to the president. The 1988 OTCA shifted these responsibilities to the USTR. The House version, better known as the Gephardt amendment after its sponsor Representative Richard Gephardt (D-Mo.), required the USTR to identify countries that consistently engage in unfair trade practices and that run an excessive trade surplus with the United States. If the foreign country did not terminate such practices within a year, the USTR was required to impose quotas, tariffs, or revoke trade concessions in order to reduce the nation's trade surplus with the United States by 10 percent annually. The Gephardt amendment passed the House by a vote of 218 to 214, with 17 Republicans in favor and 159 against, and 201 Democrats in favor and 55 against. The Senate subsequently passed a weaker version of the mandatory sanctions requirement.

Although the conference committee omitted the Gephardt amendment, it did agree to transfer the authority to retaliate against unfair trade practices under Section 301 to the USTR.[87] The Senate provision, adopted by the conference committee, required that the USTR hold public hearings on alleged unfair practices, obtain advice from the advisory committees, and request the ITC to issue an economic impact statement. If a violation were found and international dispute settlement proceedings failed to resolve the issue, the USTR could choose from a list of possible retaliatory actions.[88]

---

87. Congress had previously used administrative procedures to force the president or executive agents to take action. In the 1974 act, retaliation was left up to the discretion of the president and was subject to possible congressional disapproval. The 1979 act shifted the responsibility for determining violations away from the ITC and the Secretary of the Treasury to the USTR. In the 1984 act, Congress transferred authority to initiate investigations from the president to the USTR. On the basis of an investigation (by petition or self-initiated), and after consultations with the foreign country concerned, the USTR was required to recommend remedial actions to the president. The president could also take action on his own volition and was not required to enact the USTR's recommendations. House Conference Committee, *Omnibus Trade and Competitiveness Act of 1988*, 100th Cong., 2d sess., H. Conf. Rept. 576, 551.

88. The USTR was empowered to suspend, withdraw, or prevent the application of trade agreement concessions with the foreign country, impose duties or other restrictions on the goods

Once the USTR made its determination, the new Section 301 required the president to implement these recommendations without modification. Previously, Congress had set guidelines for industries to receive compensation, subject to presidential discretion which may or may not be vetoed by Congress. Now for the first time Congress mandated that the president take actions against a country which discriminated against U.S. goods.

5.1.5. Summary

This admittedly lengthy historical overview shows that there is a long tradition in U.S. trade policy of delegating authority to the executive branch to negotiate reciprocal concessions. From the late 1800s through 1930, a number of specific precedents were set, including countervailing duty laws, antidumping ordinances, and congressional vetoes over certain executive actions. Seen in this light, the 1934 RTAA represents a great leap forward in congressional delegation, but it is not wholly unconnected to previous trade policy.

There then followed a series of renewals of the president's negotiating authority, which were anything but automatic. In many instances, as in the one-year extensions of authority in 1947, 1953, and 1954, Congress strongly contested the president's use of his discretionary authority. When imports threatened sensitive domestic industries, Congress introduced new forms of import relief (the escape clause and the peril point provision) to protect disaffected constituents. At each turn, the authorizing legislation showed the effects of partisan conflict and a willingness on the part of legislators to design complex procedures that protected specific industries.

The generous delegation of authority in the 1962 Trade Expansion Act was followed by a complete absence of delegation from 1967 to 1973. The modern era of trade institutions was then inaugurated with the 1974 Trade Reform Act, which continued to delegate large amounts of authority to the president, but created elaborate procedures through which Congress could check the use of this authority and through which industries could petition for relief. After the 1974 act, the president could no longer enter into international trade agreements by proclamation alone; instead, he would need the consent of Congress. Standards by which industries qualified for import relief were weakened, and a series of advisory committees was instituted to enfranchise the private sector into the decision-making process.

Over the years, Congress has also shown its willingness to adjust delegation procedures in response to changing circumstances. In 1983, for instance,

---

and services, enter into binding agreements to eliminate or phase out any burden or restriction, or compensate the United States with trade benefits. The Omnibus Trade and Competitiveness Act, Pub. L. No. 100-418, §1301, 102 Stat. 1131 (1988).

the Supreme Court declared the legislative veto unconstitutional. Congress responded by changing the veto procedure, substituting a joint for a concurrent resolution to disapprove presidential actions. As with any piece of legislation, the president could veto the disapproval resolution and Congress could then override the veto by a two-thirds majority vote. Clearly, this weakened Congress's influence on trade policy, including, for example, its ability to force the president to retaliate against unfair trade practices. To compensate for this shift in authority, Congress transferred away from the president to the USTR the authority to initiate unfair trade practice decisions. In 1988 Congress went even further, making the USTR responsible for determining violations and for retaliating against such practices.

In short, there seems to be good evidence that Congress retains influence in trade policy. It has shown willingness to delegate power to the president, but it has been just as willing to restrict or revoke this authority if the president strays too far from congressional preferences. There is also evidence of continuing partisan conflict over tariff and trade policy. Unlike the late nineteenth and early twentieth centuries, however, this conflict is not tied directly to setting tariff rates. The Democrats and Republicans still oppose each other on trade legislation, but instead of having easily identifiable positions on the tariff, they fight over how much authority to delegate to the president and the awards given to industries. More discretionary power has been delegated to a president of the same party as the majority in Congress, and less to one of the opposing party.

Thus institutions would seem to be much more malleable than presidential dominance scholars would suggest. Nonetheless, it could be argued that these restrictions on delegation are not as effective as they seem. If the real responsibility of making trade policy lies with the president, congressional constraints may not change outcomes. In this case, the limitations on the president's authority may be for credit-claiming purposes, so that legislators can shift the blame for negative outcomes to the executive branch. Therefore, in the next section, I test whether levels of delegation do respond to protectionist pressures and partisan politics, and whether changes in delegation have an appreciable impact on levels of protection.

5.2. Econometric Analysis

The historical evidence seems consistent with the hypothesis that delegations of power occur most frequently when Congress and the presidency are controlled by the same political party. When this has been the case, Congress has tended to grant authority to the president with minimal restraints, as in 1934 and 1962. Otherwise, Congress either has refused to delegate authority, as from 1967 to 1973, or has imposed tight restraints on the use of this authority, as in the 1974 trade act. In this section, I provide empirical support for Propositions 2A and 2B, which make explicit predictions concerning the design of trade institutions and their effect on trade policy outcomes. In chapter 3, I argued that legislators are more willing to delegate authority to an executive sharing similar preferences. If partisan affiliation can be viewed as a proxy for preferences, then it follows that legislators delegate more authority when there is unified partisan control of government than when there is divided government. The empirical findings indicate that Congress has indeed increased the discretionary authority of presidents from the same party and decreased the latitude of presidents from the opposing party. I further show that more restrictive institutional arrangements are associated with higher levels of protection.

5.2.1. Explaining Delegation: Testing Proposition 2A

As noted, Congress frequently imposes provisions that force the president, the International Trade Commission (ITC), or the United States Trade Representative (USTR) to comply more closely with congressional views. Clearly, some of the pressure for these provisions comes from import-sensitive industries lobbying for relief from foreign competition and, as discussed in chapter 4, this pressure should rise as economic conditions worsen. But part of the willingness of legislators to limit executive authority also stems from whether Congress believes that the president will accurately reflect members' concerns. The model presented in chapter 3 asserts that the amount of authority that Congress is willing to delegate to the president depends on whether the legislative and executive branches are controlled by the same party. I now proceed to empirically test this hypothesis, Proposition 2A, with data drawn from the 1890 to 1990 period.

Data
Table 5.3 defines and provides descriptive statistics for the variables used in the analysis. The dependent variable, DELEGATION, is the discretionary authority delegated to the president in trade legislation. It can take on three possible values: 1 if the legislation increases the president's discretionary authority; 0 if there is no change; and −1 if the legislation represents a decrease in the president's authority. Table 5.4 shows the major trade acts from 1890 to 1990 and indicates whether the legislation increased or decreased the president's latitude to set policy. Congress increased the president's discretionary authority in seventeen cases, restricted the actions of the president in seven cases, and left the president's authority unaltered in seventy-seven cases. This method of coding the dependent variable is consis-

tent with the model presented in chapter 3, which defines more delegation as an increase in the president's ability to move policy away from the status quo.

For these 101 years, then, I code whether legislation promoted, restricted, or left unchanged the president's authority to affect trade policy. There are several potential weaknesses in measuring discretionary authority along these lines. Delegated authority is multidimensional, and in some cases, Congress extends existing tariff-cutting authority but imposes restrictions on

TABLE 5.3. Descriptive Statistics, 1890–1990

Variable Name	Description	Mean	S.D.
AVGTOTAL	Duties collected as a percent of the value of total imports.	12.3%	7.8%
GNP	Gross National Product in billions of 1982 dollars.	1,342.97	1,133.54
UNEMPLOY	The unemployment rate.	7.05%	5.0%
PPI	Producer Price Index (1982=100).	32.49	28.75
DELEGATION	Dummy variable equal to 1 if the president's discretionary authority increases; 0 if there is no change; and -1 if the president's discretionary authority is decreased.	0.09	0.47
DIVIDED	Dummy variable equal to 1 if Congress and the presidency are controlled by opposing parties; 0 if there is split partisan control of Congress; and -1 if Congress and the presidency are controlled by the same party.	-0.40	0.85

Sources: Tariff Data—U.S. Bureau of the Census (1975), *Historical Statistics of the United States,* Series U 207–12; and U.S. Bureau of the Census (1991), *Statistical Abstract.* Political Data—U.S. Bureau of the Census (1975), Series Y 204–10; Stanley and Niemi (1988); and Ornstein, Mann, and Malbin (1992). Economic Data—*Economic Report of the President* (1975–1991); and U.S. Bureau of the Census (1975), Series D 11–25 and E 52–63. Early GNP estimates calculated from Balke and Gordon (1989).

TABLE 5.4. Trade Legislation, Divided Government, and Delegation, 1890–1990

Legislation	President	House	Senate	Divided	Delegation
1890 McKinley Tariff Act	Rep	Rep	Rep	Unified	Increased
1894 Wilson-Gorman Tariff Act	Dem	Dem	Dem	Unified	Decreased
1897 Dingley Tariff Act	Rep	Rep	Rep	Unified	Increased
1909 Payne-Aldrich Tariff Act	Rep	Rep	Rep	Unified	Decreased
1913 Underwood Tariff Act	Dem	Dem	Dem	Unified	Increased
1922 Fordney-McCumber Tariff Act	Rep	Rep	Rep	Unified	Increased
1930 Smoot-Hawley Tariff Act	Rep	Rep	Rep	Unified	Increased
1934 Reciprocal Trade Agreements Act	Dem	Dem	Dem	Unified	Increased
1937 Extension of the RTAA	Dem	Dem	Dem	Unified	Increased
1940 Extension of the RTAA	Dem	Dem	Dem	Unified	Increased
1943 Extension of the RTAA	Dem	Dem	Dem	Unified	Increased
1945 Extension of the RTAA	Dem	Dem	Dem	Unified	Increased
1948 Extension of the RTAA	Dem	Rep	Rep	Divided	Decreased

Legislation				
1949 Extension of the RTAA	Dem	Dem	Dem	Unified	Increased
1951 Extension of the RTAA	Dem	Dem	Dem	Unified	Decreased
1953 Extension of the RTAA	Rep	Rep	Rep	Unified	Increased
1954 Extension of the RTAA	Rep	Rep	Rep	Unified	Increased
1955 Extension of the RTAA	Rep	Dem	Dem	Divided	Increased
1958 Extension of the RTAA	Rep	Dem	Dem	Divided	Decreased
1962 Trade Expansion Act	Dem	Dem	Dem	Unified	Increased
1974 Trade Reform Act	Rep	Dem	Dem	Divided	Increased
1979 Trade Agreements Act	Dem	Dem	Dem	Unified	Increased
1984 Trade and Tariff Act	Rep	Dem	Rep	Split	Decreased
1988 Omnibus Trade and Competitiveness Act	Rep	Dem	Dem	Divided	Decreased

the use of this authority, such as a congressional veto or reporting require-ments. At other times, even though Congress allows the president to negotiate trade agreements, it shifts the locus of decision-making authority on some issues away from the president to other agencies. Furthermore, legislators may change the criteria of those determinations to make it easier or harder for the president to disregard agency decisions. Thus, the fact that Congress does or does not grant the president negotiating authority reveals little about whether the institutions that govern trade policy are more or less restrictive. Taking into account these difficulties, I classify trade acts according to whether their overall effect was to increase or decrease the level of presiden-tial discretion in setting trade policy.

The independent variables include both demands for protection and the current political environment. I measure aggregate economic conditions by the real gross national product (GNP), the constant dollar producer price index (PPI), and the unemployment rate (UNEMPLOY). These variables are similar to those used in most economic analyses of the tariff and are included to make my results comparable with previous studies.[89] In some cases, I transform these variables to improve the overall fit of the economic model. This pro-vides the strongest test for Propositions 2A and 2B, which assert that political factors also influence tariff rates.

As indicated in chapter 4, it is usually postulated that a downturn in business conditions, represented by a decrease in GNP, leads workers and industries to demand higher protection, so the sign on this variable should be positive. Similarly, affected industries intensify their efforts for protection the higher the unemployment rate, so UNEMPLOY should be negatively corre-lated with delegation. The effect of rising price levels on the demand for protection, however, is ambiguous. Bohara and Kaempfer (1991a) argue that higher prices may lead consumers (voters) to demand less protection in order to reduce inflation. On the other hand, rising prices may also cause a flood of imports, thereby fueling complaints from adversely affected industries, lead-ing to increased pressures for protective tariffs. I thus make no prediction as to the sign of the coefficient on this variable.

To measure partisan conflict between Congress and the president, I create a variable labeled DIVIDED. In a given year, if Congress and the administra-tion are controlled by opposing parties (divided government), this variable takes on the value 1. If exactly one chamber of Congress and the administra-tion are controlled by the same party (split partisan control), the variable is assigned the value 0. Finally, if both houses of Congress and the president are controlled by the same party (unified government), the variable takes on the

89. Magee, Brock, and Young (1989) and Bohara and Kaempfer (1991a; 1991b) employ similar measures. The economic variables are estimated in logarithms to smooth the series and are lagged by one year. The political variable is also lagged by one year.

value -1. In the sample there are sixty-five cases of unified partisan control, twelve cases of split partisan control of government, and twenty-four cases of divided government. If Proposition 2A is correct, this variable should have a negative effect on delegation.

Ordered Probit Estimates and Discretionary Authority
Proposition 2A asserts that legislators will delegate more authority to a president with preferences over trade policy more similar to their own. Congress will then give the president less discretionary authority during times of divided government than when there is unified partisan control of government.

The basic equation to be estimated incorporates both the political and economic determinants of delegation:

$$\text{DELEGATION}_t = \alpha + \beta_1 \Delta \text{GNP}_t + \beta_2 \Delta \text{UNEMPLOY}_t$$

$$+ \beta_3 \Delta \text{PPI}_t + \beta_4 \Delta \text{DIVIDED}_t + \epsilon_t. \quad (5.1)$$

Recall from appendix 3.2 that $\partial d^*/\partial P < 0$, implying that the president's discretion rises as the policy differences between Congress and the president decrease. Thus I expect a negative relation between divided government and delegation. Also note that while the model relates levels of conflict to levels of discretion, the dependent variable DELEGATION is the change in discretion from one year to the next. To be consistent with the theoretical model, then, I difference the right-hand side variables only.[90]

Equation 5.1 can be estimated by ordinary least squares methods, with the predicted coefficients interpreted as the marginal change in the probabilities that delegation increases, decreases, or remains the same. This *linear probability* model, however, imposes the rather severe assumption that, on average, increases in delegation are equal but opposite to decreases in delegation. It may also produce negative variances and predicted probabilities less than 0 or greater than 1.

A more natural method is to estimate equation 5.1 by an *ordered probit* model, which always produces predictions between 0 and 1. This approach is used when the categories of the dependent variable are inherently ordered, as they are here. It falls between regular probit models, which ignore the ordering of the dependent variable, and linear probability models, which assume that the increment from one category to the next is exactly equal.

---

90. The model developed in appendix 3.2 relates discretion to the policy preferences of Congress and the executive. Economic effects can be incorporated into this model without qualitatively changing the previous results if the impact of the economic variables is additively separable from the political variables. That is, changes in economic conditions are assumed to shift the ideal points of Congress and the president in the same direction and by the same amount.

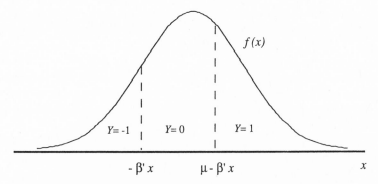

Fig. 5.2. Probability distribution of ordered probit estimates

To understand the logic of a probit estimator, consider again equation 5.1. DELEGATION can take on three different values: increase (1), no change (0), and decrease (-1). Of course, the discretionary authority actually given to the president is a continuous variable, ranging from complete authority, $d = R$, to no authority, $d = 0$, borrowing the terminology from the appendixes to chapter 3. If we could observe this authority directly, we could apply standard regression methods to equation 5.1, but since its exact value cannot be determined, we approximate it with a category variable, and the appropriate estimating technique is an ordered probit.

In more technical terms, we can think of the discrete dependent variable Y_i (DELEGATION) as being the realization of a continuous, but unobserved, variable Y_i^*. As illustrated in figure 5.2, the relationship between the categories of Y_i and the values of Y_i^* are:

Y_i = decrease if $Y_i^* < 0$;

   no change if $0 \leq Y_i^* \leq \mu$;

   increase if $Y_i^* > \mu$.

Probit estimators assume that Y_i is represented by the cumulative normal distribution:

$$\text{Prob}(Y_i = j) = \Phi(\mu_j - \beta'x_i) - \Phi(\mu_{j+1} - \beta'x_i)$$

where μ_j and μ_{j+1} denote the upper and lower threshold values for category j. The probit equation estimates the components of β and μ by maximum likelihood, from which the underlying probabilities can be calculated.

Results

The results of the ordered probit estimation are presented in table 5.5. They show that institutional restraints do respond to both economic conditions and divided partisan control of government. Column 1 tests the simple economic model, omitting the political variable. The results suggest that changes in unemployment and price levels are negatively and significantly related to the president's discretionary authority at the 5 percent level, indicating that in times of economic expansion Congress is more willing to delegate power to the president than in times of economic downturns. GNP is not a significant determinant of delegation but has the expected sign.

TABLE 5.5. Ordered Probit Estimates of Discretionary Authority

Dependent Variable: DELEGATION

Independent Variable	Model 1	Model 2
CONSTANT	1.56	1.66
	(7.37)**	(7.66)**
ΔGNP	1.45	0.24
	(0.52)	(0.088)
ΔUNEMPLOY	-0.69	-0.93
	(-1.85)**	(-2.29)**
ΔPPI	-3.60	-3.04
	(-2.47)**	(-2.30)**
ΔDIVIDED		-0.46
		(-2.84)**
μ	2.63	2.75
Number of Observations	99	99
Log Likelihood	-63.73	-61.11
Percentage Correctly Predicted	79.80	80.81

Note: t-statistics in parentheses. Standard errors computed from analytic first and second derivatives (Eicker-White).

* $\alpha < .10$. ** $\alpha < .05$.

The key result appears in column 2, when divided partisan control of government is added to the equation. As in column 1, economic conditions tend to affect the willingness of Congress to delegate authority. But even after accounting for aggregate economic conditions, divided government is negatively and significantly related to the extent of delegation, as predicted by Proposition 2A. Thus, the impression from the historical overview that institutions respond to partisan conflict is borne out in the statistical analysis.[91]

In an ordered probit analysis, the β coefficients cannot be interpreted as the marginal effects of the independent variables on delegation. To discern the complete effects of a multinomial independent variable like DIVIDED on the amount of delegation, additional calculations are required. For a three category dependent variable, we need two cut points in the normal distribution, as shown in figure 5.2. Given estimates $\hat{\mu}$ and $\hat{\beta}$, and for any values of the independent variables x, these cut points occur at $0 - \hat{\beta}'x$ and $\hat{\mu} - \hat{\beta}'x$. To estimate the effects of divided government on DELEGATION, we set all other independent variables equal to their mean values and then let DIVIDED range from -1 to 0 to 1.

The results are presented in table 5.6.[92] The top row of the table shows that when DIVIDED is equal to -1, the cut points of the normal distribution are -2.053 and 0.701. Consulting a standard normal table, this indicates that the area in the left tail of the curve shown in figure 5.2 is 0.020, the area in the middle region is 0.738, and the area in the right tail is 0.242. In other words, when there is unified government there is a 2.0 percent chance that Congress will decrease delegated authority, a 74 percent chance of no change in delegated power, and a 24 percent chance of an increase in authority. The next two rows of the table replicate this analysis for the cases of split and divided partisan control of government.

From the results in table 5.5 above, it is clear that divided government makes delegations of authority less likely and restrictions more likely. The last three rows in table 5.6 confirm these results. As we move from unified to divided government, the probability of delegating less power rises, while the probability of delegating more power falls. To be precise, a change from unified to divided government increases the probability that Congress will restrict the president's authority by about 11 percent and decreases the probability that his authority will be expanded by about 19 percent.

Interestingly, the table also shows that no action, DELEGATION = 0, is most likely under split or divided control of government (82.2 and 81.9

---

91. A number of sensitivity tests were conducted to determine whether these results are robust to different specifications of divided government; for example, the consequences of distinguishing only between unified versus divided government were examined. These variations led to qualitatively similar results.

92. See Greene 1990, 703–6 for details.

TABLE 5.6. Effects of Divided Government on Discretionary Authority

Category	$0 - \hat{\beta}'x$	$\mu - \hat{\beta}'x$	Prob[DEL=-1]	Prob[DEL=0]	Prob[DEL=1]
DIVIDED = -1	-2.053	0.701	0.020	0.738	0.242
DIVIDED = 0	-1.598	1.156	0.055	0.822	0.123
DIVIDED = 1	-1.142	1.612	0.127	0.819	0.054
Change: -1 to 0 Unified to Split			0.035	0.084	-0.119
Change: 0 to 1 Split to Divided			0.072	-0.003	-0.069
Change: -1 to 1 Unified to Divided			0.107	0.081	-0.188

percent, respectively). That is, institutional innovation appears most fre-quently when both branches of the federal government are controlled by the same party. This should not be surprising; under unified government Congress is more inclined to increase the president's discretionary authority, and the president will certainly not be averse to accepting it. In times of divided government, however, Congress is less likely to extend the president's author-ity, despite the president's wishes to the contrary. This was the case from 1967 to 1973, when the Democratically controlled Congress refused to extend Nixon negotiating authority.

The implications of the analysis are twofold. First, there is a constitu-ency basis for congressional design of trade institutions. These findings con-tradict the notion that Congress delegates authority to shift blame to the president or other administrative agencies, thereby insulating itself from pro-tectionist demands. This blame-shifting argument has been advanced by Dest-ler (1986a) and, in a similar context, by Fiorina (1982). If this were so, congressional delegation would increase as general economic conditions worsen. In fact, my findings regarding the economic variables show just the opposite: Congress is less willing to give the president discretionary authority when there is a downturn in the economic business cycle. Of course this assumes that decreasing discretionary authority leads to greater protection; this claim will be investigated in the following section.

Second, the design of trade institutions reflects partisan conflict between Congress and the president. In times of divided partisan control of national government, Congress will delegate less authority to the president than in times of unified government. The interesting implication, as mentioned above, is that procedural innovations that increase the president's discretion-ary authority will occur during times of unified government. The first delega-tion in 1890, the RTAA in 1934, and the first multilateral negotiating author-ity in 1962 all took place under unified partisan control. One notable exception was the 1974 Trade Reform Act, which was enacted when the Republicans controlled the presidency and the Democrats, Congress. But although this act increased the president's discretionary authority, it was much more restrictive than previous postwar delegations in that it required congres-sional approval of presidential trade proposals.

Finally, the results presented here address the effects of divided govern-ment on policy outcomes, a subject that has recently received considerable attention.[93] The most comprehensive study to date is by Mayhew (1991), who concludes that in the postwar era divided government makes no difference for the number of important pieces of legislation enacted. My analysis suggests that although the number of laws passed under divided and unified govern-

---

93. See Cox and Kernell 1991 and Fiorina 1992.

ment may be similar, the substance of these policies may be quite different. Specifically, this section implies that partisan conflict affects the institutional constraints Congress places on authority delegated to the executive branch. I now turn to the impact these institutions have on policy outcomes.

5.2.2. Effects of Delegation on Tariffs: Testing Proposition 2B

As suggested by the history of trade legislation, delegations of power in the post-1934 period were instituted in order to reduce the overall level of protectionism. If these procedures had real effects on outcomes, then we should observe a correlation between delegated power and tariff levels. This section tests Proposition 2B, which states that delegations of authority actually do produce lower tariffs, and that restrictions on authority are associated with higher tariffs.

Data
The empirical analysis covers the period from 1949 to 1990. The dependent variable, AVGTOTAL, is the level of protection, measured as the ratio of the value of duties collected to the value of total imports. Figure 5.3 shows the tariff trend for this period. The analysis is limited by the difficulty of measuring aggregate levels of protection. One important problem is the recent proliferation of nontariff barriers (NTBs). Unfortunately, accurate estimates of NTBs are not available for the sample period. The dependent variable does identify barriers to trade resulting from increases in the actual tariff rate, as well as certain NTBs, such as the imposition of anti-dumping or countervailing duties, the granting of affirmative escape clause actions, and other forms of protection that result in higher tariffs. The measure does *not* capture the barriers to trade due to voluntary export restraints, orderly marketing arrangements, or quotas. Nor does it identify the more oblique but equally pervasive impediments, such as labeling requirements and health and safety standards, that raise the costs of imports and in some cases prohibit them altogether.[94]

The independent variables capture both economic and political determinants of protection. To measure aggregate economic activity, I again use real gross national product (GNP), the unemployment rate (UNEMPLOY), and the constant dollar producer price index (PPI). The descriptive statistics are provided in table 5.3 above. To capture the effect of the president's discretionary authority on the tariff, I include DELEGATION, the dependent variable in the previous section, as an explanatory variable of the tariff here. Proposition 2B asserts that the more leeway the president is given, the lower will be the levels

---

94. See appendix 5.3 for a further discussion of the variables used in this analysis.

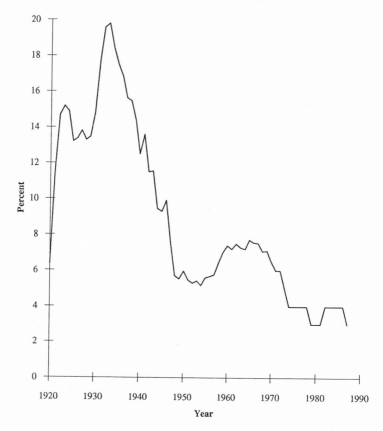

Fig. 5.3. Average tariff, 1920–90

of protection. If this prediction holds, then DELEGATION (the president's discretionary authority) will be negatively related to the tariff.

Estimation

The basic estimation technique used to test Proposition 2B is ordinary least squares. As explained in chapter 4, the tariff series shows a unit root.[95] Since the economic variables are not cointegrated, we must correct for nonsta-

---

95. For the sample period, I again tested the null hypothesis that $\rho = 1$. The resulting t-statistic is -1.02. Thus I cannot reject the hypothesis of a unit root at the 5 percent level. After first differencing the dependent variable, the estimated t-statistic is now 6.75. This time I can reject the hypothesis that the differenced tariff series has a unit root at the 5 percent significance level.

tionarity by estimating the equation in first differences.[96] Recall that DELE-GATION is the change in discretion from one year to the next; therefore, it need not be differenced again. The basic model to be estimated, then, is defined as follows:

$$\Delta \text{AVGTOTAL}_t = \alpha + \beta_1 \Delta \text{GNP}_t + \beta_2 \Delta \text{UNEMPLOY}_t$$

$$+ \beta_3 \Delta \text{PPI}_t + \beta_4 \text{DELEGATION}_t + \epsilon_t. \quad (5.2)$$

Equation 5.2 asserts that changes in tariff levels respond to changes in demands for protection and the president's discretionary authority to set trade policy.

In chapter 4, I argue that changes in the tariff in the late nineteenth and early twentieth centuries also reflected constituency interests and partisan control of government. During that period, the Republicans championed the protective tariff, the Democrats adopted a free trade platform, and whenever a new party took control of national government there was a change in tariff policy. Thus, the party in office had an immediate and direct effect on policy outcomes.

In the post-1934 period, however, partisan effects on trade legislation have not been so apparent. Trade policy is no longer made in the congressional arena; rather, legislators have chosen to delegate the authority to set specific tariff rates to the president and executive agencies. Destler (1986a; 1991) even argues that in the postwar era, trade policy is a nonpartisan issue. This chapter asserts that partisan conflict still matters, but the effects of party competition now appear indirectly, through the institutions that legislators create to govern the policy-making process. The DELEGATION variable captures these partisan effects as they now work through trade institutions.

Results

Table 5.7 reports the results of estimating equation 5.2. Column 1 includes only the economic variables; it shows that the price level is negatively and significantly correlated with the tariff. GNP is also negatively correlated, but the coefficient is insignificant. Unemployment is positively correlated and insignificant.[97] Notice that the constant term is positive but insignificant. This result is rather surprising: the constant term in a differenced equation is the trend of the dependent variable, and figure 5.3 shows a rather considerable

---

96. As in chapter 4, all reported standard errors and variances are White heteroskedastic-consistent estimates.

97. Bohara and Kaempfer (1991a) find similar results.

decline in the tariff series. Analysis of the covariance matrix, however, indicates that for the sample period GNP is correlated with both the constant term and the unemployment rate. Column 2 omits GNP from the equation; the results show that unemployment is now positively and significantly correlated with the tariff at the 5 percent level, inflation remains significant at the 10 percent level, and the trend is now negative, but again insignificant.

Columns 3 and 4 incorporate DELEGATION into the analysis and provide a test of Proposition 2B. Column 3 shows that changes in GNP and the price level are significant determinants of the tariff. Unemployment is not significant in this instance. Again, omitting GNP from the equation, as shown in column 4, changes the sign of the trend variable. The price level remains significant, as does the unemployment rate. My main results, however, are

TABLE 5.7. Least Squares Estimates of the Effect of Delegation on the Tariff

Dependent Variable: ΔAVGTOTAL

	Model 1	Model 2	Model 3	Model 4
Independent Variable				
CONSTANT	0.023	-0.0011	0.032	-0.00074
	(0.92)	(-0.10)	(1.24)	(-0.071)
ΔGNP	-0.67		-0.85	
	(-1.00)		(-1.28)*	
ΔUNEMPLOY	0.045	0.12	0.040	0.13
	(0.73)	(3.10)**	(0.62)	(3.39)**
ΔPPI	-0.44	-0.37	-0.49	-0.40
	(-1.44)*	(-1.32)*	(-1.63)**	(-1.42)*
DELEGATION			-0.024	-0.021
			(-2.10)**	(-1.91)**
Number of Observations	42	42	42	42
R^2	.17	.15	.19	.18
D.W. Statistic	1.74	1.69	1.82	1.75

Note: t-statistics in parentheses. Standard errors are White heteroskedastic-consistent estimates.

* $\alpha < .10$. ** $\alpha < .05$.

not sensitive to the model specification. In either case, the coefficient on the institutional variable is significant at the 5 percent level and has the sign predicted by Proposition 2B. These results suggest that, in the sample period studied, increasing the president's discretionary authority on average decreased the tariff rate.

5.2.3. Discussion

The analysis in this section links partisan conflict, institutional constraints, and trade policy outcomes. There are two central findings. First, the amount of discretionary authority given to the president reflects both constituency demands for protection and partisan conflict between Congress and the president. As economic conditions worsen and as we move toward periods of divided government, legislators grant the president less discretion to make trade policy. Second, in the postwar period, the president's leeway in setting policy proved to be a significant determinant of the tariff rate. Increases in discretionary authority were associated with decreases in the tariff, and as the president's discretion became more limited, the tariff increased.

One goal of my empirical analysis is to systematically code administrative procedures. Although the terms of delegation are often discussed as important factors shaping policy, rarely are they codified and subjected to rigorous econometric analysis. Clearly my method of coding delegation is only approximate. Ideally, one would like a continuous measure of the president's discretionary authority instead of the discrete measure adopted here. Such a scale, however, inevitably introduces bias into the analysis, as reliable indices are notoriously difficult to construct. Nonetheless, the coarser measure used here yields considerable variation over time that can be explained in part by the political variables suggested by my theoretical model.

5.3. Conclusion

Although Congress delegated considerable amounts of power to the president, especially after 1934, it never abdicated its control of trade policy. Every law that gave the executive branch some measure of authority also placed constraints and limits on that authority in at least one of four ways.

First, Congress places direct limits on what the president can and cannot do. For instance, it has restricted the scope of negotiating authority by limiting the president to agreements that only deal with tariff barriers. Congress also limits the amount by which the president can change policy, as in the RTAA, which allowed for tariff reductions up to 50 percent. Further, it has imposed conditions on the timing of tariff reductions, such as the staged reductions mandated by the 1955 extension of RTAA. And at times, legislators have even reserved certain articles from consideration altogether, as lumber was exempted from the 1988 U.S.-Canada Free Trade Agreement.

Second, Congress has not always delegated power directly to the president. It has created instead a series of executive agencies subject to congressional approval and oversight that are charged with providing certain information and services. Thus, the president cannot independently set trade policy; rather, these agencies hold hearings, make determinations, and suggest courses of action. Starting with the Tariff Board in 1909 and continuing with the Tariff Commission, the International Trade Commission, the Special Trade Representative, and the USTR, Congress has been careful to ensure that executive decision making conforms to specified standards. Currently, for example, the USTR, appointed with the advice and consent of the Senate, is empowered to conduct all international negotiations.

Third, Congress has defined the process by which trade negotiations are conducted. In creating fast track procedures, for example, legislators allow the president easier passage of trade agreements. Fast track stipulates simple majorities and a closed rule, as opposed to the two-thirds requirement of treaties or the possibility of amendment in normal legislative procedures. The price of these procedural advantages, however, is greater congressional control over the negotiating process, including numerous veto points and consultation requirements. The politics of fast track and its application to specific trade negotiations will be discussed at length in the next chapter.

Fourth, Congress has created detailed procedures and criteria by which industries can obtain special protection. The peril point provision aided industries whose livelihood was threatened by import competition; the national security provision protected industries deemed vital to national defense; trade adjustment assistance and the escape clause were made available to industries faced with restructuring problems as a result of international competition; and anti-dumping laws and countervailing duty procedures provide relief for industries damaged by unfair trade practices. The largest point of contention in this category is what degree of latitude will be left to the president in addressing industry exemptions. Some laws have provided that the president need merely state his reasons for overriding aid to specific industries, others have allowed for a congressional veto of presidential inaction, and in the most extreme case the Super 301 clause actually mandates presidential retaliation in certain circumstances.

Given that Congress spends enormous time and energy designing these institutions of delegation, it would be odd if these institutions had no effect on trade policy. And indeed we have seen in the empirical section that greater institutional constraints on the president's authority do lead to more protectionist policies. Further, Congress is less willing to delegate power to presidents of the opposing party. Thus, the partisan competition over tariff policy, which was supposedly killed by the passage of the 1934 RTAA, was reincarnated in partisan battles over the extent of the discretionary authority given to the president.

APPENDIX 5.1: CLASSIFICATIONS OF TRADE AGREEMENTS

To examine the relation between procedures and policy outcomes, I coded international trade agreements from 1925 to 1978 that entered into force for that year. I determined the type of procedure by the legal authority through which the agreement was enacted.

Prior to 1946, I used as my primary source the *United States Treaties and Other International Agreements, 1776–1949*. After 1946, I used as my primary source the State Department document *International Agreements Other Than Treaties, 1946–1978: A List with Citations of Their Legal Bases*.

Definitions

Prior Legislation—Under this heading, agreements are made under and within the framework of prior legislation either specifically authorizing the making of agreements or establishing policies or authorizing programs, projects, and procedures that require agreements to effectuate their purposes.

Subsequent Legislation—Under this heading are agreements made effective through subsequent legislation, that is, agreements not authorized by prior legislation but made effective through legislation approving such agreements, implementing the provisions thereof, or otherwise enabling or sanctioning the fulfillment of the purposes thereof.

Legislation and Treaty—Under this heading are agreements made within the framework of treaty provisions and made effective, in whole or in part, in accordance with legislation applying to the agreements or the subject matter thereof.

Treaty—Under this heading are agreements made within the framework of treaty provisions without prior or subsequent legislation relating to the agreements or the subject matter thereof, or made effective by the approval and entry into force of treaties dealing with the subject matter of the agreements.

Partly Legislation and/or Treaty and Partly Constitutional Authority—Under this heading are agreements made in part on the basis of the existence of prior or subsequent legislation, and/or in part on the existence of prior or subsequent treaty provisions and in part on the authority and powers of the president under the Constitution. The constitutional powers of the president are considered only to the extent that such authority and powers are deemed to be the primary basis for the agreement.

Constitutional Authority—Under this heading are agreements entered pursuant to, and deriving their effectiveness from, the authority and powers of the president under the Constitution.

Legislation	Delegated Authority	Restrictions	Retaliation	Import Relief
1890 McKinley Tariff Act	Reciprocal trade provision.	Limited to certain articles.	*LFT* President may suspend duty-free treatment when unreasonable and unequal duties are imposed.	
1894 Wilson-Gorman Tariff Act	Reciprocal trade provision repealed.			
1897 Dingley Tariff Act	Reciprocal trade provision. Reduction of duties by treaty.	Limited to certain articles. No reductions of duties by more than 20%. No transfers from the dutiable to the free-list. Agreement not to exceed 5 years.	*LFT* President may suspend duty-free treatment when unreasonable and unequal duties are imposed. *CVD* Secretary of Treasury to impose additional duty equal to the net amount of subsidy.	

1909 Payne-Aldrich Tariff Act	Reciprocal trade provision repealed. Max-Min Tariff: President imposes minimum duty when equivalent concessions are made; maximum duty otherwise.		
1913 Underwood Tariff Act	Reciprocal trade provision.	Congressional approval required.	
1916 Anti-Dumping (Revenue) Act			AD Individuals could sue for triple damages.
1921 Emergency Tariff and Anti-Dumping Act			AD Secretary of Treasury imposes duty equal to the difference between the sale and market price.
1922 Fordney-McCumber Tariff Act	Equalization of the costs of production: President proclaims	Tariff Commission recommends tariff adjustment.	LFT President may exclude articles from entry if

(continued)

Legislation	Delegated Authority	Restrictions	Retaliation	Import Relief
	changes in tariff rates to equalize costs of production in foreign and home market.	Increases or decreases not to exceed 50%.	Tariff Commission determines unfair competition. *CVD* President proclaims duty to offset subsidy, not to exceed 50% or less than 10% ad valorem. *AD* Secretary of Treasury imposes duty equal to the difference between the sale price and the foreign market value.	
1930 Smoot-Hawley Tariff Act	Equalization of the costs of production.	Tariff Commission recommends tariff adjustment. Increases or decreases not to exceed 50%. No transfers from the dutiable to free-list.	*LFT* President may exclude goods from entry if the Tariff Commission determines unfair competition. *CVD* President proclaims	

		duty to offset benefit, not to exceed 50% ad valorem. After proclamation, if discrimination persists, the president may exclude articles from importation.
1934 Reciprocal Trade Agreements Act	Reciprocal trade provision.	No increase or decrease more than 50%. No transfer from dutiable to free-list. Negotiating authority terminates in 3 years.
1937 Extension of the RTAA	Reciprocal trade provision.	Negotiating authority terminates in 3 years.
1940 Extension of the RTAA	Reciprocal trade provision.	Negotiating authority terminates in 3 years.
1943 Extension of the RTAA	Reciprocal trade provision.	Negotiating authority terminates in 2 years.
1945 Extension of the RTAA	Reciprocal trade provision.	No increase or decrease to exceed 50% of existing rates or 75% of 1934 rates.

(continued)

Legislation	Delegated Authority	Restrictions	Retaliation	Import Relief
1948 Extension of the RTAA	Reciprocal trade provision.	No transfers from the dutiable to the free-list. Negotiating authority terminates in 3 years.		*Peril point provision:* President submits a list of articles to Tariff Commission for possible tariff reduction. Tariff Commission determines the point at which tariff reductions would seriously injure an industry. If the president's actions differ from the commission's recommendation, he must report to Congress.
		Negotiating authority terminates in 1 year.		
1949 Extension of the RTAA	Reciprocal trade provision.	Negotiating authority terminates in 2 years.		Peril point provision repealed.
1951 Extension of the RTAA	Reciprocal trade provision.	Negotiating authority terminates in 2 years.		Peril point provision. *Escape Clause:* President may restrict

		concessions if imports injure domestic industry.
		Tariff Commission makes determination.
		President must report to Congress if actions differ from Tariff Commission's determination.
		Escape Clause
		Tariff Commission publishes findings immediately.
1953 *Extension of the RTAA*	Reciprocal trade provision.	Negotiating authority terminates in 1 year.
1954 *Extension of the RTAA*	Reciprocal trade provision.	Negotiating authority terminates in 1 year.
1955 *Extension of the RTAA*	Reciprocal trade provision.	No decreases greater than 15% of existing rates.
		No increases greater than 50% of the 1945 rates.
		Staged tariff reductions, not to exceed 5% per year.
		No concessions that impair national security.
		Annual reports.

(continued)

Legislation	Delegated Authority	Restrictions	Retaliation	Import Relief
1958 Extension of the RTAA	Reciprocal trade provision.	Negotiating authority terminates in 3 years. No decreases to exceed 20% of the existing rate. No increases to exceed 50% ad valorem of 1934 rates. Staged reductions. National security provision.		Peril point provision. *Escape Clause:* President's actions subject to a two-house override by two-thirds vote.
1962 Trade Expansion Act	Reciprocal trade provision. Eliminate duties on articles with tariffs less than 5%. Dominant supplier authority: If U.S. and the EEC make up 80% of world trade, then tariffs can be eliminated.	Negotiating authority terminates in 4 years. No decreases to exceed 50% of existing rates. No increases to exceed 50% of the 1934 rates. STR chief negotiator (shifted authority away from the State Department) Congressional delegates to participate in negotiations. Staged requirements.	*LFT* President could suspend concessions if country discriminates against the U.S.	Peril point provision repealed. *Escape Clause* Injury must be in *major part* the result of import concessions. Two-house override by majority vote of presidential actions that differ from Tariff Commission's determinations.

| 1974 Trade Reform Act | Fast track authority:
President negotiates agreements to reduce tariff and nontariff barriers.
GSP authority for 10 years:
Duty-free treatment of certain goods imported from less developed countries.
Balance of payments authority. | National security provision.
Consultations:
Tariff Commission
Executive Departments
Public Hearings
Negotiating authority terminates in 5 years.

No decreases to exceed 40% of existing rates.
No increases to exceed 50% of existing rates.
Staged reductions over 10 years.
Congressional approval required.
Negotiating authority terminates in 5 years. | *LFT*
301 provision:
President authorized to retaliate against unfair trade.
Presidential actions subject to a two-house override by majority vote.
CVD
Determinations subject to a one-house override by majority vote. | *TAA*
Assistance granted to firms and workers if trade concessions are major cause of injury.
Escape Clause
Criteria changed from imports being a *major cause* to a *substantial cause* (important but not less than any other cause) of injury.
Presidential actions subject to a two-house override.
TAA
Criteria changed from imports being a *major cause* to *contributing importantly* to injury.
Assistance extended to communities. |

(continued)

Legislation	Delegated Authority	Restrictions	Retaliation	Import Relief
1979 *Trade Agreements Act*	Fast track authority extended.	Created sectoral advisory committees. President must consult with congressional committees one month before submitting implementing legislation. Negotiating authority terminates in 8 years.	*LFT* 301 provision: Retaliation subject to a material injury test (changed from imports being a substantial cause). *AD* ITC conducts material injury test. *CVD* ITC conducts material injury test. American Selling Price (ASP) repealed.	Reauthorized for 8 years.
1984 *Trade and Tariff Act*	GSP authority extended for 8-1/2 years.	Expanded advisory committees. Fast track authority subject to veto by the Ways and Means and	*LFT* 301 provision: Broadened the definition of unfair trade acts.	

1988 Omnibus Trade and Competitiveness Act	Fast track authority ex- tended.	Reverse fast track: Congress can repeal fast track procedures by majority vote. Negotiating authority terminates in 3 years, with a pos- sible 2-year exten- sion.	Finance Committees. Shifted the authority to initiate investi- gations from the president to the USTR. Presidential actions subject to a two- House override by the adoption of a *joint* disapproval resolution (changed from *concurrent*).	*LFT* Super 301 provision: Shifted determina- tions away from the president and to the USTR. Retaliation manda- tory if the USTR issues a positive finding. Definition of unfair trade broadened.	*TAA* Reauthorized for 2 years. Benefits extended to secondary workers.

Note: AD=Anti-dumping; CVD=Countervailing Duty; GSP=Generalized System of Preferences; ITC=International Trade Commission; LFT =Less than Fair Trade; STR=Special Trade Representative; USTR=United States Trade Representative.

APPENDIX 5.3

This appendix provides additional discussion of the variables used to test Proposition 2B. A noticeable feature of the average duty on total imports, shown in figure 5.3, is the sharp drop in the tariff rate in the post–World War II era. Although the tariff rose soon after the war, it never again reached prewar levels. The downward trend in the tariff coincides with and is generally thought to be due to the emergence of U.S. international economic dominance and the General Agreement on Tariffs and Trade (GATT). However, the decline in the tariff has not been uniform over time. The analysis presented in section 5.2.2 examines the effects of macroeconomic conditions and domestic political institutions in explaining variations around this trend.

The study covers the years 1949 to 1990. Although delegations of authority to the president started in 1890, the historical review notes that until 1934 most tariff rates were set by legislative decree. Thus, the institutions of delegation would have only a marginal effect on tariffs before 1934. The period 1934 to 1948 is excluded from the sample for two reasons. First, with the onset of the Great Depression, international trade virtually collapsed. Second, the United States and its trading partners continued in a state of near autarky during World War II. The political and economic havoc created by the depression and the war swamp the effects my model predicts.[98]

As discussed in chapter 4, two alternative tariff measures are commonly used: an unweighted average tariff rate or an average tariff rate weighted by the share of each good in total dutiable imports (AVGDUTY). These measures ignore duty-free imports and thus exaggerate the impact of rate changes and understate the impact of coverage (goods affected by tariffs) changes on the total value of imports. The import-share-weighted average used in this chapter (AVGTOTAL) is sensitive to changes in share weights as well as changes in tariff rates (see Gardner and Kimbrough 1989).

As I noted, it would be preferable to include NTBs in the dependent variable. However, accurate NTB measures are difficult to calculate. Most studies that incorporate estimates of nontariff measures into the analysis use the number of actions before the ITC as a dependent variable (Goldstein and Lenway 1989; W. Hansen 1990; Moore 1992). One problem with these studies is that it is questionable to pool data across periods characterized by significant changes in the institutional arrangements underlying ITC decisions. Other studies calculate nontariff barriers in terms of coverage. The dependent variable is whether an industry is covered by a nontariff measure. Usually, studies employing this measure are cross-sectional, or compare the change in an industry's coverage from one period to the next. Nearly all industries, however, are covered by some form of NTB. Thus this measure makes it difficult to differentiate between those industries that receive significant NTB protection and those for which barriers to trade are minimal. Nonetheless, using estimates of industries covered by nontariff measures, Ray (1981a) and Marvel and Ray (1983) find that tariff and nontariff barriers are largely complements and shaped by similar forces. These preliminary findings suggest that the analysis presented here may not be affected by the exclusion of NTBs.

---

98. Bohara and Kaempfer's (1991a) analysis of the tariff rate controls for these effects by including a dummy variable for the Great Depression.

CHAPTER 6

Fast Track Procedures and Policy Outcomes

If you let me write the procedure, and I let you write the substance, I'll screw you every time.
— Representative John Dingell (D-Mich.)

The past few chapters have asked first if institutions influence outcomes, or if trade policy is driven purely by preferences, as claimed by pressure group models. Chapter 4 argues that the institutions through which preferences are aggregated, in particular political parties, do impact policy outcomes. Next we asked if these institutions have changed over time, or if they are permanent, as suggested by the presidential dominance school. Chapter 5 shows that over the last century institutions have changed significantly along two dimensions. First, the nature of partisan competition shifted after 1934, from the setting of individual tariff rates to defining the conditions by which power is delegated to the president. Second, the institutions that govern this delegated authority have also changed. At times, legislators have granted the president great latitude to set policy independent of congressional interference; at other times, legislators have severely restrained the president's discretionary authority. Moreover, not only have the terms of delegation changed, but they have done so in a predictable way in response to economic and political factors (i.e., business cycles and divided government). In the postwar era, this authority has directly influenced policy outcomes, with tariff rates increasing as the president's discretionary authority decreases.

This chapter addresses the last step in linking preferences, institutions, and outcomes by showing how specific institutional arrangements affect policy. I examine fast track procedures for implementing international trade agreements, which, as mentioned in chapter 5, give legislators the opportunity to vote on presidential trade proposals. I then analyze the influence of these procedures in shaping the U.S.-Canada Free Trade Agreement (FTA) and the North American Free Trade Agreement (NAFTA). The details of these cases are consistent with Proposition 3 in chapter 3, which states that an ex post veto may force the executive to accommodate congressional demands.

In general, however, it is difficult to determine the effect of institutions on outcomes. Pastor (1983, 179), Destler (1986a, 67), and Goldstein (1986, 162), for instance, argue that members have ceded much of their legislative authority over international trade policy to the president because fast track procedures restrict Congress to an up-or-down vote. These authors recognize that Congress can exert some influence over outcomes through fast track procedures, but they maintain that legislators are, for the most part, passive when confronted with presidential trade proposals. They take as evidence of this passivity the large margins by which legislators pass international trade agreements, such as the 1979 Tokyo rounds, which the House and the Senate approved by votes of 395 to 7 and 90 to 4, respectively.

It may or may not be true that fast track procedures influence the president's ability to set policy, but it is impossible to determine the extent of this influence simply by looking at the final votes on the implementing bill or observing whether Congress exercises its ex post veto. For example, although the budget often passes by overwhelming majorities, Congress certainly plays a role in allocating federal appropriations and spending.[1] The more contentious issues may be hidden in prior, closer votes on procedural motions or key amendments. Furthermore, the effect of a given procedural arrangement may vary considerably from one instance to the next. Consider a legislative veto procedure like fast track. Depending on the preferences of the relevant actors and the initial status quo policy, the discussion of Proposition 3 defines cases in which it appears as if the president has complete control over policy; cases in which the president will have some control but will yet face congressional constraints; and cases in which the president will have no power at all to change policy.

To understand the effects of institutions on particular policy outcomes, then, one must first understand the procedures themselves and why Congress designed them. These procedural arrangements define a sequence of events and strategies available to each player at the various stages of the decision-making process. Next, for a particular example, one must show how this strategic interaction shaped behavior and the outcome. Sometimes, procedures will be used in an obvious manner, such as when a president vetoes a bill. Sometimes, they will not be so clear cut, such as when the mere threat of a veto induces changes in the behavior of other actors. Without careful analysis of the exact sequence of events, one may miss key influences of procedures on policy.

To this end, the next section provides an overview of fast track implementing procedures. For convenience, fast track is divided into ex ante and ex post stages. The following section traces the effects of fast track at each step of the

---

1. See Kiewiet and McCubbins 1991 for an analysis of budget procedures and their effects.

negotiation and implementation of the U.S.-Canada Free Trade Agreement. I show that these procedures allowed certain groups influence in the decision-making process and that the possibility of a congressional veto forced the president to accommodate protectionist demands. Section 6.3 examines the application of fast track procedures to the North American Free Trade Agreement (NAFTA) and recent developments surrounding its passage. The last section assesses the progress of the U.S.-Canada FTA and presents my conclusions.

6.1. The Politics of Fast Track

The 1974 Trade Reform Act revised and expanded the institutional structure by which U.S. trade policy is made. For the first time, Congress authorized the president to enter into trade agreements to reduce nontariff barriers as well as tariffs. But in granting this authority, Congress also established special procedures for implementing international trade agreements. These procedures have come to be known as the "fast track."

Fast track reduces the uncertainty that an agreement, once entered into, will be approved. It stipulates that an agreement needs only a majority in both houses of Congress to be enacted, whereas a treaty requires two-thirds of the Senate to be ratified. This degree of consensus may prove difficult to obtain, as happened with the Senate's failure to enact the 1979 East Coast Fishing Treaty between the United States and Canada, which divided the fish and scallops in the Georges Bank area off the coast of Maine.[2] Moreover, fast track limits the amount of product-specific protectionism that results when Congress makes trade legislation itself, as noted in the 1930 Smoot-Hawley Tariff Act and, to a lesser extent, the 1967 Kennedy rounds.[3] Once the agreement is formally submitted by the president to Congress, debate is limited and the legislation is considered without the possibility of amendment.

Fast track procedures serve three functions. First, they provide Congress with a veto over executive actions. As mentioned in chapter 5, Congress retains three checks over the president's negotiating authority. First, if either the House Ways and Means Committee or the Senate Finance Committee passes a disapproval resolution within sixty days, the president will be denied fast track authority. Second, if both houses pass a resolution within any sixty-

---

2. *Congressional Quarterly Weekly Report*, May 28, 1983, 1058.

3. The 1967 Kennedy rounds provide an example of the conflict that can occur between Congress and the president when enacting a trade agreement. As discussed in chapter 5, a heated debate broke out between Congress and the administration over the repeal of the American Selling Price. The end result was numerous exemptions and special provisions to compensate industries hard pressed by imports. *Congressional Quarterly Weekly Report*, February 2, 1968, 156.

day period stating that the president has failed to keep legislators informed, then fast track authority is repealed (reverse fast track). And third, Congress has its up-or-down vote over the final agreement.[4]

Second, fast track procedures provide Congress with information. Members of Congress participate directly in international negotiations and can thereby monitor the actions of the executive branch. This is an example of so-called police patrol oversight, wherein members of Congress directly review and oversee the actions taken by the president or an executive agency. Congress also creates executive agents, so-called fire inspectors, such as the United States Trade Representative (USTR), who oversee other agencies and report directly to Congress. Furthermore, Congress enfranchises constituents into the decision-making process, through private sector advisory committees and public hearings, so that if the executive takes actions that are objectionable, the interest group can seek remedy from the agency, the courts, or from Congress itself. Such indirect monitoring is commonly known as "fire-alarm" oversight (see McCubbins and Schwartz 1984).

Third, and closely related to the previous point, fast track procedures help members of Congress define their preferred policy. They let legislators know what the president or executive agency is doing (direct and indirect oversight) and inform the president or agency and members of Congress about what policies are electorally acceptable. By requiring studies and reports with specified criteria, by mandating public hearings, and by enfranchising private sector advisory committees into the decision-making process, legislators can determine which groups benefit from the agreement and which groups are injured.

Figure 6.1 divides fast track procedures into ex ante requirements, which constrain the executive's discretionary authority before and during international negotiations, and ex post requirements, which give Congress an opportunity to "amend" or veto the agreement. Ex ante requirements include the initial vote over the use of fast track procedures, congressional monitoring and

---

4. There is a fourth potential check on presidential use of fast track. Congress has the constitutional authority to change the rules for considering legislation at any time by majority vote. Legislators explicitly protected this right by including in the 1974 act the provision that fast track procedures "were an exercise of the rulemaking power of the House of Representatives and the Senate, respectively, and as such they are deemed a part of the rules of each House . . . with full recognition of the constitutional right of either House to change the rules (so far as relating to the procedure of that House) at any time, in the same manner and to the same extent as in the case of any other rule of that House." The Trade Act of January 3, 1975, Pub. L. No. 93-618, §151, 88 Stat. 2001. In fact, Congress has revoked similar expedited procedures for other trade related issues, as it did in the 1990 debates over extending most-favored-nation status to China. See House Rules Committee, *Disapproving the Extension of Fast Track Procedures to Bills to Implement Trade Agreements Entered into after May 31, 1991,* 102d Cong., 1st sess., H. Rept. 63, pt. 1, 6.

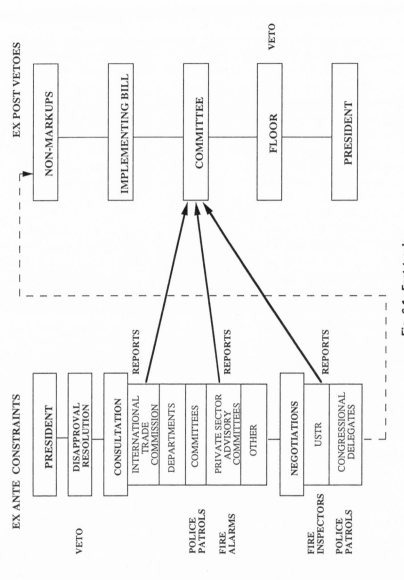

Fig. 6.1. Fast track

advice, consultation with executive departments and private sector advisory committees, and public hearings. Ex post requirements include "non-markup" sessions (drafting of the implementing legislation) and congressional approval procedures. In this section, I describe each of the steps in fast track. My purpose is to show that Congress has considerable input in the decision-making process, much more than is generally recognized by cursory treatments of fast track.

6.1.1. Ex ante Requirements: Constraints on Administrative Action

With the 1974 procedural reforms, Congress strengthened its oversight role in negotiating and implementing foreign trade policy. To further safeguard producer and consumer interests, Congress created a complete prenegotiation advisory system that increased the participation of the public, members of Congress, and various government agencies in the negotiation process. It also designated the USTR as the focal point in the executive branch for executing trade policy.

The Disapproval Resolution
At the outset, the president faces a possible veto of the proposed fast track procedures. Before beginning negotiations under fast track, the president must notify the Senate Finance Committee and the House Ways and Means Committee. If either committee passes a resolution within sixty days disapproving the negotiations, fast track implementing procedures do not apply. The committees determine whether traditional methods, such as introducing separate legislation or the treaty process, are preferable to the use of fast track.

Since the president must specify the objectives of the proposed negotiations and the issues that will be covered, Congress can force the administration to make concessions at this initial stage, such as removing certain articles from negotiations or making the agreement contingent on other factors. Congress can thereby limit not only which agreements the president can negotiate and the method by which an agreement becomes law, but also the content of those negotiations.

Consultation and Advice
Perhaps the most interesting feature of fast track procedures is the extensive prenegotiation advisory system. Congress established an elaborate "fire-alarm" oversight mechanism that incorporates the private sector, government agencies, and even congressional committees in developing international trade agreements. These consultations serve two purposes. First, groups sen-

sitive to or threatened by the proposed agreement are given an opportunity to express their concerns and seek compensation. Second, negotiators learn from these consultations which are the industries that, if ignored, may lobby members of Congress to veto any eventual agreement. The requirements for consultation and advice are defined as follows.

Before any proposed trade agreement is negotiated, the president must furnish the International Trade Commission (ITC) with a list of articles to be discussed. Within ninety days, the ITC advises the president about the probable economic effects on labor, consumers, and industries that produce similar or directly competitive articles. The ITC also conducts any additional investigations requested by the president or the USTR.[5] Further, the president consults with the Agriculture, Commerce, Defense, Interior, Labor, State, and Treasury Departments, the USTR, and each congressional committee having jurisdiction over legislation affected by a trade agreement.[6]

Private sector advisory committees play a central role in the consultation stage. The Trade Reform Act establishes an institutional framework that gives representative elements from the private sector an opportunity to express their views to U.S. negotiators. These committees inform and advise the president about negotiating objectives and bargaining positions before entering into an agreement, the operation of any agreement once entered into, and other matters that arise in connection with the development, implementation, and administration of U.S. trade policy.[7] This elaborate advisory system keeps legislators informed of executive actions, and lets the president and members of Congress know which constituents would be adversely affected by the proposed agreement.[8] Special interest groups can then seek remuneration either through administrative procedures, such as the escape clause or unfair trade practices provisions, or by directly pressuring legislators for exemptions.

There are four types of private sector advisory committees. First, the Advisory Committee for Trade Policy and Negotiations is composed of forty-five members, including representatives of state and local governments, labor, industry, agriculture, small business, service industries, retailers, and consumer interests. The committee is broadly representative of the key sectors and groups in the economy. Its members are recommended by the USTR and appointed by the president for a two year term. Second, the president can

---

5. The content of the ITC's reports are codified at 19 U.S.C.A. §2151(d) (1989).

6. Requirements for such consultation are codified at 19 U.S.C.A. §2112–52 (1989).

7. The Trade and Tariff Act of October 1984, Pub. L. No. 98-573, §306, 98 Stat. 3011. Codified at 19 U.S.C.A. §2155(c)(3) (1989). Hereinafter the 1984 Trade and Tariff Act.

8. See House Ways and Means Committee, *Trade Reform Act of 1973*, 93d Cong., 1st sess., H. Rept. 571, 39; Trade Act of January 3, 1975, Pub. L. No. 93-618, §135(d), 88 Stat. 1997; and Senate Finance Committee, *Trade Act of 1974*, 93d Cong., 1st sess., S. Rept. 1298, 101. Hereinafter the 1974 Trade Reform Act.

establish General Policy Advisory Committees for industry, labor, agriculture, services, investment, defense, and other interests. Its members are appointed by the USTR in consultation with the department secretaries. Third, the president can establish Sector or Functional Advisory Committees, which represent all industry, labor, agricultural, or service (including small business) interests affected by the agreement. Its members are also appointed by the USTR in consultation with the department secretaries. Fourth, the president can establish State and Local Government Policy Advisory Committees, which provide advice on overall policy objectives.

To the maximum extent practicable, the USTR keeps members of the advisory committees informed before and during negotiations. In addition, committee members may be designated as advisors to a negotiating delegation and participate in international meetings. However, members of the advisory committee may not speak or negotiate for the United States.[9] In addition to the private sector and state and local government advisory committees, the president provides private organizations with another opportunity to submit trade information and policy recommendations. Before entering into negotiations, the president holds public hearings on any matter relevant to the proposed trade agreement, including any article under consideration for modification and any concessions that should be sought by the United States.

Negotiations

The next stage in the process is the actual negotiations. The Trade Expansion Act of 1962 established the Special Representative for Trade Negotiations as the official who acts for the president in representing the United States in all international trade negotiations. Thus, it is the USTR, not the president, who in effect negotiates all international agreements.

The explicit intention of the House Ways and Means Committee in establishing the trade representative was to create a "focal point in the executive branch for responsibilities for carrying out the authorities delegated to the President by the Congress under trade agreement legislation."[10] Additionally, the trade representative was created to "down-play the strictly foreign policy orientation that trade agreement negotiations had been subjected in the past to under the leadership of the Department of State."[11]

The 1974 Trade Reform Act established the Office of Special Represen-

---

9. Codified at 19 U.S.C.A. §2155(k) (1989).

10. House Ways and Means Committee, *Trade Reform Act of 1973*, 93d Cong., 1st sess., H. Rept. 571, 40.

11. The Office of the Special Representative of Trade Negotiations was established under Exec. Order No. 11,075, 28 *Fed. Reg.* 473 (1963), as amended by Exec. Order No. 11,106, 28 *Fed. Reg.* 3911 (1963). House Ways and Means Committee, *Trade Reform Act of 1973*, 93d Cong., 1st sess., H. Rept. 571, 40.

tative for Trade Negotiations as an agency in the Executive Office of the President. The Ways and Means Committee sought to

> reaffirm its belief that a strong and independent office, headed by a Government official reporting directly to the President and responsible to the Congress, is the best means of assuring that in trade policy matters the United States is speaking with one strong voice on behalf of the executive branch and that positions taken accurately reflect the intent of Congress.[12]

The office is headed by the USTR, who is appointed by the president with the advice and consent of the Senate.[13]

To provide for careful and continuous congressional oversight, the 1974 Trade Reform Act allows congressional delegates, accredited as official advisors, to participate directly in international negotiations.[14] At the beginning of each congressional session, the Speaker of the House of Representatives, upon recommendation of the chair of the Ways and Means Committee, and the president of the Senate, upon the recommendation of the chair of the Finance Committee, appoint delegates. The USTR keeps each official adviser informed of the progress of negotiations.

Reports

The Advisory Committee for Trade Policy and Negotiations, each general advisory committee, and each sector or functional advisory committee meet at the conclusion of negotiations for each trade agreement and each submits a report to the president, the Congress, and the USTR. The reports from the Advisory Committee for Trade Policy and Negotiations and the general advisory committees state whether and to what extent the agreement promotes the economic interests of the United States and achieves the principal negotiating objectives set out in the prenegotiation consultations. These reports further state whether the agreement provides for equity and reciprocity within sectors and the extent to which their advisory opinion was included in the actual negotiations.

In addition to the advisory committee reports, the president submits to Congress an annual report on the progress of trade agreements under negotiation and on the national trade policy agenda. The USTR consults periodically

---

12. House Ways and Means Committee, *Trade Reform Act of 1973*, 93d Cong., 1st sess., H. Rept. 571, 40.

13. Pursuant to the authority granted under section 141 of the 1974 Trade Reform Act, and as defined in section 1 of Exec. Order No. 11,846, 40 *Fed. Reg.* 14,291 (1975).

14. The Trade Act of January 3, 1975, Pub. L. No. 93-618, §161, 88 Stat. 2008; Senate Finance Committee, *Trade Reform Act of 1974*, 93d Cong., 2d sess., S. Rept. 1298, 113.

with the congressional committees regarding overall objectives and priorities, and she reports directly to the Finance and Ways and Means Committees.[15]

Reverse Fast Track
Another safeguard Congress has over the president's exercise of delegated authority is the threat to repeal fast track negotiating privileges through a "reverse fast track."[16] If the president fails to meet the requirements for consultation with congressional committees, and if both the House and the Senate pass a disapproval resolution within any sixty-day period, fast track procedures for implementing an international trade agreement will be repealed, thereby effectively terminating the negotiations. In the House, a resolution of disapproval must be introduced by the chair or ranking minority member of the Ways and Means *or* Rules Committees, and it must be reported by both the Ways and Means *and* the Rules Committees. In the Senate, a resolution of disapproval must be an original resolution of the Finance Committee. Congress considers these resolutions under expedited procedures, which limit debate and prohibit amendments.

The threat of withdrawing fast track procedures does not imply that the president will accede to all the concerns expressed by the private sector advisory committees. It does, however, encourage the president to consult with members of Congress and keep them informed as to what actions are taken. The possibility that Congress will use its veto power provides a credible threat over executive actions and ensures that many of the concerns expressed during the prenegotiation stage will be reflected in the final agreement.

6.1.2. Ex post Requirements: Congressional Approval Procedures

After the negotiations have been concluded, the president must give Congress ninety days' notification before formally signing an international agreement. During this period, the president consults with the House Ways and Means Committee, the Senate Finance Committee, and every other committee that has jurisdiction over legislation affected by the agreement. These consultations address the nature of the agreement, how and to what extent the agreement achieves trade policy objectives, and all other matters relating to the

---

15. The secretary of the treasury and ITC face similar reporting requirements. The content of the annual reports is codified at 19 U.S.C.A. §2213(a) (1989).

16. This provision was first introduced in the Omnibus Trade and Competitiveness Act, Pub. L. No. 100-418, §1003, 102 Stat. 1131 (1988). Hereinafter the 1988 OTCA. For a discussion, also see House Conference Committee, *Omnibus Trade and Competitiveness Act of 1988*, 100th Cong., 2d sess., H. Conf. Rept. 576.

implementation of the agreement. In addition, the president's notification is accompanied by private sector reports, which give the committees an opportunity to examine the agreement before it is signed and to consider the legislative changes needed to implement the agreement.

Once the USTR enters into an official trade agreement with a foreign country or countries and the president signs it, the process is far from over. In many ways, it has only begun. The agreement must still be codified into an actual bill (the implementing legislation) and passed by Congress.

Congressional Committees: The Non-Markups

Before the formal introduction of the bill, congressional committees draft the implementing legislation in collaboration with the administration. Although there is no deadline for when the president must submit the implementing bill, thirty days before he does so, the president must consult with the Ways and Means and Finance Committees.[17] These informal consultations between the executive and the congressional committees, commonly called "non-markup" sessions, give committee members an opportunity to protect domestic industries that would otherwise be injured by more open competition. Although technically no amendments are allowed, committee members consider the draft bill and make "recommendations" regarding changes in domestic law required to meet the obligations of the international agreement and any additional provisions needed to either compensate or exempt disaffected groups. After the Ways and Means and Finance Committees have concluded their own "non-markups," they meet in a "non-conference" to reconcile the differences between their bills. These activities perform the function of the markup sessions and conference committees in the normal legislative process. The only difference is the timing; they take place before legislation is actually introduced. Congress thereby shapes the implementing legislation without violating its commitment not to amend the agreement once it is formally introduced.

The Implementing Bill

Fast track procedures require a final up-or-down vote on legislation within ninety days from when the bill is introduced.[18] After entering into the agree-

---

17. Committee hearings and consideration of possible legislative changes usually begin prior to the president actually signing the formal agreement. As discussed above, the 1979 trade act more carefully defined these consultations to ensure that all international agreements considered under fast track would take effect only by an act of Congress.

18. This assumes that the measure is introduced as a revenue-implementing bill. In this case, as with all revenue bills, the House must consider the legislation first, then the Senate takes up the measure. If the agreement is introduced as a nonrevenue measure, then, the House and Senate consider the bill simultaneously and there is a sixty-day time limit.

ment and consulting with the appropriate congressional committees on how to "package" the legislation, the president sends a copy of the final legal text of the agreement to the House of Representatives and to the Senate. The implementing legislation includes a draft of the bill, a statement of any necessary administrative action, and a summary of the effects the agreement will have on existing legislation.[19] The implementing bill is then introduced in the House and the Senate by the Majority and the Minority Leaders. Next, the Speaker of the House and the president of the Senate refer the implementing bill to the Ways and Means and Finance Committees and to other committees of either chamber with jurisdiction over the legislation affected by the agreement. If at the end of forty-five days the bill has not been reported, the committees are automatically discharged from further consideration of the bill.[20] After the House passes the enacting legislation, the Senate committees have an additional fifteen days to report the bill.

Floor Consideration

Finally, the bill must pass by a majority vote in the House and Senate. Time limits on floor consideration are enforced and no amendments are permitted. On or before the fifteenth day after the bill has been reported or discharged from committee, each chamber is required to vote on final passage of the bill. Debate on the House and Senate floor is limited to not more than twenty hours, which is divided equally among proponents and opponents.[21] A motion to recommit the bill is not in order.

6.1.3. Summary

Fast track procedures for the consideration of international trade agreements shield legislation from amendments and filibusters. These procedures allow members of Congress to overcome the collective dilemma of legislative logrolls (discussed in chapter 3) that they face when passing trade legislation. At the same time, fast track procedures reduce the uncertainty over whether an international trade agreement will be enacted. In restricting themselves to the fast track, however, members of Congress do not just reserve for themselves the symbolic role of critic and issuer of statements, as presidential dominance models claim. The trade agreement negotiated by the USTR and signed by the president is not necessarily what Congress enacts into law; trade accords are not self-executing. At each point in the negotiation and implementation process, Congress can sway the outcome. The Ways and Means and Finance Committees can veto fast track procedures. The USTR consults with congres-

---

19. Codified at 19 U.S.C.A §2112(e) (1989).
20. The 1974 Trade Act, Pub. L. No. 93-618, §151(e), 88 Stat. 2003.
21. The 1974 Trade Act, Pub. L. No. 93-618, §151(e)(1), 88 Stat. 2003.

sional committees before and during the negotiations. Members actively participate in the negotiations. Congressional committees draft the implementing legislation. And finally, a majority in Congress must approve the agreement. The final policy outcome is the result of each of these procedural points.

6.2. Fast Track and the U.S.-Canada Free
Trade Agreement

In the mid-1980s, when the United States and Canada first began considering a free trade agreement, they had the world's largest bilateral trade, totaling $166 billion in 1987. About 73 percent of Canada's total exports of merchandise and about 66 percent of its total imports were accounted for by the United States. On the other hand, the United States sold 24 percent of its merchandise exports to Canada and purchased 17 percent of its total imports from Canada. Total bilateral foreign direct investment exceeded $68 billion. The advantages of a free trade zone were obvious.

Barriers to entering into such an agreement were also evident. Canadian tariffs on U.S. dutiable exports averaged 10 percent, compared to an average U.S. tariff of 3 percent on dutiable imports from Canada. The Canadian government's presence in the Canadian economy was extensive. It ran the country's major airline, the railroad, telephone services, and an oil company. Government programs also benefited the lumber industry, beer producers, and hog growers. These industries lobbied against a free trade agreement, which would eliminate government subsidies.

On the American side of the border, too, were sources of strong opposition to the free trade agreement. The potato farmers of Aroostook County, Maine, once "the potato capital of the world," faced increased competition from imported Canadian potatoes. Washington State lumbermen complained of unfair Canadian trade practices in the form of government-subsidized stumpage fees. Truckers, oil companies, airlines, uranium miners, border television stations, gas companies, and magazine publishers all criticized Canadian trade practices.[22] United States companies filed numerous unfair pricing and subsidy cases against Canada, including commodities such as salted codfish, red raspberries, and pork products. A true free trade agreement would therefore require major changes in domestic legislation on both sides of the border.

In the end, the Free Trade Agreement (FTA) managed to negotiate a gradual reduction of all tariffs on bilateral trade. Tariffs on about 10 percent of all dutiable items imported from Canada—including articles such as data processing and telecommunications equipment, motorcycles, whiskey and rum, raw hides, leather, and furs—were terminated when the FTA was imple-

---

22. *Congressional Quarterly Weekly Report,* May 28, 1983, 1058.

mented. The rest of the tariffs on dutiable items were to be phased out. Thirty-five to 40 percent of all dutiable goods had their tariff rates lowered over five years with reductions of 20 percent each year. The remaining tariffs on Canadian imports are being phased out over ten years.

The FTA also eliminated some nontariff barriers, liberalized certain restrictions on investment and services, and established a binational system for review of national determinations on unfair pricing and subsidy practices. The FTA eliminated some quotas on poultry and eggs, relaxed U.S. health and safety standards on Canadian exports of pork products, and removed the duty remissions program for motor vehicle parts. It prohibited future Canadian and American laws and regulations from discriminating against providers of services, such as construction, tourism, insurance, telecommunications, wholesale and retail trade, management and other business services, and computer and some professional services.

Numerous provisions were also included in the FTA to compensate economic interests, such as agriculture, mining, and fishing, that would be injured by increased imports. Moreover, a number of industries were exempt from tariff reductions altogether. For example, plywood retained the existing tariff rates until a common performance standard between the two countries could be arranged. The FTA required the president to negotiate reciprocal quotas on potatoes and voluntary export restraints on steel. Temporary duties on fruits and vegetables were also imposed. And a provision required the president to take retaliatory measures if Canada enacted fish landing requirements. New England sardine and herring canneries, who depend upon Canadian raw fish, were thereby protected from possible Canadian export controls. The agreement also incorporated numerous procedures to protect industries, including rules-of-origin requirements for duty-free entry and studies on beef, dairy, egg, automotive products, and numerous natural resources. These studies could then be used by industries to qualify for import relief under the escape clause and unfair trade provisions.

Overall, the FTA was fairly successful in creating a harmonized system of customs classification and in eliminating tariffs on most product categories over ten years.[23] With regard to nontariff barriers, however, the results have been decidedly mixed. The agreement provided for changing only a few explicit regulations. To ensure congressional approval, many of the most contentious issues were left to be resolved either through dispute-settlement mechanisms or in future negotiations (O'Halloran and Noll 1991). The FTA

---

23. Indeed, in May, 1990, the United States and Canada agreed to accelerate the elimination of tariffs on over four hundred products. See Message of the President of the United States, *United States-Canada Free Trade Agreement Biennial Report*, 102d Cong., 1st sess., H. Doc. 36, January 30, 1991.

reduced minor trade irritants between the two countries, such as tariff barriers, and some uncertainty in dealing with domestic trade regulations. But clearly, fewer gains were made than had been expected. To explain why the FTA took the shape it did, we must examine the negotiation and implementation of the agreement.

6.2.1. Negotiating the U.S.-Canada Free Trade Agreement

On December 10, 1985, President Reagan formally notified Congress that he intended to negotiate a bilateral free trade agreement with Canada. The initial goal of the president was to reduce general tariff barriers and thereby open Canadian markets to U.S. exports. Reagan specifically highlighted government procurement and funding programs, air transport, energy trade, high technology goods and related services, and intellectual property rights.[24]

To most of the administration, especially USTR Clayton Yeutter, the proposal was largely noncontroversial. The administration's request was nonetheless almost disapproved. In the hearings before the Finance Committee, various senators expressed concerns about the possible adverse effects of the agreement. For example, Senator Russell Long (D-La.) protested the effects increased Canadian imports of oil and natural gas would have on domestic industries. Senator Max Baucus (D-Mont.) and Senator Robert Packwood (R-Oreg.) expressed concern over effects on the lumber industry. Senator George Mitchell (D-Maine) protested the Canadian diversion program for its potato farmers.[25] The Senate Finance Committee's threat to reject fast track authority could have ended the negotiations before they began. Along with the particularistic concerns expressed by some senators, the committee's hostility toward the proposed trade talks also reflected a broader concern by Senator John C. Danforth (R-Mo.) and other congressional leaders over the Reagan administration's incoherent trade policy (Tobin 1987).

On April 23, 1986, the Senate Finance Committee rejected a resolution of disapproval by a 10–10 tie, thereby granting permission to the White House to begin trade talks with Canada under fast track procedures.[26] But the administration's close victory occurred only after considerable concessions. For example, to win over the pivotal votes of Senator Steven Symms (R-Idaho) and Senator Packwood, President Reagan was forced to pledge to

---

24. See the "Joint Canada–United States Declarations on Trade and International Security" (March 18, 1985), in Reagan 1985, vol. 1, 307.

25. Senate Finance Committee, *Proposed Negotiations of the United States–Canada Free Trade Agreement,* 99th Cong., 2d sess., S. Hrg. 743.

26. *Congressional Quarterly Weekly Report,* April 25, 1986, 905–6.

resolve the lumber dispute, a historical point of contention between the United States and Canada.[27]

The second step in negotiating the agreement is consultation among the administration, Congress, and representatives of various special interests. In the hearings on the U.S.-Canada Free Trade Agreement before the Senate Finance Committee, the advisory committees expressed concern over numerous areas, such as subsidies for the lumber industry, diversion programs for potato farmers, high Canadian tariffs, the treatment of foreign investment, trade in services, protection of intellectual property rights, and various forms of government assistance at both the federal and provincial level. Specific industries that opposed the agreement included New England potato farmers and the steel, uranium, and plywood industries.[28]

The administration consulted closely with the appropriate committees throughout the negotiating process and when drafting the formal language of the agreement. Many of the concerns raised by Congress and the private sector advisory committees, such as the temporary duties on fruits and vegetables, were included in the agreement signed by President Reagan and Prime Minister Mulroney, thus attesting to congressional influence.

6.2.2. Implementing the U.S.-Canada Free Trade Agreement

On January 2, 1988, Prime Minister Mulroney and President Reagan signed the U.S.-Canada Free Trade Agreement. Congressional committees, in collaboration with the president, then turned to the task of drafting the implementing legislation. Ways and Means and Finance, joined by seven other House committees and five other Senate committees, had to agree on language that would bring domestic legislation into conformity with the president's proposal. From February to May of 1988, the committees held public hearings, "non-markup" sessions, and a "non-conference" to reconcile the differences between the House and the Senate. Numerous provisions were introduced into the legislation, such as mandatory retaliation against Canadian export controls on fish, the requirement to negotiate potato-import quotas, size limitations on imported crustaceans (lobsters), and aid to the uranium industry.

---

27. The issue was temporarily resolved on December 30, 1986. Canada imposed a 15 percent tax on exports of softwood lumber to the United States until fair pricing standards could be agreed upon. See "The Memorandum of the Export of Softwood Lumber Products from Canada" (December 30, 1986), in Reagan 1986, vol. 2, 1653. See also *Congressional Quarterly Weekly Report*, April, 25, 1986, 905–6.

28. Senate Finance Committee, *Proposed Negotiations of the United States–Canada Free Trade Agreement*, 99th Cong., 2d sess., S. Hrg. 743.

Senators Danforth and Baucus of the Finance Committee also introduced an amendment to the implementing bill that addressed Canadian subsidies. The Danforth-Baucus Amendment for nonferrous smelters contained three major provisions. First, the amendment defined as one of the primary nego-tiating objectives the elimination of subsidies. Second, it included a provision to terminate the agreement if progress was not made toward removing such unfair trade practices. And third, it included an interim procedure to monitor Canadian subsidies and impose offsetting duties or take other action under U.S. trade law. This measure was drafted for nonferrous metals, but it could be extended to other industries faced with similar difficulties, such as coal.

The Canadians protested the Finance Committee's recommendation be-cause it singled them out from other countries that partake in similar trade practices. A compromise was reached, and the provision was broadened to cover other countries with which the United States might enter into similar agreements. The Finance Committee also pushed the administration to inter-pret the terms of the agreement so as to impose restrictions on Canadian wheat imports if domestic farmers were threatened.[29]

In the non-conference between the Ways and Means and Finance Com-mittees, only two issues remained unresolved and were therefore left to the discretion of the administration: the Senate's lobster proviso and the Senate's recommendation that, as a condition of the FTA taking effect, the national Canadian government would assure compliance by the provincial govern-ments. In the final implementing legislation, both recommendations were excluded.[30]

Only after both the House and the Senate committees informally ap-proved the bill did the president formally introduce the implementing legisla-tion to Congress. In submitting the implementing bill, the president is not bound by the recommendations made at the non-markup stage. Nonethe-less, the agreement must still be approved by both chambers of Congress, and if the president does not accept the committees' recommendations, strong opposition is likely on the House and Senate floor. To win support for the final legislation, therefore, the administration often accedes to protectionist demands.

For instance, Senator Domenici (R-N.Mex.) almost derailed the FTA because it exempted Canada from import restrictions on unprocessed ura-nium.[31] In response, the administration suggested including a $1.75 billion bailout proposal for the uranium industry to buy off opposition from Baucus, Domenici, and other western Republican senators. This proposal was deleted

29. *Congressional Record,* 100th Cong., 2d sess., 1988, 134, pt. 127:S12789–91.
30. *Congressional Quarterly Weekly Report,* May 28, 1988, 1446.
31. *Congressional Record,* 100th Cong., 2d sess., 1988, 134, pt. 16:S1460.

from the final bill, however, at the insistence of Senator Bentsen and Representative Rostenkowski, the Democratic chairs of the Finance and Ways and Means Committees.[32]

On August 9, 1988, the House passed the FTA by a vote of 366 to 40. One month later, by a 83 to 9 margin, the Senate also approved the implementing legislation. Finally, on September 28, 1988, President Reagan signed the bill implementing the U.S.-Canada Free Trade Agreement.

The lopsided vote in the House and Senate, however, suggests neither indifference toward the agreement nor members' blindly following the president's initiative. Congress devoted an enormous amount of time and attention to the trade agreement. Senators and representatives had the opportunity to pander to constituency pressures during the negotiation and drafting process. By the time the trade agreement reached the House and Senate floor, though, only a few members actually voted against the legislation.

6.2.3. Summary

The U.S.-Canada Free Trade Agreement was designed in part to achieve the maximum leverage for American exports entering Canada. The FTA also provided either protection or compensation to those industries that would have difficulty competing in more open markets. These measures allowed members of Congress and the president to grant benefits to constituents who wanted improved access to foreign markets, a visible solution to the highly visible and politically salient problem of the mounting trade deficit, and compensation to those industries adversely affected by lower tariffs. Some of these payoffs, as in the case of the plywood industry, came as a promise to negotiate for the removal of foreign subsidies. Other payoffs came in the form of administrative protection. The FTA also contained an enormous number of exception clauses that granted short-term protection to damaged industries: reciprocal potato quotas, voluntary export restraints for steel, fish-landing requirements, and so forth. The final outcome was a broad compromise between Congress and the president, and the nature of this bargain was structured by the implementing process.

One way to measure Congress's influence in the decision-making process is to compare the U.S.-Canada Free Trade Agreement with the concurrent 1988 Omnibus Trade and Competitiveness Act (OTCA). Although the FTA was passed under fast track and the OTCA was passed under normal legisla-

---

32. Although the uranium industry did not receive its bailout proposal, it was eligible for special protection under the monitoring program. Also, the lobster provision was later included in an amendment to the Magnuson Fishery Conservation Act, which limited the size of lobster imports into the United States. See Pub. L. No. 101-224, §8, 103 Stat. 1905–7 (1989).

tive procedures, the acts were very similar in their primary objectives and in the groups that received import relief. Both acts sought to remove barriers to exports in services, finance, and intellectual property by using the U.S. market as a lever. In the end, similar economic interests received compensation for import injury from both acts, such as agriculture, industry, and mining. Remuneration included exemptions for certain industries, delay through staging requirements, direct recompense to groups adversely affected by an increase in imports, and protection through administrative procedures.

The mechanism for achieving the objectives of the United States was also much the same in both cases: the incentive of more open or continued favorable access to the U.S. market in exchange for access to foreign markets. A central purpose of the 1988 OTCA was to use the U.S. economy as a lever to obtain access to foreign markets through mandatory retaliation against unfair trade practices. In the OTCA, Congress specified as its primary negotiating objectives the removal of barriers to foreign direct investment, access to high technology, trade in services, and the strengthening of intellectual property rights.[33]

As in the U.S.-Canada Free Trade Agreement, Congress sought to compensate constituents injured by more open import competition, including imports from Canada. For example, Congress repealed the windfall profits tax on oil, thereby compensating oil producers for increased competition from low-priced Canadian oil and crude imports.[34] In addition, the act expanded triggered market loans and export enhancement programs for agriculture, granted price supports for sunflower and cottonseed, and included an export incentive program for dairy products.[35] As an obvious payoff to the lumber industry, faced with rising Canadian imports, Congress extended the Agricultural Export Credit Program to wood products.[36]

The OTCA also authorized numerous studies, including Canadian wheat import licensing requirements, dairy products, meat, poultry, egg products, and roses.[37] As in the FTA, these studies could then be used as evidence for import relief under the escape clause and unfair trading practices provisions. Overall, these numerous similarities between the FTA and the OTCA suggest that fast track procedures can be an effective mechanism for enfranchising interest groups into the negotiating process. I now turn to the lessons that can be learned from the implementation of the U.S.-Canada FTA for the North American Free Trade Agreement.

---

33. The 1988 Trade Act, Pub. L. No. 100-418, §1101, 102 Stat. 1121.
34. The 1988 Trade Act, Pub. L. No. 100-418, §1941, 102 Stat. 1322.
35. The 1988 Trade Act, Pub. L. No. 100-418, §4301, §4302, §4308, 102 Stat. 1395–99.
36. The 1988 Trade Act, Pub. L. No. 100-418, §4401, 102 Stat. 1400.
37. The 1988 Trade Act, Pub. L. No. 100-418, §§4501–9, 102 Stat. 1403–6.

6.3. Fast Track and the North American Free
Trade Agreement

As the U.S.-Canada Free Trade Agreement was drawing to a close, talk of a North American Agreement between the United States, Canada, and Mexico was gaining momentum. The incoming Bush administration saw NAFTA as the flagship of its economic program. But the problems of enacting an agreement with Mexico proved formidable.

Since Mexico joined GATT in 1986, it had undergone a dramatic liberalization of its economy. The average Mexican tariff had fallen from 100 percent in 1981 to 25 percent in 1985 to 10 percent today. Privatization of the economy had also occurred. In December, 1982, the Mexican government owned 1,115 firms. As of February, 1990, 73 percent of these firms were privatized or were in the process of being sold to private investors. Foreign direct investment regulations had been dramatically relaxed. Since 1986, foreign investment into Mexico had tripled, with U.S. investors accounting for 63 percent of this increase. Direct trade in goods and services between the United States and Mexico had also increased. United States exports to Mexico had risen 132 percent from $12.4 billion dollars in 1986 to $28.4 billion in 1990. On the other hand, imports from Mexico had increased 79 percent from $17.1 billion to $30.2 billion during the same time period.

Extending the free trade zone to south of the border had a number of advantages. Mexico was America's third largest trading partner after Canada and Japan. A free trade agreement among the United States, Canada, and Mexico would create the world's largest trading block, with 360 million producers and consumers and a total output of almost $6 trillion. Although Mexico had recently liberalized its markets, American exporters still faced tariffs two-and-a-half times the average U.S. tariff. A free trade agreement would eliminate these barriers.

For the most part, the primary objectives of the Bush administration in negotiating a free trade agreement with Mexico were similar to those of Reagan in entering into the FTA with Canada: to reduce tariff and nontariff barriers, harmonize government regulations, protect intellectual property rights, liberalize foreign investment regulations, and loosen government procurement rules. The administration also emphasized the expansion of trade in services, telecommunications, and financial services. Moreover, agreement would offer an opportunity to further liberalize trade with Canada, it would stabilize investment opportunities in Mexico, and it would lock in reforms toward trade liberalization.

As in the U.S.-Canada agreement, impediments existed to creating a free trade zone, and in the case of Mexico, these barriers were even more pronounced. One aspect that facilitated the success of the FTA with Canada was the roughly similar health and safety standards, labor laws, and environmental regulations shared by the two countries. Such similarity did not extend to Mexico. For example, at the time, Mexico used pesticides prohibited in the United States and Canada. Mexico had less stringently enforced environmental and health and safety regulations, which raised fears of border pollution and industry flight. Increased trade between the United States and Mexico led to a number of legitimate concerns over the impact on the environment, consumer safety, and health and sanitary standards. Environmentalists feared that further liberalization of commerce might lead to political pressures to loosen American standards so as to compete with cheaper Mexican imports. For example, since 1988, with the imposition of more stringent air quality control standards in the Los Angeles basin, over forty furniture manufacturers had moved to the border region in Mexico. American unions feared that industries would likewise relocate to take advantage of cheaper labor and less stringent environmental laws, leading to a further loss of American jobs and environmental degradation.

Besides differences in domestic regulations, two further reasons made the negotiations with Mexico problematic. First, protectionist pressures had risen as trade issues moved to the forefront of the national political debate. The country faced a recession, which made more industries sensitive to import competition. The most vocal opposition to the proposed free trade agreement came from fruit and vegetable producers, textile and apparel manufacturers, auto suppliers, and the steel industry, all of whose products competed directly with Mexican imports. This opposition was even more difficult to ignore in hard economic times. Congress had become more protectionist as well. When the House and the Senate agreed to consider the Canadian FTA under fast track, Republicans were the majority party in the Senate. This explains the strong emphasis in the U.S.-Canada agreement on western and agricultural interests, regions that are staunchly Republican. In 1990, however, the Democrats commanded a majority in both houses; consequently, the areas of importance were eastern manufactures and the rust belt. Traditional Democratic constituencies in these areas (steel, textile, and auto producers) were experiencing economic difficulties and voiced strong opposition to NAFTA.

Second, institutional changes gave Congress more leverage in the negotiation process. The main procedural change since the passage of the FTA was the introduction of reverse fast track, which allows Congress to pass a resolution revoking fast track authority. This provision was introduced largely in response to the Reagan administration's failure to consult with congressional leaders during the negotiation of the U.S.-Canada FTA. As explained above, if the president does not accommodate key congressional concerns, members can suspend fast track and amend the agreement. These procedural changes and increasing protectionist demands made the implementation of NAFTA even more precarious than the U.S.-Canada agreement.

6.3.1. Getting Congress to Go Along

Experience with Canada demonstrated that to defuse domestic political opposition, many sectors, such as auto products, textiles, and fruits and vegetables, that compete directly with Mexican imports would be off-limits to trade liberalization or barriers would have to be gradually reduced. In the case of NAFTA, getting Congress to go along with the administration's proposal proved even more difficult. Not only did the president have to hurdle the Ways and Means and Finance Committees' disapproval resolution, but he also had to get Congress to extend fast track for an additional two years. This necessity gave Congress as a whole, rather than just the Ways and Means and Finance Committees, the opportunity to extract promises from the administration in return for the president being able to negotiate the U.S.-Mexico agreement under fast track authority.[38]

The Disapproval Resolution
Despite the manifold differences between the two countries, on June 11, 1990, President Bush and Mexico's President Salinas issued a joint statement of their intent to negotiate a free trade pact. On August 21, 1990, President Salinas wrote to Bush proposing that the United States and Mexico negotiate a free trade agreement. A month later, Bush notified the Ways and Means and Finance Committees of the proposed agreement. He thereby triggered a sixty-day legislative clock, during which time the committee could review the proposed negotiations with Mexico and, if either committee so chose, disapprove the application of fast track procedures.[39]

In Senate Finance Committee hearings on February 6 and 20, 1991, most members, particularly those from border states, such as Finance Committee Chairman Senator Bentsen (D-Tex.) and Senator Domenici (R-N.Mex.), expressed support for the negotiations with Mexico. Nonetheless, numerous concerns were raised about U.S. businesses relocating to Mexico to take advantage of inexpensive labor and lax environmental laws. For instance,

---

38. If the president is denied fast track negotiating procedures, he would then be forced to negotiate a treaty, which requires approval of two-thirds of the Senate to be ratified, or to send Congress separate implementing legislation that could be freely amended.

39. The sixty-day time limit in fast track procedures refers to sixty *legislative* days. Thus, when Bush submitted the proposal to Congress in September, 1990, the time limit expired in February of the following year. On February 5, 1991, the president informed Congress that the United States, Canada, and Mexico would proceed with trilateral negotiations.

Senator Donald W. Riegle, Jr. (D-Mich.) raised concerns about possible industry flight, citing the average wage differential as $10.47 in the United States to 57 cents in Mexico. Louisiana Democrat John B. Breaux said that U.S. companies must invest in costly new equipment to comply with stringent clean air standards, whereas these industries would not face such steep costs in Mexico.[40] Even those who supported the agreement like Chairman Bentsen called for improvements in Mexican infrastructure and laws governing intellectual property, pharmaceutical products, and software.

The House Ways and Means Committee raised similar concerns. Representative Bill Thomas (R-Calif.) reflected the California fruit and vegetable growers' concern about the effects of increased Mexican competition. More strident opposition came from Midwestern members who feared that companies would move to take advantage of the cheap Mexican labor pool. Representative Donald J. Pease (D-Ohio) argued that not only low-wage U.S. industries but high-wage and some high-skill industries would be attracted by Mexico's increasingly sophisticated work force. Jobs especially vulnerable included the electronics and automobile industries.[41]

The sixty-day legislative review period expired on February 27, 1991, with neither committee voting to deny fast track authority. Although there were numerous concerns about the effects of free trade with Mexico, there was little likelihood that either Ways and Means or Finance would exercise its option and block the talks. The real battle would come over the procedural matter of whether to extend fast track authority.

Extending Fast Track Authority
As outlined in chapter 5, the 1988 Omnibus Trade and Competitiveness Act extended fast track authority for three years, with the possibility of an additional two years if the president requested authority by March of 1991 and if neither house passed a resolution disapproving the extension. Congress had until June 1 to block fast track extension; after that, fast track procedures would continue automatically for two more years. The original intent of Congress in providing the short time period was to ensure that the Uruguay round GATT negotiations were making significant progress and to give U.S. negotiators bargaining leverage.[42]

This procedural measure had the unanticipated effect of allowing Congress the opportunity to further set guidelines for the president in negotiating the North American agreement. The Democratically controlled Congress took the opportunity of the renewal of fast track to ensure that many of the most

---

40. *Congressional Quarterly Weekly Report*, February 9, 1991, 362.
41. *Congressional Quarterly Weekly Report*, February 23, 1991, 453.
42. *Congressional Quarterly Almanac 1988*, 209.

controversial issues—the environment, labor concerns, and workers' rights—
were written directly into the authorizing legislation.

On March 4, 1991, Bush requested the extension of fast track procedures.[43] This set up a strange scenario in which organized labor, environmental groups, and human rights activists formed a loose coalition in opposition to
extending fast track authority. The AFL-CIO strongly opposed the talks and
made defeating the fast track a top priority. Environmental groups warned that
a U.S.-Mexico free trade agreement would exacerbate pollution along the
border and create pressure to weaken U.S. environmental laws as businesses
relocated to take advantage of lax Mexican enforcement of its pollution controls. Human rights advocates worried that poor working conditions in Mexico would result in lower health and safety standards for American workers.

The administration lobbied hard for the fast track extension, seeing the
procedure as crucial to the success of the negotiations. But this required that
the president make concessions to key congressional leaders. By early May,
USTR Carla Hills had met individually with about 150 members of Congress,
including two-thirds of the Senate. Bush met with key Democrats Bentsen,
Rostenkowski, and House Majority Leader Gephardt (D-Mo.) to discuss the
extension of fast track. To counter the attacks made by labor and environmen-
talist groups and quench congressional opposition, on May 1, 1991, the
administration put forth an "action plan," containing three main points.[44]

First, President Bush pledged that NAFTA would include transition and
safeguard provisions. As in the FTA, most Mexican and U.S. tariff and
import barriers would be reduced gradually, allowing industries time to adjust
to stiffer competition. Also, the agreement would include escape clause and
"snapback"[45] provisions, which allow for the temporary restoration of duties
or other barriers if domestic industries are injured by imports from Mexico or
Canada. In addition, the president promised that the agreement would include
strict rules-of-origin provisions to prevent third countries from funneling their
goods through Mexico to evade U.S. tariffs. For automotive imports, the
administration would seek a domestic-content rule of more than 50 percent.

Second, the president promised to work with Congress in designing a
trade adjustment assistance program to provide services to workers displaced
by imports resulting from the trade pact. In addition, the administration excluded from the talks labor mobility and U.S. immigration laws, except with
regard to a few managerial services. Furthermore, the plan directed the Labor
Department to sign an agreement with the Mexican government providing for

---

43. Message from the President of the United States: *The Extension of Fast Track Procedures,* 102d Cong., 1st sess., H. Doc. 51, March 4, 1991.

44. *Weekly Compilation of Presidential Documents* 27, no. 18 (May 3, 1991), 523–56.

45. If domestic producers were injured by imports, the tariff rate would "snap back" to the
rate prior to the agreement. A similar clause was included in the U.S.-Canada FTA.

cooperation in areas of occupational health and safety, workers' conditions, child labor law, and labor statistics. Enforcement of these regulations would also be reviewed.

The third central issue the president's action plan addressed was the environment. The administration vowed not to negotiate lower standards than were currently in law in the areas of pesticides, energy conservation, toxic waste, and health and safety. Furthermore, the administration promised to maintain the right to bar entry of products that did not meet these standards. As a payoff to environmentalists, the administration would begin parallel negotiations on a series of environmental problems between the United States and Mexico. Further, the president invited environmental experts to participate in the policy-making process to ensure that efforts to liberalize trade were consistent with sound environmental practices.

With the action plan, the administration succeeded in driving a wedge between organized labor and some environmental organizations, thereby diffusing much of the congressional opposition. Appeased by the president's promises to prevent further environmental degradation and to include them in the negotiation process, environmental leaders withdrew their opposition to the extension of fast track. Still not satisfied with the president's assurances, labor continued to fight against the extension, although the defection of the environmentalists was a serious blow to their cause. This episode is typical of bargaining under fast track. The president traded off the gains and losses from meeting certain interest group demands in order to win congressional support. Congress, on the other hand, by extracting public promises from Bush on contentious provisions, strengthened its bargaining position vis-à-vis the administration.

The plan received quick endorsement from key Democrats Rostenkowski and Bentsen, who indeed had helped draft Bush's plan. At their insistence, for example, the administration softened its stance against government assistance to workers who may lose their jobs as a result of the trade agreement. Gephardt also announced that he would support Bush's request for a fast track extension, although he reiterated his position that Congress could still reject the agreement outright or simply invoke reverse fast track and permit amendments *after* the pact had been negotiated.[46]

The Ways and Means Committee met on May 14 to consider a resolution introduced by Byron L. Dorgan (D-N.Dak.) to deny the extension of fast track procedures. If the disapproval resolution passed, its effect would be to restore normal congressional procedures for the consideration of legislation to implement trade agreements. The committee rejected the measure by a vote of 9 to 27 and reported it unfavorably to the full House. The House on May 23

46. *Congressional Quarterly Almanac 1991*, 119.

also rejected the disapproval resolution, 192 to 231. The Republicans voted 21 in favor and 140 against, while the Democrats voted 170 in favor and 91 against the resolution. (One independent member voted in favor of the resolution.) The House then approved a nonbinding resolution, sponsored by Rostenkowski and Gephardt, by a 329 to 85 vote, emphasizing that Congress could suspend fast track if the administration did not keep its promise to include adequate protection for U.S. workers, industries, and the environment.[47]

The Senate Finance Committee similarly voted 3 to 15 to reject the disapproval resolution introduced by Ernest Hollings (D-S.C.) and reported the measure unfavorably. The full Senate also voted to reject the resolution by a vote of 36 in favor and 59 against. Only 5 Republicans voted for the resolution and 36 voted against. The Democrats were more divided on the issues, with 31 voting in favor of the resolution and 23 against. Thus, through bargaining and strategic concessions, the president was able to keep NAFTA on track.

In extending fast track authority, labor and environmental groups successfully lobbied Congress for amendments to the authorizing legislation. Labor won promises of retraining grants, and environmentalists received assurance that no environmental degradation would result from NAFTA. Majority Leader Richard Gephardt, who made the U.S.-Canada FTA a central issue in his unsuccessful 1988 presidential campaign, continued to promote industries' positions concerning "unfair" trade practices. Even in supporting the extension of fast track authority, he threatened that "if the administration trades away American jobs, or tolerates pollution or abuse of workers, Congress can and will amend or reject the agreement."[48] The 1988 procedural innovation, the reverse fast track, made Gephardt's threat to amend or veto the treaty credible.

6.3.2. The "Final" Agreement

In August, 1992, the Democrats renewed pressures on the free trade agreement, now in the final stages of negotiation. As the administration pushed to complete the agreement before the November elections, Gephardt accused the Bush administration of ignoring promises to clean up the border region with Mexico, preserve U.S. health and safety laws, assist workers who could lose their jobs as a result of lowering trade barriers, and help industries threatened by Mexican imports. On August 6, 1992, the House voted unanimously to warn President Bush again that it would not tolerate any pact that would

---

47. *Congressional Quarterly Weekly Report*, May 18, 1991, 1257–60.
48. *Congressional Quarterly Weekly Report*, May 11, 1991, 1181.

weaken U.S. health, safety, labor, or environmental laws.[49] Supporters of the nonbinding resolution wanted to demonstrate that congressional approval of NAFTA was not guaranteed.

As the House passed the nonbinding resolution, the administration was finishing negotiations with Canada and Mexico.[50] On September 18, 1992, Bush formally notified Congress of his intent to sign the free trade agreement with Canada and Mexico, submitting the text of the agreement and the advisory committee reports.[51] Many of the concerns raised by Congress during the debates surrounding the extension of fast track were reflected in the negotiated agreement, although perhaps not to the extent that some members would have liked.[52]

We recall that the president's notification must be accompanied by private sector reports and that there are three types of advisory committees. The largest, the Advisory Committee for Trade Policy Negotiations (ACTPN), strongly endorsed NAFTA and recommended that it be signed by the president and implemented by the Congress. The report nonetheless expressed disappointment with the energy section, which failed to open trade and investment in Mexico's electricity, petrochemical, gas, and equipment markets. The committee was also dissatisfied that further progress had not been made toward liberalizing agricultural trade between the United States and Canada. The two labor representatives on the ACTPN disagreed with the majority report, stating that protections for workers and the environment were not adequate, and urged Congress to reject the agreement. In addition to the ACTPN report, the president's notification was accompanied by reports from seven policy advisory committees. Six of the seven committees supported NAFTA; the labor committee opposed it. Also submitted were reports by thirty technical and sectoral advisory groups.

As expected, the biggest winners were the telecommunications, financial, investment, and insurance industries. The agreement would eliminate restrictions on American sales to and investment in the Mexican market for telecommunications equipment and services. Also, Mexican domestic content rules, requiring that a certain value of a product be locally manufactured, would be eliminated, as would export performance standards. The agreement

---

49. *Congressional Quarterly Weekly Report,* August 1, 1992, 2258.

50. It should be noted that two bilateral free trade agreements do not equal one trilateral agreement. The number of outstanding nontariff barrier issues among the three countries meant that a significant number of compromises still had to be reached to create a three-nation free trade zone.

51. Under law, the president is required to wait at least ninety days after notification before formally signing the agreement.

52. For an overview of these provisions, see the "Report of the Administration on the North American Free Trade Agreement and the Actions Taken in Fulfillment of the May 1, 1991 Commitments." Released by the USTR, September 18, 1992.

strengthened intellectual property rights and relaxed land transportation barriers. In addition, about 65 percent of U.S. industrial and agricultural exports to Mexico would be eligible for duty-free treatment immediately. The remaining tariffs would be reduced gradually.

As in the U.S.-Canada FTA, certain sectors would also be hurt. To compensate these industries, the agreement allowed for the phaseout of U.S. duties over fifteen years. Industries that are now heavily protected from Mexican competition, such as glassware, ceramic tile, watches, and certain footwear, were eligible for this extended reduction period. Agricultural items entitled to protection included orange juice, peanuts, sugar, broccoli, cucumbers, asparagus, dried onion and garlic, and cantaloupes. NAFTA also provided a ten-year phaseout of duties for dyes, ball bearings, bicycles, leather goods, most chemicals, and some agricultural products like eggplant, chili peppers, squash, and watermelons. In the textile and apparel sector, U.S. tariffs and quotas would remain in place for up to ten years.

In addition to the staged tariff reductions, the agreement included numerous safeguards to protect domestic industries. It contained a snapback provision that allows the United States to return to the rates in force prior to the agreement for up to three years—four years in extremely sensitive products—if the industry could prove that increased imports caused or threatened to cause serious injury. These safeguards, however, were linked to compensation provisions. The agreement stated that a country taking an action under the snapback clause must compensate the country whose exports were affected; if no compensation was agreed upon, the affected country could retaliate by imposing an equivalent tariff.

Fulfilling a commitment made to congressional leaders in his action plan, Bush proposed a new federal program, Advancing Skill through Education and Training (ASETS), for retraining and providing temporary assistance to workers who lose their jobs in industries facing international competition. The program would receive a budget of $2 billion a year, tripling the funding of the current trade adjustment assistance program.

One of the most contentious issues in the negotiations concerned domestic rules of origin. These rules prevent products manufactured outside North America from using Mexico or Canada as a pass-through into the United States. In most cases, the rules of origin would be determined not by an ad valorem scaling, as in the U.S.-Canada agreement, but by the level of processing. For example, in computers, the "motherboard" must be assembled in North America to receive duty-free treatment; and in textile products, goods must be made from the yarn-spinning stage forward to be eligible. The auto industry proved most difficult. The United States and Canada already have a domestic content requirement for automobiles set at 50 percent. Under the new agreement, autos entering the United States would come in duty-free as long as 62.5 percent of their value was attributable to North American parts and manufacture. The agreement also removed the "roll-over" or the "all-or-nothing" provision that led to the controversy over whether Honda cars produced in Canada were eligible for preferential treatment, as explained below.

As negotiated, the agreement maintained existing U.S. federal and state health, safety, and environmental standards, and preserved the right to ban nonconforming imports. States and cities were free to enact environmental regulations stricter than international or national standards. Thus, states like California, with higher environmental codes, could exclude goods not meeting those standards without being charged for violating the agreement.

The administration released the text of the agreement in the beginning of September, bringing strong opposition from Congress. In hearings before the Senate, Carla Hills faced charges that the administration failed to uphold its agreement on the environment and worker assistance. Max Baucus (D-Mont.), chairman of the Senate Finance Trade Subcommittee, asserted that "the agreement simply does not pay adequate attention to job displacement or environmental concerns."[53] Gephardt called on the Bush administration to stop efforts to win congressional approval for the agreement. He asserted that NAFTA should be renegotiated to strengthen protection for U.S. workers whose jobs would be threatened by expanded competition with Mexico.

These strong protests from Democratic leaders may have been politically motivated. At the time, President Bush was using NAFTA as a major issue in his bid for reelection. For example, Clinton at first refused to commit himself on NAFTA, prompting Bush's taunt that Clinton suffered from "straddle sores."[54] When Clinton conditionally endorsed NAFTA, he claimed that "the shortcomings in the agreement are really a reflection . . . of the shortcomings in the Bush economic policy."[55] In the end, Bush lost a tumultuous election in which Texan Ross Perot won 19 percent of the vote, mostly from traditionally Republican constituents. Bush's defeat created a strange scenario: when the agreement was formally signed on December 17, 1992, the task of implementing NAFTA fell to a president of the opposite party.

6.3.3. Clinton Takes Over

Despite his initial waverings on the campaign trail, once in office Clinton supported NAFTA as long as acceptable side agreements on labor and the environment could be negotiated. In addition to the supplemental agreements,

53. *Congressional Quarterly Weekly Report,* September 12, 1992, 2699.
54. *Congressional Quarterly Weekly Report,* September 12, 1992, 2699.
55. *Congressional Quarterly Weekly Report,* October 10, 1992, 3137.

Clinton proposed five unilateral measures as part of the overall NAFTA package:

1. Trade adjustment assistance to workers and communities adversely affected by imports;
2. Protection of the environment through cleanup and investment;
3. Assistance for farmers hurt by imports;
4. The right for citizen-initiated suits against other countries' environmental practices; and
5. Protection for workers against strike breakers.

With a Democratic president in the White House, opposition to the trade agreement weakened somewhat. Senator Donald Riegle, Jr. (D-Mich.), a longtime NAFTA foe, dropped efforts to derail fast track procedures and instead sent Clinton a letter cosigned by twenty-four Democrats urging the president to negotiate tough side agreements. In the House, Representative Gephardt also softened his opposition, describing the pact as "a reasonable and good thing for the United States, Mexico, and Canada to do." Six environmental groups reached a compromise with the administration, agreeing to support the pact if adequate environmental safeguards could be negotiated. And the AFL-CIO's executive council decided to continue pressing for broad side agreements rather than try to kill the pact altogether.[56]

6.3.4. Diluting the Opposition

Just as the administration seemed to be reining in the opposition, a monkey wrench was thrown into the works. On June 30, 1993, U.S. District Judge Charles R. Richey ruled that all trade agreements must include an environmental impact statement (EIS), as required under the 1970 National Environmental Policy Act (NEPA). Richey argued that since the agreement was negotiated by the USTR, the completion of negotiations constituted a "final agency action." Furthermore, since NEPA requires that an environmental impact statement accompany all legislative proposals, he reasoned, NAFTA should contain one, too.[57] The Clinton administration immediately appealed the verdict, hopeful that it would be reversed in time to pass NAFTA by the year's end.

---

56. *New York Times*, May 11, 1993, D1. See also *Congressional Quarterly Weekly Report*, March 20, 1993, 661.

57. Although the decision failed on several points of administrative law, Judge Richey did correctly adduce in his decision that trade negotiations are essentially a congressional prerogative, not a matter of presidential foreign policy. That is, the president's authority in trade policy is delegated authority working through the office of the USTR.

Late in the summer of 1993, considerable doubt still surrounded the ultimate passage of the agreement. Not only was the environmental impact ruling still lingering in the air, but former presidential candidate Ross Perot and organized labor were conducting a vigorous campaign against the pact. The anti-NAFTA forces, which included House Majority Whip David Bonior (D-Mich.) and Majority Leader Richard Gephardt, predicted that the agreement would cost millions of American jobs (the famous "giant sucking sound"), ruin the environment, and infringe on U.S. sovereignty. Labor leaders also threatened to withhold campaign contributions and volunteer support from any candidate who voted for NAFTA.

The Clinton administration, at first slow to respond to the anti-NAFTA offensive, began its counterattack by announcing the signing of three side agreements on September 14. The two major agreements dealt with environmental and labor issues. They established commissions to investigate lax enforcement of domestic environmental and labor laws. If informal negotiations failed to resolve the dispute, a bi- or tri-national arbitration panel would be established. These panels would conduct investigations into possible violations and, if necessary after a lengthy negotiation process, apply trade sanctions to any country that failed to comply with its recommendations. The third supplemental agreement established a working group to investigate surges in imports that damage or threaten to damage any domestic industry. In such cases, tariffs would temporarily revert to their previous levels, as provided in the emergency relief provisions of the agreement.

While the side agreements were being negotiated, two facts became apparent. First, countries were reluctant to relinquish any control over their internal labor markets to a supranational panel. Second, U.S. environmental groups proved to be more willing than their labor counterparts to work with the administration in formulating an acceptable deal. In the end, then, the environmental side agreement negotiated by the administration was stronger than the labor agreement. A country's environmental practices could be challenged on any grounds, while labor practices could be disputed only if they pertained to worker safety, child labor, or minimum wage issues. Also, once an environmental protest was lodged, an investigation would begin automatically unless two of the three countries objected. On the other hand, convening a labor panel required the active assent of two out of three countries. Consequently, a number of major environmental groups, including the Audubon Society and the National Resources Defense Council, supported the agreement, while labor leaders only intensified their opposition.

The administration's offensive received another boost on September 24, when a three-judge panel ruled unanimously to overturn the lower court's EIS decision. Two of the judges did so on the grounds that the 1946 Administrative Procedure Act (APA) does not apply to the president. They argued that the final-agency action being challenged was the submission of NAFTA to Congress by the president, and that presidential actions are not reviewable under the APA. The third judge agreed with the ruling, but in addition argued that no agency action could be considered final if it required subsequent congressional approval.[58] Thus entering the final stage of implementation, the administration had successfully addressed most environmental concerns, but still had to overcome stiff labor opposition.

6.3.5. The Final Push

With legal concerns now set aside, the House Ways and Means and Senate Finance committees began drafting the implementing legislation through the informal non-markup process. As explained earlier, fast track allows for congressional input before the president formally sends the trade agreement to Congress. Thus, non-markups substitute for the usual congressional amendment process. Since the Senate was expected to pass the bill with little objection, the administration's attention focused on winning over marginal Democrat and Republican votes in the House. There were three main methods for accommodating members' demands: add-on amendments to the implementing legislation, last-minute deals with Mexico, and promises by the Clinton administration for specific benefits.

The non-markup sessions, which started September 28 and continued throughout the month of October, produced many suggested amendments to the original agreement. For example, Tennessee representatives inserted an amendment protecting brand-name distilled spirits from trademark infringements. Only whisky produced in Tennessee could be labeled "Bourbon Whisky" or "Tennessee Whisky."[59] Another amendment stated that no accelerated reductions in tariffs of any sort could be negotiated without the approval of U.S. producers. To prevent Australian or New Zealand beef from entering the United States through Mexico, stringent record-keeping rules were devised. Makers of household appliances, concerned that Mexican producers retained an unfair advantage in the form of higher tariffs, pushed for easier relief under snapback proceedings. Trade in tomatoes, peppers, fresh fruits, vegetables, and cut flowers was to be monitored, in case import levels rose suddenly. And imported peanuts were to be held to the same rigid standards as domestically grown peanuts.

All the above suggestions were included in the final legislation.[60] Two notable amendments, however, were not adopted by the administration. One

---

58. *New York Times*, September 25, 1993, 9.

59. Similar protection was added for Canadian Whisky and Tequila.

60. See Message from the President of the United States, *North American Free Trade Agreement*, 103d Cong., 1st sess., H. Doc. 159, November 4, 1993.

proposed to guarantee worker retraining benefits for five years. The administration retained its original proposal of eighteen months, promising that a new comprehensive retraining program would be enacted by 1995. The second amendment, proposed by Senator Baucus (D-Mont.), would restore Super 301 procedures, which had expired in 1990.

A number of last-minute deals were also negotiated directly between the United States and Mexico. The two countries agreed to begin negotiations immediately after NAFTA went into force to accelerate tariff reductions on brandy, wine, car window glass, household appliances, and bed frames, where U.S. producers felt that reciprocal concessions had not been obtained. A North American Development Bank was established to provide border cleanup and development funds. At the behest of Representative Esteban Torres (D-Calif.), the bank was given an initial endowment of $4 billion. Frozen orange juice also received special concessions: if prices declined for five consecutive days, the extra imports from Mexico would revert to the rates enforced prior to the agreement. And representatives from Louisiana and Maryland were appeased by an understanding that imported products containing high fructose corn syrup would count against Mexico's sugar quota.[61]

Finally, a number of unilateral promises from Clinton bought the support of many legislators. Representative Floyd Flake (D-N.Y.) received assurances that a small business administration pilot program would be established in his Queens district.[62] Representative Peter King (R-N.Y.) was assured that a dredging project in his Long Island district, which the Army Corps of Engineers had threatened to cancel, would live to see the light of day. Clinton also promised delegates from Oklahoma and Georgia that he would seek retaliatory actions under Section 22 of the U.S.-Canada FTA if a compromise could not be reached on Canadian wheat subsidies and increased peanut shipments. And the administration wooed Florida representatives by promises to protect tomato growers from increased Mexican exports.[63]

On November 4, 1993, the president formally submitted the implementing legislation to Congress. This action started the expedited legislative clock for considering NAFTA under a closed rule. As late as a week before the scheduled November 17 House vote, NAFTA opponents claimed sufficient strength to defeat the agreement. But the deals and accommodations listed above, typical of the bargaining process under fast track, had the desired effect: when the day of the vote came, the White House was confidently predicting victory.

The final tally was 234 to 200 in favor of NAFTA. Republicans supplied

---

61. A large sugar refinery resides in the district of Benjamin Carding (D-Md.).

62. *Congressional Quarterly Weekly Report*, November 20, 1993, 3179.

63. *Congressional Quarterly Weekly Report*, November 20, 1993, 3179.

the majority of the pact's support: they voted 132 to 43 in favor, while the Democrats voted 102 to 156 against. Proponents of the agreement came mainly from the South and West: 63 percent of southern representatives and 65 percent of western representatives voted in favor. On the other hand, 65 percent and 52 percent of northeast and midwest representatives, respectively, voted against. After his ill-fated debate with Vice President Al Gore, Ross Perot ceased to be a major factor; even in those districts that were heavily pro-Perot in the 1992 election, a large majority of representatives supported the pact.[64]

After the dramatic House campaign, Senate action on the implementing legislation proved anticlimactic. On November 20, the Senate passed NAFTA by a vote of 61 to 38 with minimal debate. Partisan breakdown of the Senate vote mirrored the earlier House vote: Democrats cast their ballots 27 to 28 against the pact, while Republicans voted 34 to 10 in favor. Finally, on December 8, 1993, President Clinton signed the agreement into law.

6.4. Conclusion

For most commentators, U.S. trade policy begins and ends with the executive branch. They analyze the relation of trade policy to the president's agenda, the role of executive branch negotiators in constructing trade agreements, and trade policy as an extension of the president's overall foreign policy goals. Congress, on the other hand, is seen as playing only a minor role in shaping trade policy. Having delegated its powers to the president, Congress is reduced to criticizing from the sidelines.

This chapter challenges the conventional wisdom, arguing that Congress continues to affect policy through the procedures it designs. Thus, to explain U.S. trade policy one must examine the process by which it is made. Currently, the relevant process is fast track, which prohibits amendments during floor consideration of the bill, but still gives members of Congress the opportunity to influence the final implementing legislation at the non-markup stage. The question is not whether Congress or the president dominates decision making; clearly, both branches of government play an integral role in trade policy formation. The relevant question is how does Congress structure the delegation of authority to control policy without reverting to legislative logrolls?

By examining fast track and two accords negotiated under these procedures, I have shown that Congress can use veto threats to force the president to accommodate protectionist demands. In the U.S.-Canada FTA, key legislators won concessions in the form of short-term exemptions and administrative

---

64. *Congressional Quarterly Weekly Report*, November 20, 1993, 3182.

protection. In the U.S.-Mexico FTA, the Bush administration promised to negotiate complex side agreements on environmental and labor issues in return for continued fast track authority, and Clinton was forced to make numerous last-minute concessions to garner congressional support. One interesting way to judge the effect of fast track procedures on policy outcomes is to see how the U.S.-Canada agreement has fared since its enactment. Has the agreement effectively eliminated tariff and nontariff trade barriers, or have political pressures forced an unraveling of these gains?

The U.S.-Canada Free Trade Agreement took effect on January 1, 1989, and thereby established the world's largest and most comprehensive bilateral free trade area. Over $200 billion of goods and services flowed between the United States and Canada in 1989. In the same year, bilateral trade in goods alone reached $167 billion, an increase of about 9 percent over 1988, despite a slowdown in both economies. The main success of the agreement has been the reduction of tariff barriers between the two countries. Indeed, in May, 1990, the United States and Canada agreed to accelerate the elimination of duties on over four hundred products, accounting for almost $6 billion in bilateral trade. This accelerated reduction was achieved with the cooperation and strong support of affected private-sector interests on both sides of the border, the Canadian government, and Congress.[65]

On some issues, however, agreement remains elusive. One example is wood items. According to American lumber producers, the Canadian government, which owns about 90 percent of Canadian timber, uses noncompetitive appraisal and selling methods that result in stumpage fees (costs of raw timber) far below U.S. prices and a "fair" market value. These methods give the Canadian lumber industry a competitive advantage. But it is unclear that they constitute improper subsidization, because Canadian timberland may have a lower opportunity cost than U.S. forests. Nonetheless, in 1986 the American lumber industry filed an unfair trade practice suit against Canada and obtained a 15 percent surcharge on Canadian softwood lumber exports into the United States. This tax would be phased out proportionately as Canadian federal and provincial governments increased the charges imposed on softwood lumber production.[66] The recent decision by Canada to cancel the tax on its lumber exports to the United States has reignited this long-standing argument between the two countries. Far from being resolved, this issue, which almost caused the Senate Finance Committee to refuse to grant fast track authority in 1986, is very much alive today.[67]

---

65. Message from the President of the United States, *United States-Canada Free Trade Agreement Biennial Report*, 102d Cong., 1st sess., H. Doc. 36, January 30, 1991.

66. See "The Memorandum of the Export of Softwood Lumber Products from Canada" (December 30, 1986), in Reagan 1986, vol. 2, 1653.

67. *Wall Street Journal*, September 14, 1991, A12.

Nontariff barriers are more difficult to negotiate than tariffs because reducing them involves changing complex domestic legislation, such as health, safety, and product standards. The plywood case nicely illustrates the problems that the United States and Canada face in harmonizing domestic performance standards and trade regulations. Canadian building codes prohibit the use of C- and D-grade plywood in the construction of Canada Mortgage and Housing Corporation–financed houses. Canada maintains that plywood containing D-grade veneer is liable to delaminate because larger knots are allowed in that grade. As a result of this regulation, 60 percent of U.S.-manufactured plywood is denied entry into Canada. In response, the United States has exempted plywood from the agreement and retained high protective tariffs until a common performance standard could be arranged.[68] However, little progress has been made toward changing domestic legislation.

In a continuing effort to remove such trade restrictions, the United States and Canada established both formal and informal dispute-settlement mechanisms. The informal panels consist of working groups of U.S. and Canadian officials who attempt to find a mutually acceptable compromise on outstanding trade issues. The formal panels were established to replace judicial review of anti-dumping and countervailing duty decisions made by U.S. or Canadian bureaucracies. For instance, when the ITC ruled that red raspberries imported from Canada were indeed being dumped on the U.S. market, the Canadians challenged this determination and appealed it to a binational panel. The Canadians won, and the ITC was directed to revise its earlier finding.

To date, the informal panels have settled only two disputes: salmon and lobsters. On the other hand, over two dozen cases have been appealed to the formal panels, including some of the issues that have long plagued U.S.-Canada trade relations: the plywood lumber case, the red raspberry case, the alcoholic beverages case, and the pork case.[69] In fact, the latter case came perilously close to nullifying the entire free trade agreement. After the United States lost the initial panel ruling on frozen and fresh pork, it appealed the decision to an extraordinary challenge committee. When the United States lost again, there were some indications that it might disregard the challenge committee's recommendations. Had the United States done so, the FTA allowed for the possibility that Canada could cancel the entire agreement. In the end, the United States conceded and, though expressing disappointment, promised to abide by the determination.[70]

Without a doubt, the FTA has reduced minor trade irritants on both sides

---

68. See House Ways and Means Committee, *Written Comments on the United States–Canada Free Trade Negotiations*, 99th Cong., 2d sess., 1986, Committee Print 16.

69. See O'Halloran and Noll 1991 for a detailed discussion of these panels.

70. See panel decisions USA-89-1904-06 and USA-89-1904-11. For a discussion see the *New York Times*, June 15, 1991, 17.

of the border, such as tariff barriers. It has also reduced the uncertainty in dealing with domestic trade regulations, such as anti-dumping and counter-vailing duty decisions. However, the preceding discussion suggests that many of the most contentious trade issues were left unresolved because the agreement had to pass through Congress. Rather than risk legislative opposition to the final proposal, the president excluded these issues from the agreement altogether. Although the FTA has not completely unraveled due to these lingering issues, fewer gains have been made than expected.

The implementation of NAFTA faces similar problems. Interestingly, NAFTA has also included a trilateral settlement mechanism. As in the FTA, anti-dumping and countervailing duty decisions can be appealed to the panel, as can disagreements over environmental and labor standards. But, also as in the FTA, many traditional disputes have remained unresolved. The most important of these is the fact that the countries have such widely varying health, safety, and labor regulations.

The agreement made no attempt to harmonize or introduce common performance standards. Rather, each country retains its own regulations, and imports will be permitted only if they meet those standards. The dispute-settlement mechanism should prevent the manipulation of environmental regulations for the sole purpose of excluding imports, but these standards none-theless act as de facto trade barriers. In the future, the lack of uniform regulations will continue to cause friction on a number of fronts. Certain regulations, such as laws prohibiting the use of banned pesticides or underage labor, cannot be enforced merely by inspecting products at the border. Compliance with these provisions will require the inspection of agricultural fields and working conditions. As long as such invasive on-site inspection remains impractical, these environmental and health regulations will continue to be contentious issues.

Overall, this chapter suggests that Congress influences trade policy be-fore, during, and after the implementation of an agreement. Before implementing an agreement under fast track, Congress has an initial veto over the use of expedited procedures, legislators directly monitor negotiations, and advisory committees keep members informed of any possible adverse effects. During implementation, Congress drafts the necessary legislation through the non-markup process and can veto the final agreement. After implementation, Congress continues to influence the course of trade policy by establishing dispute-settlement mechanisms to mediate conflicts arising under the agreement and to address issues left unresolved in the negotiations. Thus, fast track procedures, though designed to avoid legislative logrolls and facilitate the elimination of trade barriers, nonetheless attenuate possible gains by allowing legislators to protect special interests.

CHAPTER 7

Conclusion

The forces brought to bear on democratic government are not wholly beyond conscious control. The subject is, therefore, one of the greatest in modern politics. To manage pressures is to govern; to let pressures run wild is to abdicate.

—E. E. Schattschneider, *Politics, Pressure, and the Tariff*

Over a half century ago, Schattschneider realized that the legislative process has an important bearing on policy outcomes. In line with modern theories of legislative behavior, he asserted that the committee system gives inordinate influence to well-organized special interests. In the absence of strong party discipline in Congress, tariff legislation is characterized by "reciprocal non-interference" or universalism in which "each industry is encouraged to seek duties of its own and induced to accept the incidental burdens of the system without protest" (Schattschneider 1935, 284). Unless protectionist interests could be divided, Schattschneider argued, the inevitable result would be high protective tariffs. Under the prevailing system, he foresaw no significant reversal of this trend that would bring about a move toward freer trade.

As Schattschneider concluded his study of the 1930 Smoot-Hawley Tariff Act, however, Congress did change the system. The 1934 Reciprocal Trade Agreements Act (RTAA) embodied exactly the political strategy that Schattschneider thought necessary to isolate protectionist demands. The act offered inducements to exporting interests to support lower tariffs and thereby balanced the pressures placed upon members of Congress. Moreover, the RTAA delegated authority to the president, who is better able to play interests off against each other because his constituency is larger. The subsequent lower tariffs and the move toward freer trade is attributed largely to this institutional change.

One of the central arguments of this book is that trade policy since 1934 can be explained by the rich set of procedural arrangements that have taken shape over the past half century and have led to dramatically lower trade barriers. This is not to say that pressure politics is no longer important. On the contrary, pressures continue to affect outcomes, but their influence is now felt indirectly through procedures rather than directly on tariffs. Moreover, these institutional arrangements have changed over time, reflecting both constituency demands and partisan politics between Congress and the president.

It is not always easy, however, to untangle the effects of various institutions merely by observing results. A single institutional arrangement may lead to very different results, depending on the preferences of Congress and the president relative to current policies. At times policy outcomes may seem as if the president dominates decision making. Other times, aggressive special interests working through their representatives or the courts seem able to thwart the president's free trade initiatives. Thus, it is important to understand the details of the decision-making process, why legislators designed the process in this way, and the effects of these procedures on policy. For this reason, I have not only provided a detailed account of trade institutions and how they have changed over time, but also examples of how these procedures translate into policy outcomes.

To draw out the broader implications of the preceding analysis for the study of American politics, I address three questions in this conclusion:

1. What is the relation between interest groups and parties?
2. What is the effect of divided government on delegation?
3. What forces shape the congressional design of bureaucracy, and how do these procedures influence outcomes?

7.1. Interest Group Politics and Political Parties

A wealth of descriptive evidence suggests that political parties are an important organizing principle in Congress (Ripley 1967; Peabody 1976; Sinclair 1983; and Rohde 1990). However, empirical evidence of partisan effects on policy has proved elusive. Krehbiel (1990, 2) even casts doubt on the notion that political parties play an independent role in structuring legislators' behavior, presenting this challenge to party models: "Is there systematic, as opposed to anecdotal, support for the widespread belief that parties in Congress use resources and exercise parliamentary rights for partisan purposes *above and beyond what party-free theories predict?*" (emphasis in original). This is indeed the crucial question. The historical literature is rich with examples of party politics influencing the tariff, but there are surprisingly few empirical studies that support these claims. Even Magee, Brock, and Young (1989), who explicitly model political parties, conflate interest groups with voters and do not address the deeper issues of parties as coalitions.

Chapter 4 argues that even after accounting for changes in constituency demands, partisan control of government had a significant effect on tariff policy in the era after Reconstruction until 1934. Furthermore, political parties enacted tariff policies that differed significantly from one another and that benefited certain producer groups at the expense of others. This last finding points toward the importance of coalition building for party cohesion.

For example, in the late nineteenth and early twentieth centuries, interests were polarized on the tariff issue: manufacturers favored high protective tariffs, whereas agricultural groups pushed for lower tariffs on consumer goods. This clear separation of interests explains why partisan effects were easily discernible during this period. The two major parties divided along similar lines, with the Republicans representing protectionists and the Democrats, free traders. Referring back to figure 3.2, the parties' platforms diverged widely on the tariff issue, and therefore policy oscillated as one party replaced another in control of national government. As long as the parties were committed to enacting their platform once in office, a change from one party to the next brought a dramatic change in policy above that explained by changes in the median voter alone.

In the early 1920s, however, this contour of preferences began to change. At the end of World War I, a worldwide collapse of agriculture prices put intense economic pressure on American farmers. As prices remained depressed, farmers, too, began to lobby for protective legislation. Consequently, tariff laws became progressively more protectionist. This trend culminated in the 1930 Smoot-Hawley Tariff Act, which, as explained in chapter 5, had begun as an agricultural relief measure. Thus, the two parties' positions on the tariff moved closer together, with high tariff demanders predominating in both parties.

As the constituency bases of the parties began to coalesce, the policies they enacted became more similar. Indeed, by the post–World War II period, the political parties had actually switched positions on trade policy. Republicans now embraced free trade, and the Democrats, protectionism (Wade and Gates 1990). The implication for empirical party analysis, then, is that studies of legislative behavior may miss partisan effects by not distinguishing policy issues on which the parties take competing positions from those on which their positions overlap.

7.2. Divided Government and Delegation

A large and growing literature examines the effects of divided government on policy. These studies analyze the relation between divided government and patterns of electoral competition (Jacobson 1990), the number of major pieces of legislation enacted (Mayhew 1991), state-level policy (Fiorina 1992), and federal budget deficits (McCubbins 1991).[1] In this book, I argue that divided government has a subtle but important effect on policy through the willingness of Congress to design procedures that delegate authority to the president.

For instance, the 1934 Reciprocal Trade Agreements Act (RTAA) marks a watershed in American trade history. Congress delegated more authority to the president under fewer guidelines than ever before. Arguably, after the passage of the RTAA, Congress committed itself to a trade policy in which tariffs were set by executive agreement, rather than legislative enactment. But Congress nonetheless remained active in trade policy-making. The decision to delegate was not the final word. Rather, it presented Congress with a different series of questions: when to delegate, how much power to delegate, and what constraints to place on delegation.

In designing the institutions that structure delegation, legislators face constituency pressure for protectionism. Although they have incentives to avoid caving in to these demands, legislators are also unwilling to give the executive complete control over trade policy. Congress's solution has been to temper its delegation, diluting it with procedures through which industries can seek compensation from the adverse effects of increased competition. Thus, instead of Congress legislating itself out of the business of making product-specific trade laws, it has gone into the business of procedural protectionism. The battleground has shifted from legislators' fighting among themselves over specific tariff rates to their fighting with the executive over how much leeway the president will have to set policy.

Hence, the nature of partisan competition over trade policy in modern times has changed. The debate now centers on how much authority to delegate to the president, and the similarity of preferences between Congress and the president is an important factor in this decision. Congress will therefore be more likely to delegate power to a president of the same party than to a president of the opposing party. That is, restraints imposed on the president's discretionary authority will be stronger under conditions of divided government than when there is unified government. A more constrained president implements policies closer to the congressional norm of high tariffs.

As discussed above, in the period from post-Reconstruction to 1934 partisan competition directly influenced the tariff, and national elections that brought a change in partisan control also brought a change in trade policy. However, with the delegation of authority in the post-1934 era, the influence of party has become more obscure, as party competition now centers on the design of procedures that govern how policy will be made. Thus, partisanship matters, but in a much more subtle way than before. It is reflected in the

---

1. For a overview of the effects of divided government on a wide range of issues, see Cox and Kernell 1991, and for a concise summary of the scholarly literature see Fiorina 1992.

procedural restraints placed on the president and thereby indirectly shapes policy outcomes.

7.3. Trade Politics as Regulatory Politics

What is apparent from the detailed historical analysis presented in chapter 5 is that Congress spends an enormous amount of time debating the design of trade institutions and has created a complex web of regulatory procedures through which industries can petition for import relief. Although it is not usually thought of as such, trade policy has essentially become regulatory policy. Congress has designed a series of executive agencies, such as the ITC and the USTR, which implement legislative guidelines regulating trade policy. These include enforcing anti-dumping and countervailing duty codes and granting industry waivers under escape clause and trade adjustment assistance provisions. The 1988 Trade and Competitiveness Act alone was over a thousand pages long, including such detailed procedures as Super 301 and reverse fast track. In addition, many regulatory determinations are subject to an ex post veto, like countervailing duty decisions and the extensions of most-favored-nation status.

The rise of procedural protectionism carries important implications for interest group influence on regulatory agencies regarding trade policy. Recently, several studies (Destler 1991; Goldstein and Lenway 1989) have argued that interest groups have little influence on the regulatory process.[2] These studies conclude that policy is insulated to a large degree and that these regulatory mechanisms act as a means to diffuse protectionist demands.

By contrast, this book argues that interest group influence has already been incorporated into the regulatory process through the procedures that govern administrative decision making. That is, the standards by which industries qualify for government assistance, whether it be anti-dumping actions or trade adjustment assistance, are themselves the result of the political process. Thus interest group influence may be apparent not at regulatory proceedings, but rather in the standards of proof applied at these proceedings. For instance, the debate over the American Selling Price (ASP) method of customs evaluation was fueled by conflicts over industry demands for protection. ASP resulted in higher tariffs for certain chemical and footwear products by requiring that higher American prices be used as the basis of comparison. Similarly, the argument over whether import relief, such as escape clause actions, should be conditioned on a firm's ability to show that increased imports caused serious injury or merely a loss of sales is really an argument over how hard or easy it will be for firms to obtain regulatory exemptions from tariff reductions.

---

2. W. Hansen (1990) is one notable exception.

Seen in the context of trade policy as regulatory policy, what is important about fast track procedures is that they make even the negotiation of international agreements into regulatory-like proceedings.[3] For example, as discussed in chapter 6, Congress has created a congressional agent within the executive office of the president, the USTR, who negotiates international trade accords and is responsive to congressional concerns. Expanded advisory committees and numerous consultation and reporting requirements force the executive to engage in something akin to notice-and-comment rulemaking. Congressional delegates are required to be present at negotiations as a form of direct oversight. And the extensions of fast track authority have included extra points at which Congress can exercise a legislative veto. Whereas trade negotiations were once seen as one of the president's diplomatic functions, they are now treated much as any other executive branch regulatory proceeding.

The result of this shift has been to enfranchise Congress and special interests into the negotiation and implementation of trade agreements. Advisory committees must be consulted before and during the negotiations. The president must hold public hearings and give interested parties the opportunity to offer suggestions and advice. And Congress holds hearings in which experts and representatives from affected industries have the chance to voice any concerns. As a result, in many cases the president will be forced to accommodate the demands of certain interests in order to assure final passage of the implementing legislation. For instance, the U.S.-Canada Free Trade Agreement included reciprocal potato quotas, voluntary export restraints on steel, and fish landing requirements. Thus, instead of allowing the president to remain above the fray, brokering protectionist and free trade concerns, these procedures enmesh him in the parochial interests of legislators and force him to accede to protectionist demands.

Congress walks a fine line in regulating trade policy. On one hand, Article I, Section 8, of the Constitution empowers Congress to "impose duties and regulate commerce with foreign nations." On the other hand, Congress may best exercise its authority by delegating power to the president. If, as Schattschneider claims, to govern is to manage pressures, then Congress will continue to govern by creating procedures to control trade policy through, not despite, delegation.

---

3. There are of course elements of trade policy that fall more naturally under the purview of foreign policy, such as export controls of sensitive technology or economic embargoes. These topics are peripheral to my analysis of the domestic components of trade policy-making.

References

Alchian, Armen A. 1958. "Uncertainty, Evolution, and Economic Theory." *Journal of Political Economy* 58:211–21.

Alchian, Armen A., and Harold Demsetz. 1972. "Production, Information Costs, and Economic Organization." *American Economic Review* 62:777–95.

Alchian, Armen A., and Harold Demsetz. 1973. "The Property Rights Paradigm." *Journal of Economic History* 33:16–27.

Alesina, Alberto, and Jeffery Sachs. 1988. "Political Parties and the Business Cycle in the United States, 1948–1984." *Journal of Money, Credit, and Banking* 20:63–82.

Arrow, Kenneth J. 1951. *Social Choice and Individual Values.* New Haven: Yale University Press.

Austen-Smith, David. 1991. "Rational Consumers and Irrational Voters: A Review Essay on Black Hole Tariffs and Endogenous Policy Theory, by Stephen Magee, William Brock and Leslie Young, Cambridge University Press, 1989." *Economics and Politics* 3:73–92.

Austen-Smith, David, and Jeffrey Banks. 1989. "Electoral Accountability and Incumbency." In *Models of Strategic Choice in Politics*, ed. Peter Ordeshook. Ann Arbor: University of Michigan Press.

Baack, Bennett D., and Edward J. Ray. 1983. "The Political Economy of Tariff Policy: A Case Study of the United States." *Explorations in Economic History* 20:73–93.

Baack, Bennett D., and Edward J. Ray. 1985. "Special Interest and the Adoption of the Income Tax in the United States." *Journal of Economic History* 45:607–25.

Baldwin, Robert E. 1985. *The Political Economy of U.S. Import Policy.* Cambridge, MA: MIT Press.

Baldwin, Robert E. 1988. *Trade Policy in a Changing World Economy.* Cambridge MA: MIT Press.

Balke, Nathan S., and Robert Gordon. 1989. "The Estimation of Prewar Gross National Product: Methodology and New Evidence." *Journal of Political Economy* 97:38–92.

Baron, David. 1989. "Service-Induced Campaign Contributions, Incumbent Shirking, and Reelection Opportunities." In *Models of Strategic Choice in Politics.*, ed. Peter Ordeshook. Ann Arbor: University of Michigan Press.

Baron, David. 1991a. "Spatial Electoral Competition and Campaign Contributions with Informed and Uninformed Voters." Research Paper No. 1174, GSB Research Paper Series, Stanford University.

Baron, David. 1991b. "Majoritarian Incentives, Pork Barrel Programs, and Procedural Control." *American Journal of Political Science* 35:57–90.

Baron, David, and Jongryn Mo. 1991. "Campaign Contributions and Party-Candidate Competition in Services and Policies." Research Paper No. 1151, GSB Research Paper Series, Stanford University.

Basevi, Giorgio. 1966. "The United States Tariff Structure: Estimation of Effective Role of Protection of United States Industries and Industrial Labor." *Review of Economics and Statistics* 48:840–52.

Bauer, Raymond, Ithiel De Sola Pool, and Lewis Anthony Dexter. 1963. *American Business and Public Policy: The Politics of Foreign Trade.* Chicago: Aldine-Atherton.

Becker, Gary S. 1983. "A Theory of Competition among Pressure Groups for Political Influence." *Quarterly Journal of Economics* 97:371–400.

Becker, Gary S. 1985. "Public Policies, Pressure Groups, and Dead Weight Costs." *Journal of Public Economics* 28:329–47.

Berry, Thomas S. 1988. *Production and Population since 1789: Revised GNP Series in Constant Dollars.* Bostwick Paper No. 6. Richmond, VA: Bostwick.

Bhagwati, Jagdish. 1988. *Protectionism.* Cambridge, MA: MIT Press.

Bhagwati, Jagdish, and Hugh T. Patrick, eds. 1990. *Aggressive Unilateralism.* Ann Arbor: University of Michigan Press.

Bidwell, Percy W. 1933. "Tariff Policy of the United States: A Study of Recent Experience." Report to the Second International Studies Conference on *The State and Economic Life,* London, June.

Bidwell, Percy W. 1956. *What the Tariff Means to American Industries.* New York: Harper and Brothers.

Black, Duncan. 1958. *The Theory of Committees and Elections.* London: Cambridge University Press.

Bohara, Alok, and William H. Kaempfer. 1991a. "A Test of Tariff Endogeneity in the United States." *American Economic Review* 80:952–60.

Bohara, Alok, and William H. Kaempfer. 1991b. "Testing the Endogeneity of Tariff Policy in the United States." *Economic Letter* 35:311–15.

Brady, David. 1973. *Congressional Voting in a Partisan Era.* Lawrence: University of Kansas Press.

Brady, David. 1988. *Critical Elections and Congressional Policy Making.* Stanford, CA: Stanford University Press.

Brady, David, Richard Brody, and David Epstein. 1989. "Heterogeneous Parties and Political Organization: The U.S. Senate, 1880–1920." *Legislative Studies Quarterly* 14:205–24.

Cassing, James, Timothy J. McKeown, and Jack Ochs. 1986. "The Political Economy of The Tariff Cycle." *American Political Science Review* 80:841–62.

Caves, Richard E. 1976. "Economic Models of Political Choice: Canada's Tariff Structure." *Canadian Journal of Economics* 9:278–300.

Cheh, John. 1976. "A Note on Tariffs, Non-Tariff Barriers and Labor Protection in the U.S. Manufacturing Industries," *Journal of Political Economy* 84:389–94.

Cohen, Stephen D. 1988. *The Making of United States International Economic Policy: Principles, Problems, and Proposals for Reform.* New York: Praeger.

Cohen, Stephen D., and Meltzer, Ronald I. 1982. *United States International Economic Policy in Action: Diversity in Decision Making.* New York: Praeger.

Congress and the Nation I, 1945–1964. 1965. Washington, DC: Congressional Quarterly Press.

Congress and the Nation II, 1965–1968. 1969. Washington, DC: Congressional Quarterly Press.

Congress and the Nation III, 1969–1972. 1973. Washington, DC: Congressional Quarterly Press.

Congress and the Nation IV, 1973–1976. 1977. Washington, DC: Congressional Quarterly Press.

Congress and the Nation V, 1977–1980. 1981. Washington, DC: Congressional Quarterly Press.

Congressional Quarterly Almanac. Various years. Washington, DC: Congressional Quarterly Press.

Conybeare, John A. C. 1991. "Voting for Protection: An Electoral Model of Tariff Protection." *International Organization* 45:57–81.

Cooper, Joseph. 1985. "The Legislative Veto in the 1980s." In *Congress Reconsidered,* ed. Lawrence C. Dodd and Bruce I. Oppenheimer. Washington, DC: Congressional Quarterly Press.

Cooper, Richard. 1973. "Trade Policy Is Foreign Policy." *Foreign Policy* 9:18–36.

Coughlin, Cletus. 1985. "Domestic Content Legislation: House Voting and the Economic Theory of Regulation." *Economic Inquiry* 23:437–48.

Coughlin, Cletus, Joseph V. Terza, and Noor Aini Khalifah. 1989. "The Determinants of Escape Clause Petitions." *Review of Economics and Statistics* 71:341–47.

Cox, Gary W., and Samuel Kernell, eds. 1991. *The Politics of Divided Government.* Boulder, CO: Westview Press.

Cox, Gary W., and Mathew McCubbins. 1986. "Electoral Politics as a Redistributive Game." *Journal of Politics* 48:370–89.

Cox, Gary W., and Mathew McCubbins. 1993. *Legislative Leviathan: Party Government in the House.* Berkeley: University of California Press.

Crabb, Cecil B., and Pat M. Holt. 1989. *Invitation to Struggle: Congress, the President, and Foreign Policy.* Washington, DC: Congressional Quarterly Press.

Craig, Barbara H. 1988. *Chadha: The Story of an Epic Constitutional Struggle.* New York: Oxford University Press.

Curtis, Thomas, and John Robert Vastine. 1971. *The Kennedy Round and the Future of American Trade.* New York: Praeger.

Demski, Joel, and David Sappington. 1987. "Delegating Expertise." *Journal of Accounting Research* 25:68–89.

Denzau, Arthur, and Michael Munger. 1986. "Legislators and Interest Groups: How Unorganized Interests Get Represented." *American Political Science Review* 80:89–106.

Destler, I. M. 1986a. *American Trade Politics: System Under Stress.* Washington, DC: Institute for International Economics.

Destler, I. M. 1986b. "Protecting Congress or Protecting Trade?" *Foreign Policy* 62:96–107.

Destler, I. M. 1991. "U.S. Trade Policy-making in the Eighties." In *Politics and Economics in the Eighties,* ed. Alberto Alesina and Jeffery Carliner. Chicago: University of Chicago Press.

Destler, I. M., and John Odell. 1987. *Antiprotection: Changing Forces in United States Trade Politics*. Washington, DC: Institute for International Economics.

Dobson, John M. 1976. *Two Centuries of Tariffs: The Background and Emergence of the U.S. International Trade Commission*. Washington, DC: Government Printing Office.

Dodd, Lawrence, and Bruce Oppenheimer, eds. 1985. *Congress Reconsidered*. Washington, DC: Congressional Quarterly Press.

Downs, Anthony. 1957. *An Economic Theory of Democracy*. New York: Harper and Row.

Eichengreen, Barry. 1989. "The Political Economy of the Smoot-Hawley Tariff." *Research in Economic History* 12:1–43.

Eisenhower, Dwight D. *Public Papers of the President of the United States: Dwight D. Eisenhower, 1953–1961*. Washington DC: Government Printing Office.

Engle, Robert, and C. W. Granger. 1987. "Co-Integration and Error Correction: Representation, Estimation, and Testing." *Econometrica* 55:251–76.

Epstein, David. 1992. "An Informational Rationale for Committee Gatekeeping Power." Ph.D. diss., Stanford University.

Evans, John. 1971. *The Kennedy Round in American Trade Policy*. Cambridge, MA: Harvard University Press.

Farrand, Max, ed. 1911. *The Records of the Federal Convention of 1787, vols. I–III*. New Haven: Yale University Press.

Feigenbaum, Susan, Henry Ortiz, and Thomas Willett. 1985. "Protectionist Pressures and Aggregate Economic Conditions: Comment on Takacs." *Economic Inquiry* 23:175–82.

Fenno, Richard E. 1978. *Home Style: House Members in Their Districts*. Boston: Little, Brown.

Ferejohn, John. 1974. *Pork Barrel Politics*. Stanford: Stanford University Press.

Finger, Michael, Keith Hall, and Douglas Nelson. 1982. "The Political Economy of Administered Protection." *American Economic Review* 72:452–66.

Finger, Michael, and Sam Laird. 1987. "Protection in Developed and Developing Countries: An Overview." World Bank, Washington, DC: Typescript.

Fiorina, Morris P. 1974. *Representatives, Roll Calls, and Constituencies*. Lexington, MA: D. C. Heath.

Fiorina, Morris P. 1981. "Universalism, Reciprocity, and Distributive Policy-Making in Majority Rule Institutions." In *Research in Public Policy Analysis and Management*, ed. John Crecine. Greenwich, CT: Jai Press.

Fiorina, Morris P. 1982. "Legislative Choice of Regulatory Forms: Legal Process or Administrative Process." *Public Choice* 39:33–66.

Fiorina, Morris P. 1991. "Divided Government in the States." In *The Politics of Divided Government*, ed. Gary Cox, and Samuel Kernell. Boulder, CO: Westview Press.

Fiorina, Morris P. 1992. *Divided Government*. London: Macmillan.

Fisher, Louis. 1972. *The President and Congress: Power and Policy*. New York: Free Press.

Fisher, Louis. 1987. *The Politics of Shared Power: Congress and the Executive*. Washington, DC: Congressional Quarterly Press.

Fudenberg, Drew, and Jean Tirole. 1991. *Game Theory*. Cambridge, MA: MIT Press.

Fuller, Wayne A. 1976. *Introduction to Statistical Time Series*. New York: Wiley.

Gallarotti, Giulio M. 1985. "Toward a Business-Cycle Model of Tariffs." *International Organization* 39:155–87.

Gallman, Robert E. 1966. "Gross National Product in the United States, 1834–1909." In *Output, Employment, and Productivity in the United States after 1800*. Studies in Income and Wealth, vol. 30. Conference on Research in Income and Wealth. New York: Columbia University Press.

Galloway, George B. 1962. *History of the House of Representatives*. New York: Thomas Y. Crowell.

Gardner, Grant W., and Kent P. Kimbrough. 1989. "The Behavior of U.S. Tariff Rates." *American Economic Review* 79:212–18.

Gilligan, Thomas, and Keith Krehbiel. 1987. "Collective Decision Making and Standing Committees: An Information Rationale for Restrictive Amendment Procedures." *Journal of Law, Economics, and Organization* 3:287–335.

Gilligan, Thomas, and Keith Krehbiel. 1989. "Asymmetric Information and Legislative Rules with a Heterogeneous Committee." *American Journal of Political Science* 33:459–90.

Goldstein, Judith. 1986. "The Political Economy of Trade: Institutions of Protection." *American Political Science Review* 80:161–84.

Goldstein, Judith. 1988. "Ideas, Institutions and American Trade Policy." In *State and American Foreign Economic Policy*, ed. G. John Ikenberry, David A. Lake, and Michael Mastanduno. Ithaca, NY: Cornell University Press.

Goldstein, Judith, and Stefanie Lenway. 1989. "Interests or Institutions: An Inquiry into Congressional ITC Relations." *International Studies Quarterly* 33:303–27.

Gourevitch, Peter. 1986. *The Politics of Hard Times*. Ithaca, NY: Cornell University Press.

Granger, C. W. J. 1986. Developments in the Study of Cointegrated Economic Variables. *Oxford Bulletin of Economics and Statistics* 48:213–28.

Greene, William H. 1990. *Econometric Analysis*. New York: Macmillan.

Grier, Kevin, and Michael Munger. 1991. "Committee Assignments, Constituent Preferences, and Campaign Contributions." *Economic Inquiry* 29:24–43.

Haggard, Stephan. 1988. "The Institutional Foundations of Hegemony: Explaining the Reciprocal Trade Agreements Act of 1934." In *The State and American Foreign Economic Policy*, ed. G. John Ikenberry, David Lake, and Michael Mastanduno. Ithaca, NY: Cornell University Press.

Hamilton, Alexander, John Jay, and James Madison. 1787. *The Federalist*. New York: Modern Library.

Hansen, John Mark. 1990. "Taxation and the Political Economy of the Tariff." *International Organization* 44:527–51.

Hansen, Wendy. 1990. "The International Trade Commission and the Politics of Protection." *American Political Science Review* 84:21–46.

Hardin, Garrett. 1968. "The Tragedy of the Commons." *Science* 162:1243–48.

Hardin, Russell. 1971. "Collective Action as an Agreeable n-Prisoners' Dilemma." *Behavioral Science* 16:472–81.

Hardin, Russell. 1982. *Collective Action.* Baltimore, MD: Johns Hopkins University Press.

Hasbrouck, Paul DeWitt. 1927. *Party Government in the House of Representatives.* New York: Macmillan.

Hilsman, Roger. 1958. "Congressional-Executive Relations and the Foreign Policy Consensus." *American Political Science Review* 52:725–44.

Holmström, Bengt. 1979. "Moral Hazard and Observability." *Bell Journal of Economics* 10:74–91.

Hufbauer, Gary, Diane Berliner, and Kimberly Elliott. 1986. *Trade Protection in the United States.* Washington, DC: Institute for International Economics.

Jacobson, Gary C. 1990. *The Electoral Origins of Divided Government.* Boulder, CO: Westview Press.

Johnson, Loch K. 1984. *The Making of International Agreements: Congress Confronts the Executive.* New York: New York University Press.

Johnston, John. 1984. *Econometric Methods.* New York: Macmillan.

Joskow, Paul, and Roger Noll. 1981. "Regulation in Theory and Practice: An Overview." In *Studies of Public Regulation,* ed. Gary Fromm. Cambridge, MA: MIT Press.

Kahn, Alfred. 1988. *The Economics of Regulation: Principles and Institutions.* Cambridge, MA: MIT Press.

Kanodia, Chandra. 1987. "Stochastic Monitoring and Moral Hazard." *Journal of Accounting Research* 23:175–93.

Kegley, Charles W., and Eugene Wittdopf. 1987. *American Foreign Policy: Pattern and Process.* New York: St. Martin's.

Kendrick, John W. 1961. *Productivity Trends in the United States.* General Series, no. 24. Princeton, NJ: Princeton University Press.

Kenkel, Joseph F. 1983. *Progressives and Protection.* New York: University Press of America.

Kiewiet, D. Roderick, and Mathew McCubbins. 1991. *The Logic of Delegation.* Chicago: University of Chicago Press.

King, Gary, and Lyn Ragsdale. 1988. *The Elusive Executive: Discovering Statistical Patterns in the Presidency.* Washington, DC: Congressional Quarterly Press.

Kingdon, John W. 1984. *Agendas, Alternatives, and Public Policies.* Boston: Little, Brown.

Kmenta, Jan. 1986. *Elements of Econometrics.* New York: McGraw-Hill.

Kramer, Gerald H. 1971. "Short-Term Fluctuations in U.S. Voting Behavior, 1896–1964." *American Political Science Review* 65:131–43.

Krehbiel, Keith. 1988. "Spatial Models of Legislative Choice." *Legislative Studies Quarterly* 13:259–319.

Krehbiel, Keith. 1990. "Where's the Party?" Graduate School of Business, Stanford University, Typescript.

Krehbiel, Keith. 1991. *Information and Legislative Organization.* Ann Arbor: University of Michigan Press.

Kuznets, Simon. 1946. *National Product since 1869*. New York: National Bureau of Economic Research.

Laird, Sam, and Alexander Yeats. 1990. "Trends in Nontariff Barriers of Developed Countries, 1966–1986." Policy, Planning, and Research Working Paper no. 137. World Bank, Washington, DC.

Lavergne, Real P. 1983. *The Political Economy of U.S. Tariffs: An Empirical Analysis*. New York: Academic Press.

Lohmann, Susanne, and Sharyn O'Halloran. 1994. "Divided Government and U.S. Trade Policy." *International Organization* (forthcoming).

Lowi, Theodore. 1964. "American Business, Public Policy, Case-Studies, and Political Theory." *World Politics*. 16:677–715.

Lutz, James M. 1991. "Determinants of Protectionist Attitudes in the United States House of Representatives." *The International Trade Journal* 5:301–28.

Mackenzie, Kenneth C. 1968. *Tariff-Making and Trade Policy in the U.S. and Canada: A Comparative Study*. New York: Praeger.

MacKinnon, James. 1991. "Critical Values for Cointegration Tests." In *Long-Run Economic Relationships: Readings in Cointegration*, ed. Robert F. Engle and C. W. J. Granger. London: Oxford University Press.

Magee, Stephen, and Leslie Young. 1987. "Endogenous Protection in the United States: 1900–1984." In *U.S. Trade Policies in a Changing World Economy*, ed. Robert Stern. Cambridge, MA: MIT Press.

Magee, Stephen, William Brock, and Leslie Young. 1989. *Black Hole Tariffs and Endogenous Policy Theory: Political Economy in General Equilibrium*. Cambridge: Cambridge University Press.

Mann, Thomas, and Norman Ornstein, eds. 1981. *The New Congress*. Washington, DC: American Enterprise Institute for Public Policy Research.

Margolis, Lawrence. 1986. *Executive Agreements and Presidential Power in Foreign Policy*. New York: Praeger.

Marks, Stephen, and John McArthur. 1990. "Empirical Analysis of the Determinants of Protection: A Survey of Some New Results." In *International Trade Policies: Gains from Exchange between Economics and Political Science*, ed. John S. Odell and Thomas D. Willett. Ann Arbor: University of Michigan Press.

Martin, Elizabeth M. 1991. "Free Trade and Fast Track: Why Does Congress Delegate?" Graduate School of Business, Stanford University. Typescript.

Marvel, Howard P., and Edward J. Ray. 1983. "The Kennedy Round: Evidence on the Regulation of International Trade in the United States." *American Economic Review* 73:190–97.

Mayhew, David. 1974. *Congress: The Electoral Connection*. New Haven: Yale University Press.

Mayhew, David. 1991. *Divided We Govern: Party Control, Lawmaking, and Investigations, 1946–1990*. New Haven: Yale University Press.

McCubbins, Mathew. 1985. "Legislative Design of Regulatory Structure." *American Journal of Political Science* 29:721–48.

McCubbins, Mathew. 1991. "Party Governance and U.S. Budget Deficits: Divided Government and Fiscal Stalemate." In *Politics and Economics in the Eigh-*

ties, ed. Alberto Alesina and Jeffery Carliner. Chicago: University of Chicago Press.

McCubbins, Mathew, Roger Noll, and Barry Weingast. 1987. "Administrative Procedures as Instruments of Political Control." *Journal of Law and Economics* 3:243–77.

McCubbins, Mathew, Roger Noll, and Barry Weingast. 1989. "Structure and Process; Policy and Process: Administrative Arrangements and the Political Control of Agencies." *Virginia Law Review* 75:431–82.

McCubbins, Mathew, and Thomas Schwartz. 1984. "Congressional Oversight Overlooked: Police Patrols versus Fire Alarms." *American Journal of Political Science* 28:165–79.

McKelvey, Richard. 1976. "Intransitivities in Multidimensional Voting Models and Some Implications for Agenda Control." *Journal of Economic Theory* 12:472–82.

McKeown, Timothy. 1984. "Firms and Tariff Regime Change: Explaining the Demand for Protection." *World Politics* 36:215–33.

McKeown, Timothy. 1986. "The Limitations of Structural Theories of Commercial Policy." *International Organization* 40:43–64.

Milner, Helen. 1988. *Resisting Protectionism.* Princeton, NJ: Princeton University Press.

Moe, Terry M. 1984. "The New Economics of Organization." *American Journal of Political Science* 28:739–77.

Moe, Terry M. 1990. "Political Institutions: The Neglected Side of the Story." *Journal of Law, Economics, and Organizations* 6:213–54.

Moore, Michael. 1992. "Rules or Politics?: An Empirical Analysis of ITC Anti-Dumping Decisions." *Economic Inquiry* 30:449–66.

Morici, Peter, ed. 1990. *Making Free Trade Work: The Canada-U.S. Agreement.* New York: Council on Foreign Relations Press.

Nelson, Douglas. 1988. "Endogenous Tariff Theory: A Critical Survey." *American Journal of Political Science* 32:796–837.

Neustadt, Richard E. 1960. *Presidential Power: The Politics of Leadership.* New York: Wiley Science Editions.

Niskanen, William A. 1971. *Bureaucracy and Representative Government.* Chicago: Aldine.

Nordhaus, William. 1975. "The Political Business Cycle." *Review of Economic Studies* 42:169–90.

O'Halloran, Sharyn. 1990. *Politics, Process, and American Trade Policy: Congress and the Regulation of International Trade.* Ph.D. diss. University of California, San Diego.

O'Halloran, Sharyn. 1992. "Congress, Parties, and the Tariff." Department of Political Science, Stanford University. Typescript.

O'Halloran, Sharyn. 1993. "Congress and Foreign Trade Policy." In *Congress Resurgent: Foreign and Defense Policy on Capital Hill,* ed. Randall B. Ripley and James M. Lindsay. Ann Arbor: University of Michigan Press.

O'Halloran, Sharyn, and Roger Noll. 1991. "Institutions as Congressional Commitments: International Trade Policy in the Postwar Liberal Era." Paper presented at the Social Science Research Council Conference on Congress and Foreign Policy, Stanford University, April.

Olson, Mancur. 1965. *The Logic of Collective Action: Public Goods and the Theory of Groups*. Cambridge, MA: Harvard University Press.

Ornstein, Norman, Thomas Mann, and Michael Malbin. 1992. *Vital Statistics on Congress: 1991-1992*. Washington, DC: Congressional Quarterly Press.

Pastor, Robert. 1980. *Congress and the Politics of U.S. Foreign Economic Policy, 1926–1976*. Berkeley: University of California Press.

Pastor, Robert. 1983. "Cry-and-Sigh Syndrome: Congress and Trade Policy." In *Making Economic Policy in Congress*, ed. Allen Schick. Washington, DC: American Enterprise Institute for Public Policy Research.

Pattison, Joseph. 1991. *Antidumping and Countervailing Duty Laws*. New York: Clark Boardman.

Peabody, Robert. 1976. *Leadership in Congress: Stability, Succession, and Change*. Boston: Little, Brown.

Peltzman, Sam. 1976. "Toward a More General Theory of Regulation." *Journal of Law and Economics* 19:211–48.

Pincus, Jonathan. 1975. "Pressure Groups and the Pattern of Tariffs." *Journal of Political Economy* 83:757–78.

Pincus, Jonathan. 1977. *Pressure Groups and Politics in Antebellum Tariffs*. New York: Columbia University Press.

Plott, Charles. 1967. "A Notion of Equilibrium and Its Possibility under Majority Rule." *American Economic Review* 57:787–806.

Porter, Kirk H. 1924. *National Party Platforms*. New York: Macmillan.

Ratner, Sidney. 1972. *The Tariff in American History*. New York: Van Nostrand.

Ray, Edward J. 1981a. "The Determinants of Tariff and Nontariff Trade Restrictions in the United States." *Journal of Political Economy* 89:105–21.

Ray, Edward J. 1981b. "Tariff and Non-Tariff Barriers to Trade in the United States and Abroad." *Review of Economics and Statistics* 63:161–68.

Ray, Edward J. 1987. "The Impact of Special Interests on Preferential Tariff Concessions by the United States." *Review of Economics and Statistics* 69:187–93.

Ray, Edward J., and Howard Marvel. 1984. "The Pattern of Protection in the Industrialized World." *Review of Economics and Statistics* 66:452–58.

Reagan, Ronald. 1985. *Public Papers of the Presidents of the United States: Ronald Reagan, 1983–91*. Vol. 1. Washington, DC: Government Printing Office.

Reagan, Ronald. 1986. *Public Papers of the Presidents of the United States: Ronald Reagan, 1983–91*. Vol. 2. Washington, DC: Government Printing Office.

Riker, William H. 1982. *Liberalism against Populism: A Confrontation between the Theory of Democracy and the Theory of Social Choice*. San Francisco: W. H. Freeman.

Ripley, Randall B. 1967. *Party Leaders in the House of Representatives*. Washington, DC: Brookings Institution.

Robinson, James. 1967. *Congress and Foreign Policy Making*. Homewood, IL: Dorsey.

Rogowski, Ronald. 1987. "Political Cleavages and Changing Exposure to Trade." *American Political Science Review* 81:1121–37.

Rohde, David. 1990. " 'The Reports of My Death Are Greatly Exaggerated': Parties and Party Voting in the House of Representatives." In *Changing Perspectives on Congress*, ed. Glenn Parker. Knoxville: University of Tennessee Press.

Romer, Christina D. 1989. "The Prewar Business Cycle Reconsidered: New Estimates of Gross National Product, 1869–1908." *Journal of Political Economy* 97:1–37.

Romer, Thomas, and Howard Rosenthal. 1978. "Political Resource Allocation, Controlled Agendas, and the Status-quo." *Public Choice* 33:27–43.

Schattschneider, E. E. 1935. *Politics, Pressure, and the Tariff: a Study of Free Private Enterprise in Pressure Politics, as Shown in the 1929–1930 Revision of the Tariff.* Hamden, CT: Archon Books.

Schlesinger, Arthur M. 1945. *The Age of Jackson.* Boston: Little, Brown.

Schlesinger, Arthur M. 1973. *The Imperial Presidency.* Boston: Houghton Mifflin.

Schofield, Norman. 1978. "Instability of Simple Dynamic Games." *Review of Economic Studies* 45:575–94.

Setser, Vernon G. 1969. *The Commercial Reciprocity Policy of the United States, 1774–1829.* New York: Da Capo.

Shepsle, Kenneth A., and Barry R. Weingast. 1981. "Political Preferences for Pork Barrel: A Generalization." *American Journal of Political Science* 25:96–111.

Shepsle, Kenneth A., and Barry R. Weingast. 1984. "Legislative Politics and Budget Outcomes" In *Federal Budget Policy in the 1980s*, ed. Gregory B. Mills and John Palmer. Washington, DC: Urban Institute Press.

Shepsle, Kenneth A., and Barry R. Weingast. 1987a. "The Institutional Foundations of Committee Power." *American Political Science Review* 81:85–104.

Shepsle, Kenneth A., and Barry R. Weingast. 1987b. "Why are Congressional Committees Powerful?" *American Political Science Review* 81:935–45.

Silbey, Joel H. 1985. *The Partisan Imperative: The Dynamics of American Politics before the Civil War.* Oxford: Oxford University.

Sinclair, Barbara. 1983. *Majority Leadership in the U.S. House.* Baltimore, MD: Johns Hopkins University Press.

Stanley, Harold W., and Richard G. Niemi. 1988. *Vital Statistics on American Politics.* Washington, DC: Congressional Quarterly Press.

Stanwood, Edward. 1903. *American Tariff Controversies in the Nineteenth Century.* New York: Russell and Russell.

Stern, Robert. 1973. "Tariff and Other Measures of Trade Control: A Survey of Recent Developments." *Journal of Economic Literature* 11:857–88.

Stewart, Charles. 1991. "Lessons from the Post-Civil War Era." In *The Politics of Divided Government*, ed. Gary W. Cox and Samuel Kernell. Boulder, CO: Westview Press.

Stigler, George J. 1971. "The Theory of Economic Regulation." *Bell Journal of Economic and Management Science* 2:3–21.

Stigler, George J., ed. 1988. *Chicago Studies in Political Economy.* Chicago: Chicago University Press.

Stone, Frank. 1984. *Canada, the GATT, and the International Trade System.* Montreal: Institute for Research on Public Policy.

Sundquist, James L. 1981. *The Decline and Resurgence of Congress.* Washington, DC: Brookings Institution.

Takacs, Wendy. 1981. "Pressures for Protectionism: An Empirical Analysis." *Economic Inquiry* 19:687–93.

Takacs, Wendy. 1985. "More on Protectionist Pressures and Aggregate Economic Conditions: A Reply." *Economic Inquiry* 23:183–84.

Taussig, F. W. 1931. *The Tariff History of the United States.* New York: Augustus M. Kelley Publishers.

Taylor, Michael. 1987. *The Possibility of Cooperation.* Cambridge: Cambridge University Press.

Terrill, Tom E. 1973. *The Tariff Politics, and American Foreign Policy 1874–1901.* Westport, CT: Greenwood Press.

Thompson, Richard. 1888. *The History of Protective Tariff Laws.* New York and London: Garland Publishing.

Tirole, Jean. 1986. "Hierarchies and Bureaucracies: On the Role of Coercion in Organizations." *Journal of Law, Economics, and Organization* 2:181–214.

Tobin, Glenn. 1987. "The U.S.-Canada Free Trade Negotiations: Gaining Approval to Proceed," Harvard University Kennedy School of Government Case Program, no. C16-87-786.0.

Travis, William. 1964. *The Theory of Trade and Protection.* Cambridge, MA: Harvard University Press.

Travis, William. 1967. *Does the American Tariff Protect Labor?* Cambridge, MA: MIT Press.

Truman, David. 1951. *The Governmental Process.* New York: Knopf.

U.S. Bureau of the Census. Various years. *The Statistical Abstract of the United States.* Washington, DC: Government Printing Office.

U.S. Bureau of the Census. 1975. *Historical Statistics of the United States, Colonial Times to 1970.* Washington, DC: Government Printing Office.

U.S. Department of State. 1950. *United States Treaties and Other International Agreements, 1776–1949.* Washington, DC: Government Printing Office.

U.S. Department of State. 1980. *International Agreements Other Than Treaties 1946–1978: A List With Citations of Their Legal Bases.* Washington, DC: Government Printing Office.

U.S. House of Representatives. Various years. *Calendars of the United States House of Representatives and History of Legislation.* Washington, DC: Government Printing Office.

U.S. President. 1975–91. *Economic Report of the President.* Washington, DC: Government Printing Office.

U.S. Tariff Commission. 1919. *Summary of the Report on Reciprocal and Commercial Treaties.* Washington, DC: Government Printing Office.

Vaccara, Beatrice. 1960. *Employment and Output in Protected Manufacturing Industries.* Washington, DC: Brookings Institution.

Wade, Larry, and John Gates. 1990. "A New Tariff Map of the United States (House of Representatives)." *Political Geography Quarterly* 9:284–304.

Wallerstein, Michael. 1987. "Unemployment, Collective Bargaining, and the Demand for Protection." *American Journal of Political Science* 31:729–51.

Webb, Michael. 1992. "The Ambiguous Consequences of Anti-Dumping Laws." *Economic Inquiry* 30:437–48.

Weingast, Barry. 1979. "A Rational Choice Perspective on Congressional Norms." *American Journal of Political Science* 23:245–62.

Weingast, Barry. 1984. "The Congressional Bureaucratic System: A Principle-Agent Perspective." *Public Choice* 41:147–91.

Weingast, Barry, and William Marshall. 1988. "The Industrial Organization of Congress." *Journal of Political Economy* 96:132–63.

Weingast, Barry, and Mark Moran. 1983. "Bureaucratic Discretion or Congressional Control: Regulatory Policymaking by the Federal Trade Commission." *Journal of Political Economy* 91:765–800.

Weingast, Barry, Kenneth Shepsle, and Christopher Johnsen. 1981. "The Political Economy of Benefits and Costs: A Neoclassical Approach to Distributive Politics." *Journal of Political Economy* 89:642–64.

Williams, James A. 1978. *The Canadian–United States Tariff and Canadian Industry: A Multisectoral Analysis.* Toronto: University of Toronto Press.

Williamson, Oliver. 1985. *The Economic Institutions of Capitalism.* New York: Free Press.

Wilson, James Q., ed. 1980. *The Politics of Regulation.* New York: Basic Books.

Wonnacott, Paul. 1987. *The United States and Canada: The Quest for Free Trade.* Washington, DC: Institute for International Economics.

Index